Hound Pound Narrative

Hound Pound Narrative

*Sexual Offender Habilitation and
the Anthropology of Therapeutic Intervention*

James B. Waldram

UNIVERSITY OF CALIFORNIA PRESS
Berkeley · Los Angeles · London

University of California Press, one of the most
distinguished university presses in the United States,
enriches lives around the world by advancing
scholarship in the humanities, social sciences, and
natural sciences. Its activities are supported by the UC
Press Foundation and by philanthropic contributions
from individuals and institutions. For more
information, visit www.ucpress.edu.

University of California Press
Berkeley and Los Angeles, California

University of California Press, Ltd.
London, England

Library of Congress Cataloging-in-Publication Data

Waldram, James B. (James Burgess).
   Hound pound narrative : sexual offender
habilitation and the anthropology of therapeutic
intervention / James B. Waldram.
      p.   cm.
   Includes bibliographical references and index.
   ISBN 978-0-520-27255-2 (cloth : alk. paper)
   ISBN 978-0-520-27256-9 (pbk. : alk. paper)
   1. Sex offenders—Canada—Rehabilitation.
2. Cognitive therapy—Canada.   I. Title.
   HQ72.C3W35   2012
   365′.661—dc23   2011047717

Manufactured in the United States of America

20 19 18 17 16 15 14 13 12
10 9 8 7 6 5 4 3 2 1

In keeping with a commitment to support
environmentally responsible and sustainable printing
practices, UC Press has printed this book on Rolland
Enviro100, a 100% postconsumer fiber paper that is
FSC certified, deinked, processed chlorine-free, and
manufactured with renewable biogas energy. It is
acid-free and EcoLogo certified.

Contents

Preface   *vii*

Acknowledgments   *xvii*

1. A Man Who Needs No Introduction   *1*

2. Goin' Down with the "Hounds"   *23*

3. Disordered Sex   *47*

4. Moral Citizenship   *76*

Moral Habilitation 1: "Stinkin' Thinkin' "   *101*

5. "It's *Your* Life Story"   *106*

Moral Habilitation 2: "How To Say 'Fuck Off' Politely"   *135*

6. "Feeding Frenzy"   *140*

Moral Habilitation 3: "Peter Meter"   *163*

7. "My Rules for Staying Out of Jail"   *166*

Moral Habilitation 4: "The Most Emotionally Draining Thing I Have Ever Done in My Life"   *184*

8. "A Pretty Shitty Place Out There"   *197*

9. "It's All in the Head"   *220*

Epilogue: Where Are They Now?   *239*

Notes   *241*

Works Cited   *245*

Index   *257*

Preface

Despite appearances, prisons are not totally impervious institutions. Each day people can be seen going in and out: guards, treatment and office staff, chaplains, police, delivery personnel, new inmate arrivals, and even inmates discharged from the institution. Nevertheless, what goes on behind those walls is largely unknown, and of little interest, to the public. Prisons are rather unique institutions in that control of both information and people is tightly restricted. Access to the residents of prisons, the inmates, or "offenders" in much contemporary discourse, is legally restricted, of course, but also controlled by fears, often unfounded, that only danger lurks there. The idea that prisons contain complex and fully functioning social worlds eludes many. Chaos and evil reign supreme, it is assumed; this is a Hobbesian realm of nasty and brutish men barely under control, ready to kill or riot at a moment's notice, always trying to escape and wreak havoc on the public. Those convicted of sexual crimes occupy a special category of evilness as well: they are morally bankrupt monsters that lurk in the shadows waiting to spring on an unsuspecting (typically) female "victim" or—even worse—a child.[1] The orderly, even banal, quotidian passage of tasks and time familiar to those on the outside is not assumed to be characteristic of our prisons.

I first encountered sexual offenders during some research in the early 1990s on the involvement of Aboriginal inmates in Aboriginal traditional treatment or "healing" programs (Waldram 1993, 1994, 1997,

1998).[2] At the time I too harbored some of these disparaging views. I thoughtlessly accepted the interpretation of the anthropologist Elliott Leyton (2001: 3), who in a study of multiple murderers argues that "the eradication of a disease requires the intensive study of all the pus and blood and deformed tissue." Leyton's metaphor is striking, and one that resonates with many: sexual offenders as "deformed tissue."

The problem for me was that at this stage in my work I knew sexual offenders only peripherally, as a by-product of my research on Aboriginal healing. Were they indeed the monsters of public discourse, one-dimensional subhumans for whom incarceration was perhaps not adequate enough punishment for their crimes? Were they the decrepit, drooling predators hiding in bushes and lurking about elementary schools? Were they sex-crazed, violent stalkers hunting suburban neighborhoods for victims? Were they social misfits, lacking the necessary skills and personalities to form normal, healthy relationships with adults? I did not readily see the "everyman" described by forensic psychologist William Marshall (1996) as the typical sex offender: the friend, the spouse, the family member, the neighbor, the co-worker. And my first encounter with a sexual offender did little to dissuade me from Leyton's view. This inmate delighted in volunteering the minute details of his sexual assault and attempted murder of a two-year-old girl. He tried to rattle me, and he was successful. I felt a rage within me, and I wanted to reach across the interview table and throttle him. After our interview, I immediately went home to my own daughters, still shocked at what I perceived then to be a complete and utter lack of humanity, a true evil. My impulse was to look the other way, to keep my girls in the safety of our home, and to expunge such images from my world.

But the disturbing images that the inmate described remained in very unsettling ways. I could not fathom how anyone could imagine, let alone commit, such heinous crimes. I was reminded of Akira Kurosawa's 1950 Japanese crime mystery film *Rashômon,* in which the murder of a samurai and the brutal sexual assault of his wife are recounted by four different characters: the murdered man (through a medium), the wife who survived the attack, the witness who found the body, and the perpetrator. The stories of all the characters prove to contradict each other; that of Tajômaru, the "bandit" accused of the crimes, is rife with internal contradiction and confusion, but it provides detail that none of the other characters can offer. Tajômaru offers a perspective that, although understandably difficult and repugnant to viewers, helps to complete this ugly picture. And this is a perspective that allows

Kurosawa to create his polyphonic telling of the crime, one that reflects yet criticizes Japanese icons of masculinity, such as those embodied within the samurai mystique. It dawned on me that anthropologists are called on all the time to offer the perspectives of real-life characters in order to contribute to the polyphonic understandings of collective behavior and human suffering and to engage in the complex and contradictory discourses that surround these. But do we do enough to bring the perspectives of the "bandits" to this disciplinary task? Do we earnestly attempt to render the seemingly unfathomable understandable so that we can better appreciate the ugliness with which we are faced? My goal here is to attempt just that.

More academically, these reflections led me to appreciate "the paradox of perpetration," in Hinton's (2005: 4) words, "to resist simple, reductive explanations" of the behavior of sexual offenders and their potential for change, to see them as complex, multidimensional human beings who often have family and people who love and care for them and who want the same things in life as the rest of us—individuals who, like us, live within a moralized social world in which they, by and large, not only see themselves in moral terms but are quite prepared to question the morality of others.

My research with sexual offenders emerged fortuitously out of a failed attempt to obtain approval of the Correctional Service of Canada (CSC) to undertake a study of a healing program designed specifically for Aboriginal sexual offenders. In conjunction with the Aboriginal Elder who ran the program, we submitted a proposal that followed the template of my earlier work in other prisons, for a project that would focus on the Aboriginal approach to healing more than on the treatment of sexual offenders per se. A research official with CSC insisted that all our transcripts be provided in raw form as part of the project, ostensibly to allow for confirmation of our data. This demand was new to me, and of course we rejected it outright on ethical grounds, so the research was abandoned. I have written about this incident in greater detail elsewhere (Waldram 1998). The key issue here is that, having prepared for this research, I had become intrigued by sexual offender treatment more generally, an interest fueled by many unsolicited opinions that what I had in mind would never work with *these* men in *this* context. I took their pessimism as a challenge! So several years later, after numerous changes in personnel at CSC and the termination of the Aboriginal-specific program, I tried again, this time requesting permission to study the mainstream sexual offender treatment unit (which houses both Aboriginal and non-Aboriginal offenders) in a facility that was at once a multiple-security-level penitentiary and a psychiatric hospital. Frankly, I was quite surprised that the response was positive. A subsequent successful grant application to the Canadian Institutes of Health Research provided the funding.

This book is the result of this study: it is an ethnography of the experience of prison-based sexual offender treatment. It is my goal to climb inside the offenders' world as much as possible, to "go down with the hounds," as one inmate describes it, and try to understand what it is like for them to be in a prison treatment program for sexual offenders. My assumption in so doing is that *how* they experience treatment very much affects what they gain from it, and little is known about this experience. My attention here is directed virtually exclusively to issues of narrative and therapeutic intervention. As in any work, other areas could have drawn my focus: the gendered dimensions to the men's crimes and earlier life experiences; the diverse and often contradictory ways in which addiction and substance abuse are related in both official and individual representations of sexual offenses; and the vocabulary of violence (how different words are strategically employed and their broader political effect, both inside and outside the prison), among others. And of course, the project could have been extended in many ways, to include, for example, a comparison with narratives of survivors of sexual assault and abuse. Ultimately, though, my research centered on the inmates' therapeutic engagement and the processes of habilitation. My reasons for this focus are varied, but foremost among them is the fact that most sexual offenders are eventually released from prison, and understanding more fully how they engage with treatment programs "on the inside" should prove relevant to what we can expect from them when they are our neighbors. Although this work offers only a partial understanding of sexual offenders and their worlds, it is hopefully a step, not toward rationalizing their reprehensible crimes or justifying their criminal acts, but toward understanding those who are cast as the most evil among us.

The research also represents a continuation of my career-long interest in what I call the anthropology of therapeutic intervention: that is, the application of the lens of anthropology—at the intersections of medical and psychological anthropology—to therapeutic contexts imbued with power relations, which often involve reluctant, recalcitrant, and otherwise difficult individuals whose participation is in some ways not entirely "voluntary," and in which the benefits are often seen to accrue more to others than to the "patient." I see this research as perhaps my ultimate challenge as an anthropologist, to enter into a world where few researchers have ever meaningfully ventured, to be accepted by members of one of society's most secretive, wary, paranoid, and despised groups, and to undertake a form of research—ethnography—that few have attempted in prison.

Ethnographers generally try to paint a sympathetic portrait of the people with whom they work. Most frequently this is relatively easy to do, as we are "'called' into the stories and lives of others by the moral process of engaged listening, the commitment to witnessing, and the call to take account of what is at stake for people" (Kleinman 1999a: 418). Despite the endless possibilities for the exoticization of the fascinating worlds of the peoples with whom we tend to work, for the most part ethnographies come by their positive portrayals honestly. Anthropologists characteristically work with victims, the oppressed, the powerless, the downtrodden; they emote an enraged sensibility toward the powerful forces that create and maintain inequality and pain. "Social suffering" is a dominant paradigm in medical anthropology these days, one that puts emphasis on health and social inequalities and violence due to broader political, economic and social processes. Some even adopt an avowedly "militant" stance (e.g., Scheper-Hughes 1995, 2004), going "undercover" to expose the outrageous actions of those who would seek to exploit and harm others for their own benefit. Such research lends itself naturally to poetic pronouncements, and where accompanied by professional-quality photographs (e.g., Biehl 2005; Bourgeois and Schonberg 2009) these can be profoundly persuasive and moving. The "people who get rubbished" (Scheper-Hughes 1997) are the common subjects of anthropological inquiry. Not so those who do the trashing.

The "social suffering" paradigm does not, of course, easily allow for a sympathetic portrayal of the perpetrators of violence. But does it allow for efforts to understand them? The few ethnographers who work with particularly nasty types—those who would generally attract little public sympathy, such as perpetrators of genocide (Hinton 2005) and hardened criminals (Rhodes 2004)—have been able to refrain for the most part from having to deal with the issue of representation. Lorna Rhodes (2001: 76), in her own prison research, expresses a kind of conventional wisdom when she suggests, "To forget one's position as an outsider is to be in danger, not only from interpersonal trouble of various kinds but, more enduringly, from alarming emotional and intellectual identifications. Here," she continues, "the ethnographic desire for (perhaps fantasized but nonetheless compelling) alignment with one's subject(s) must be relinquished or at least bracketed." Jim Thomas (1993), in his ethnographic research on inmates and prison experiences, so feared that he might romanticize them as he got to know them and their prison circumstances better that he steeled himself against any kind of emotional attachment and chose to write on topics that would be less influenced by any emerging sympathy. Such concerns as expressed by Rhodes and Thomas are understandable given public perceptions of these individuals. I wonder, however, if researchers have also avoided work with certain groups, such as prison inmates, because of assumptions that they are difficult and more problematic to work with than anyone else, that they are somehow too dangerous to get near, as if they were contagious, or even that they are less human and hence less deserving of our scholarly attention. Of what value is anthropological research that sidesteps or even denies the essentialness of establishing close relations with those we study and writing ethnography that reflects this experience-near process? To struggle against developing relationships with prison inmates is nonsensical in anthropological terms; to a priori "steel" one's self unnecessarily closes doors that should remain open. And believe me, you never, ever forget that these men have committed some very serious crimes and that at the end of the day you get to go home and they are locked up in a cell.

In this book I have chosen to be as faithful as possible to the experiences of the inmates and to present their words at length. Consequently, in the many scholarly presentations that I have given on this research (and in the reactions of some peer reviewers to submitted journal manuscripts), the issue of representation has loomed large (Waldram 2007). In my attempts to understand, analyze, and communicate the experiences of sexual offenders undergoing treatment I have been accused of being an apologist for their abhorrent behavior, a supporter of pure evil, a likely sexual offender myself ("Why study them if you are not one yourself?"), and otherwise engaged in the retraumatization of victims, at the very least by "silencing" them, that is, not including them in my research, but more significantly by "giving voice" to those who should be silenced (see Waldram 2007).

I have been chastised as well for the "tone" of my presentation of inmate's experiences. "To describe the patient's situation faithfully," writes Erving Goffman (1961: x) in his classic *Asylums,* "is necessarily to present a partisan view." I have tried here to be more than simply partisan, through the application of theoretical interpretation, but the fact remains that I must present the views of the inmates if I am to be successful in presenting an ethnography of their experiences. I believe that the best test of the validity of any ethnography is the extent to which it resonates with those who participated in the research, or other individuals who find themselves in similar circumstances. I cannot say definitively that this is the case here, as none of my participants have read the manuscript, but several individuals who have worked in prisons have read parts or heard my presentations and have remarked on my success in replicating the "feel" of prison institutional life and treatment programs. I have unabashedly made an effort to present sexual offenders' experiences and perspectives, and to this end the "tone" I employ throughout is meant to reflect these experiences as accurately as possible, both cognitively and emotionally. This may be challenging and disturbing to some readers. But I do not think striving to capture and communicate such sentiment is something anthropologists should reserve only for Trobriand Islanders, moral saints, or victims of social suffering. It serves no constructive purpose to "tone down" an inmate's outrage at being removed from the treatment program and sent back to his home prison, for instance, no matter how disagreeable that inmate is and no matter how reasonable or legitimate the prison officials' action may be. The inmate *is* angry and upset, and I see it as my job to communicate that to the best of my ability. When an inmate "laments" that he cannot have any family contact while in treatment, I must try to convey his emotional state, even though the treatment staff have very legitimate reasons for their actions. My research is not about their reasons, it is about the inmate's experiences. I anticipate most readers will appreciate my efforts here, even while they, like me, abhor the criminal acts perpetrated by these men.

So how I represent the experiences of these sexual offenders—individuals who see themselves in a moral light, just like the rest of us (Waldram 2009b)—is an enduring dilemma. And how I can do this when my research participants must remain largely invisible simply compounds the difficulty.

There are no photographs in this book. The identities of federal inmates are protected by law, and I was not allowed to photograph them or the treatment unit. I could not present complete biographies without such extensive rewriting as to render them meaningless. Therefore, by necessity, the inmate portraits I present in this book are to varying degrees fractured and distorted, going beyond the usual anthropological convention of protecting the identities of our research participants. In an effort to keep the portraits as balanced as possible, however, each inmate that appears in this ethnography has, at the very least, the bare bones of his current convictions detailed. Readers need to know my participants' relevant criminal history. However, I decline to present graphic descriptions of the crimes outside those offered in group sessions by the inmates themselves, as explored in chapters 5 through 7. I use the generic term *sexual assault* in its legal sense to refer to all manner of sexual touching, interference, forced oral, anal or vaginal intercourse, and statutory offenses, where the victim is underage and therefore unable to provide consent. Clearly working with imprisoned sexual offenders exceeds the normal ethical parameters of most anthropological work. It presents a unique challenge to the ethnographer.

My goal here is not to deliberately paint a sympathetic portrait of sexual offenders; rather, it is to understand them as much as possible in all their complexity as human beings experiencing a treatment program. There have been some good moments in their lives, moments of happiness with family and friends. There are even some good times in prison. Despite popular perceptions that all such criminals proclaim their innocence, I have found almost all willing to accept that they have also done some very bad things; they have also experienced very difficult times, often in which some very bad things have been done to them. The victim/victimizer dichotomy blurs and opens up a different kind of paradox, one that has been debated in forensic psychology circles under the label of the "cycle of violence." Victims have the public's sympathy, but the minute they victimize another person, they garner our disdain.

The irony here is that the victims are largely invisible in this work. Their identities too must be protected, of course, both legally and morally. However, largely omitting the victims from this ethnography also reflects, in my experience, the program itself, where the victim has no voice in the treatment of the offender. The victim is spoken about, even spoken for as part of somewhat bizarre role-playing exercises I will detail later, but nevertheless remains amorphically disembodied in the daily discourse of treatment. And while there are some community-based treatment programs for sexual offenders that are built upon models of restorative justice, which bring the offender and the victim together, this is not a practice typically found in penitentiaries. The victim exists entirely within the public utterances of the offender in treatment and within the private court documents and police records available to the treatment staff. Thus it is impossible in this work to do justice to the experience of the victims of these crimes.

I am often asked, "Why study sexual offenders in prison?" The one response that resonates is straightforward: most of them will be released into our communities at some point, sometimes on parole and other times without conditions as their sentences expire. Most of the men I present in this study have already been released, and some are back in prison. What happens to them in prison, especially in programs designed to "rehabilitate" them, is a crucial issue for public safety, yet we know little of their treatment experiences. The question of the efficacy of prison-based therapeutic programs for sexual offenders is also legitimately raised. Do the offenders emerge from prison as different, more morally sound and prosocial individuals? Are they "healed"? It is not my intent here to judge the efficacy of this or any other prison treatment program, but this is an area to which an anthropology of therapeutic intervention seems primed to contribute.

Acknowledgments

First and foremost I need to acknowledge the many inmates involved in the treatment program during the period of research. While I did not interview them all, and a few declined to be interviewed, they all in their own ways supported the goals of the research. I very much appreciate that they gave me their trust, a difficult thing to do in prison, and I hope that my work here meets their standards and reflects their experiences. Of course it is not possible to name any of these individuals.

I would like to extend my gratitude to various officials at the Correctional Service of Canada and the therapeutic prison where this research was undertaken, and to the staff members of the unit where I worked, for allowing me access and facilitating my research. These staff members in particular deserve special commendation; while my work here is critical, it should not be read as critical of them. They are as dedicated a group as one could imagine, working in extremely difficult circumstances with a very difficult clientele, and as a result they, too, are often the target of disparaging comments from a public that questions the legitimacy of prison rehabilitation efforts for sexual offenders. Although they were not the subjects of my research, the high degree of professionalism that they brought to their work, day in and day out, was inspiring.

Funding for the research was provided primarily by a standard grant from the Canadian Institutes of Health Research's Institute of Neurosciences, Mental Health and Addiction, for which I remain grateful. A small grant from the Community-University Institute for Social Research at the University of Saskatchewan allowed me a reduced teaching load, which was essential to facilitating the field research. Two sabbatical leaves granted by the University of Saskatchewan—both to relocate to the vibrant anthropology program at UCLA—were utilized to analyze the data from this study and complete the manuscript for this book. Jason Throop, in the Department of Anthropology at UCLA, kindly provided an introduction to senior acquisitions editor Reed Malcolm, of the University of California Press, for which I am very appreciative. Reed, in turn, has been a strong advocate for this project as it worked its way through the editorial decision-making process. Stacy Eisenstark and Suzanne Knott worked diligently with me throughout the production process, and Elisabeth Magnus helped me improve the text as copy editor. I also extend thanks to all those other individuals at the press who will have worked in some way to bring this project to fruition. In Saskatoon, I am grateful for the challenging insights of two graduate students in particular, Janice Victor and Jan Gelech, who have worked with me on the data set and analysis for several years. Ray Stephanson and Allison Muri, two colleagues in our English department, provided some valuable assistance on narrative theory. Mark Olver in the Department of Psychology helped me understand key aspects of sexual offender risk assessment. Three reviewers of this manuscript also made valuable suggestions, and these have made the work much stronger. I very much appreciate their diligence and efforts.

This ethnography is a new work, and I have not published any of the chapters elsewhere. However, the ideas expressed here represent a continuing development of my thinking on this topic, and these ideas, and perhaps a little verbatim text, may reflect some earlier publications. I wish to thank the publishers for permission to utilize ideas and passages previously published in these articles: "Moral Agency, Cognitive Distortion, and Narrative Strategy in the Rehabilitation of Sexual Offenders," *Ethos* 38 (3): 251–74 (2010); "'It's Just You and Satan, Hanging Out at a Pre-School': Notions of Evil and the Rehabilitation of Sexual Offenders," *Anthropology and Humanism* 34 (2): 219–34 (2009); "The Narrative Challenge to Cognitive Behavioral Treatment of Sexual Offenders," *Culture, Medicine and Psychiatry* 32 (3): 421–39 (2008); "Narrative and the Construction of 'Truth' in a Prison-Based Treatment Program for Sexual Offenders," *Ethnography* 8 (2): 145–69 (2007); "'Everybody's Got a Story': Listening to Imprisoned Sexual Offenders," *Qualitative Health Research* 17 (7): 963–70 (2007). Also, elements of chapter 8 are borrowed from a conference paper, "'Coming to a Theatre Near You': Community Notification and Registration Policies for Sexual Offenders," authored by myself and Janice Victor and presented at the 2009 conference of the Society for Medical Anthropology at Yale.

I would also like to acknowledge all those who have experienced the pain and trauma of sexual assault and to express my hope that the work I present here in some way helps make our communities safer, for those women and children who are a part of my life as well as yours.

Finally, I need to thank Pamela Downe for her unwavering support during the often difficult days of this research. The topic of my work was not always well received by some of my anthropological colleagues, and Pam was always there to soothe hurt feelings, to recast such disparaging responses in a broader context, and to remind me that this kind of challenging work is central to Canadian engaged anthropology. Pam also freely shared her considerable theoretical expertise and gave the final manuscript a good, critical read, for which I am very grateful.

This research was approved by the Research Ethics Board at the University of Saskatchewan and by the Research Ethics Committee of the Correctional Service of Canada. All names of research participants are fictitious, and elements of their stories are altered to protect their identities. I purposefully mix the gender identities of prison staff as well.

As always, the views expressed in this book do not necessarily reflect those of any of these individuals or agencies, and errors, omissions, or misinterpretations are my responsibility alone.

This book is dedicated to all those on both sides of the criminal justice divide who work to keep our communities safe.

CHAPTER I

A Man Who Needs No Introduction

Sam is starting to smile. It's not his "happy" smile. I have seen that smile many times over the past month since he arrived, and particularly as he worked both of the day rooms, his buoyant personality and boundless energy barely tolerated by most (something of which he seemed oblivious). No, this is his defensive smile, his "Now I'm getting pissed" smile. Lips tight together, his smile fighting off a grimace, and his face flushed. His Autobiography, of which he seemed so confident a day earlier when I interviewed him, has not gone as planned. Therapists and inmates alike, surrounding Sam in a big three-quarter crescent like vultures circling wounded prey, have questioned, challenged, and even openly scoffed as he told his life story. Sam has become rattled, confused. It has seemed at times he was about to lose control, an all-too-frequent occurrence according to his criminal record and a problem that partially explains his sexual crimes. Losing control in the group would also send a very wrong signal to the therapists who are documenting the session carefully. But how can he sit here, listening to such critical commentary on his life, and not respond? Why is he not allowed to respond? Whose story is it anyway?

Sam is in a Canadian therapeutic prison, an institution that is both prison and psychiatric hospital. He is participating in a "high-intensity" treatment program for sexual offenders designed according to the principles of Cognitive Behavioral Therapy (CBT), a standard psychotherapeutic technique that seeks to change how individuals think about or understand their life (more on this later). An Aboriginal man in his midtwenties, he is short, heavily muscled, with shoulder-length hair and a wispy moustache. Like most men in this program, he has a long record of juvenile and adult criminal offenses, in his case including assaults on his spouse and a previous conviction for sexual assault. He is now serving a three-year federal sentence—his first—for sexual assault, and he came to the treatment program a few weeks ago to join a new cohort of sixteen men. Like the others, he has "volunteered" for treatment, although he was uncertain what the experience would be like when he did so. He is already known on the sex offenders unit as a sarcastic "tough guy," a little hot-headed and belligerent if crossed, but otherwise always joking around. He has been asked to provide his "Autobiography,"[1] and now the other inmates and two psychiatric nurse therapists listen intently to it.

His life so far, he tells us, has involved bouncing back and forth between his home reserve and the city; he has committed crimes in both places and, by his own admission, is not well liked on the small reserve as a result. He is asked about this. Can he go back? You should go home and make amends, he is instructed. Does your family still want you? He responds patiently. "I think so." He finds the anonymity of the city much more appealing, however, even though he there joins the largely unemployed coterie of Aboriginal people eking out a living in a society that seems to care little for their plight. Why stay if you can't find a job? he is asked. You will surely get into trouble without work. Who are your friends in the city? Do they use? "Yes," he replies, "but I don't." "Not true," interjects a nurse, pointing to some papers in her lap. "Well," he clarifies, "I don't do drugs *anymore*." "That's because you're in jail," deadpans an inmate in response. Many laugh at the irony of this, since access to drugs in penitentiaries is often greater than on the street. Sam laughs a little too, but it is an uncomfortable laugh.

He arrived at this Autobiography session this morning with handwritten notes to use as a guide. The previous day I had asked him about his plan for his "Auto." He expressed confidence, informing me that he had worked through several drafts already and had received feedback from his primary nurse therapist, who had requested revisions and the addition of several other episodes of his life. The assistance of the therapist was important to the framing of his story. "I had a little bit of troubles and got help, like wording it and stuff. And then after they looked it over, they tell you to make some changes, and then you make some changes." It seemed to Sam that his life story had been preapproved, so he was not nervous. Despite having attended a few other "Autos" since arriving at the treatment program, and having seen how other inmates had been roasted, he seemed to feel he would make it through unscathed. Sam did not lack confidence, framed by the kind of bravado necessary for survival in prison.

Today, however, he seems visibly nervous as he faces the group. He speaks quietly at first and is asked repeatedly to speak up. He begins by discussing his family, the breakup of his parents' marriage, and some of his employment history. He also touches on the development of his sexuality, when and in what contexts he began to masturbate and when he had his first sexual encounter. Not the usual content of a life story—at least not on the outside—and a clear sign that he has been prompted. He began to masturbate at fifteen, he admits. "Not likely," suggests an inmate. "How about, like, ten?" "Okay, maybe," agrees Sam. Details about his sexual history are sparse, however, and he continues to be interrupted with some frequency by both therapists and the other inmates.

Since Sam is being vague on the details, the therapists seek clarifications, about his work and especially about his sexual activities and offenses. They glance frequently at their notes, a compendium of legal and psychological "facts" about Sam. He eyes them nervously as they do, wondering what the notes say, hoping he gets it "right." The therapists are particularly insistent that he disclose specific details about the sexual offenses, details he did not initially offer in his story. In a few instances he responds with annoyance by saying that he is going to present these details later in the presentation, implying that he is being rushed or interrupted before the narrative can unfold according to his plan. This attempt at self-rescue is met with guffaws from some men. In just a few weeks they have already learned not to believe everything Sam says.

Sam's story becomes jumbled as he introduces new details about previously narrated events, while still attempting to move the story forward. Episode laps episode, details jumble together, and Sam's attempts to clarify only obfuscate. At one point a staff member interjects that the story so far has been rather confusing. "It's *your* life story," she reminds, adding, "Try to do it in a neat, chronological way." Several other men also note that from their point of view the story is difficult to follow. Sam stares blankly at his pieces of paper, by now a somewhat disheveled mnemonic that, it seems, is starting to fail him. He stuffs the notes between his knees when one of the two therapists in the session directs him to discuss the details of his sexual crimes. There is nothing in his notes he can use now.

Sam's description of his first offense is rather evasive, and he offers up few specific details. He describes his assault of a "drunk" female acquaintance who had passed out at a party. She had "come on" to him while dancing, then again later at the house, he relates. After drinking for a while he went looking for more beer and came across her sleeping in bed in a "see-through nightgown." "Whoa," interjects an inmate, and several other heads simultaneously snap around to look not at him but at the nurses. This sounds an awful lot like "justification," I think to myself, and I suspect that others have picked this up. But Sam's primary nurse shushes the inmates and indicates to Sam that he should proceed. Sam does. He looked around for the beer, he continues to explain. Then, providing no details whatsoever, he states, "Then I assaulted her."

The quizzical look on some faces suggests that this is not an adequate explanation of the crime. There is quite a gap between looking for beer and sexual assault! And so questions follow. One inmate insists on hearing "how it actually went down." "Did you watch her for a while first?" asks another inmate, suggesting that Sam contemplated the assault before committing it. Sam continues to be evasive, saying that he just "did it." The woman woke up part way through, he clarifies, but she did not struggle or order him to stop. "Minimizing!" an inmate accuses. Did you physically hurt her? others want to know. How much had you really drunk? You must remember more than what you are disclosing. Sam retreats, insisting he can recall few details. He continues the story and explains that when he was finished assaulting the woman he told her not to tell anyone and left. He was arrested a few hours later after she contacted police.

Sam pauses before launching into an explanation of his second sexual assault. He begins slowly, explaining that when he arrived at the apartment where the offense took place he rang the buzzer. No other background information is provided. We have no idea how he came to be at this apartment. A woman answered, he continues, and asked if he was alone. He said yes. She asked again if he was alone. He said yes again. Then he was buzzed in. He climbed the stairs to the apartment and knocked on the door. Sam then backtracks, filling us in on some details. He had been drinking heavily that day and in preceding days, he explains. He starts to enumerate the different kinds of alcoholic beverages involved and their sizes and quantities. He informs us where he got them: from the liquor store, then from a friend's place. The story of this assault is clearly different from the last: the last has just been criticized for providing few specific details, but this new story is bogging down in them. Belaboring the minutiae, Sam also seems to be slowing the story down, perhaps trying to avoid getting to the part in which everyone is most interested. Others seem to sense this game as well, and a few eyes start to roll. Then the interruptions commence yet again.

Both therapists and inmates want more pertinent details and clarifications, and he is admonished many times to "explain" himself, especially in reference to the assault. The cacophony grows. At one point an inmate, seemingly angry, attempts to rescue Sam. "I'm losing track of the story," he declares, "because of all the interruptions!" Some of the issues on which the therapists want clarification have already been provided or are simply irrelevant, he continues, and Sam should be allowed to finish his presentation. After several minutes of questions and discussion, Sam is allowed to resume, and the audience goes quiet, anticipating the finale. This is what they all want to hear. It is what they want to hear every Autobiography, what every inmate in prison wants to know about all the others: "What are you in for?" While they appreciate that they have all been convicted of at least one sexual offense, they generally know little about each other or the specifics of the offenses. Personal information—such as what makes up an autobiography—is carefully guarded. Indeed, on the unit they may be surprised to encounter an acquaintance or even a friend from the penitentiary, someone who had until this point been able to hide his sexual offense from the others. Was Sam's sexual offense a "good" one or a "bad" one? I cannot help thinking there may be a titillating, pornographic element to the insistence on details, and I wonder to myself if it makes sense for inmates convicted of sexual crimes to hear such specific details of the commission of other sexual crimes.

Sam frustrates yet again, as his detailed recounting of events leading up to the offense suddenly gives way to a very thin, indeed evasive, description of the offense itself. Sam explains that he was helping a seventeen-year-old girl with her homework. (At this point in the story, no mention has been made of her existence. Men look around at each other and shrug, clearly unable to connect the victim to the other events in the story). Later when she was sleeping he assaulted her. She told him to stop. He did. Then he left and was arrested a short time later. That's all.

The Autobiography is now over. In this room, it seems the story of one's life effectively ends with the commission of the "index" offense, the one most directly relevant to the current incarceration. Little that happens subsequently in a man's life seems tell-worthy or of rehabilitative value. Prison experiences are, of course, logical material for autobiographical construction, but they are not therapeutically significant.

Several men shift in their seats, and one lets out an audible sigh as he slouches back in his chair. An air of disappointment lingers. Sam stares at his feet again. He waits for the questions, the criticism, or the advice that he doesn't want to hear.

During the question period, the control of Sam's narrative shifts perceptibly to the group as a whole. The constant interruptions during the story were just the opening salvo, after all. Sam's emotional state follows suit; he raises his voice and flashes looks of anger at his challengers. They press for details of his second conviction. Who was this seventeen-year-old girl? Was she a relative? Why would *you* be helping a "high schooler" with homework? one man asks derisively. Sam tries to explain that he almost has his grade 12, adding that he is trying to complete it in prison. "This was not about homework," states a therapist emphatically, ending this line of discussion. Sam starts to become defensive, even belligerent. When one man suggests that if Sam, like himself, does not quit drinking he will surely reoffend, Sam blurts out, "That's based on your life. That's not mine." When asked bluntly if he will quit drinking, Sam responds with an emphatic "no," a response that encourages several other men to jump into the discussion, a cacophony of voices, some in support of Sam's right to make his own choices but many more critical of his lack of insight into the negative role of alcohol in his life. Sam is then accused of being flippant, of laughing and smirking throughout and not taking the session seriously. Sam denies each accusation. Another man verbally challenges the first, saying that this is simply how Sam expresses himself when nervous. It is a matter of opinion, he says, and the first man should keep his to himself. The exchange is heated, and a therapist asks them to calm down. Sam sits back and watches for several minutes as his life is discussed.

Several inmates now accuse Sam of lacking insight and failing to disclose his thoughts and feelings at the time of the offenses. But another inmate intercedes before Sam can respond, claiming that no one knows these things and that they come to treatment programs to figure them out. Sam, making no effort to intervene, again sits back and watches the debate. This is a brief respite: he is no longer being challenged and no longer needs to defend himself. With the narrative event now completely in the group's hands, Sam actually seems content; the focus is no longer on him even as he remains the subject of the discussion. He could interject at any time but chooses not to do so. The clock creeps ever more closely to lockup time when the session must terminate for count. Saved by the bell? Not yet. There is still one more phase to survive before he is done. The therapists push forward, also mindful of the time. Predictably, perhaps, Sam's demeanor changes when the formal feedback component begins. In the ultimate blow to narrative agency, narrators are not permitted to respond, allowing the audience to have the final say in judging the merits of the Autobiography they have heard. Sam now sits back stone-faced and quiet, refusing to look at his inquisitors, while inmates and therapists lend commentary to his life. This is definitely not his happy smile he is wearing now.

Sam's experience is not unique, as I shall demonstrate in this book. His engagement with prison-based therapeutic intervention for sexual offending behavior exhibits an ongoing tension between subjective experience and personal agency, on one hand, and a positivist, science-based "best practices" model of treatment on the other. At stake here are competing versions of the "truth" of an inmate's life. This truth is laid over a factual frame, the who, what, where, when, and why that are at the core of both judicial process and autobiographical narrative, yet what these facts "look" like often diverges dramatically. These five "w's" are hotly contested, to be sure, situated as they are at the front lines of an ongoing carceral-therapeutic struggle among therapists and inmates. The picture is complicated further, however, when we add into the autobiographical mix other cognitive and affective details. "What were you thinking about at the time of the crime?" "How did that make you feel?" The manner in which the inmate presents and explains the details of his life is crucial to his success in the treatment program.

While initially enticed by the illusion of agency, the request and opportunity (and yes, the demand) to tell his story—and especially to an audience partially composed of presumably sympathetic allies—most inmates ultimately and to varying degrees come to terms with the therapeutic paradigm, some for instrumental and others for therapeutic reasons (and some for both). This authoritative paradigm is backed by a massive dossier of previously acquired information about the inmate and supported by a cognitive behavioral science treatment model that is designed to help him see how his personal narrative is problematic. He must change his story in just the right way as treatment unfolds, as the "real truth" of his life cannot be found except through the therapeutic filter of treatment. Sam needs no "introduction" because his life is already known and understood; its significant factual details are in the existing judicial and correctional files, and its meaning is clearly articulated within the theoretical model of treatment. His "type" is known and understood. While he may assert his subjectivity and agency to define the relevant facts of his own life and their meaning, if he decides that a positive evaluation in the program is important, then resistance to the treatment team's efforts to rebuild his narrative is counterproductive. Why? Well, this *is* a prison, and many people—correctional officers, therapists, psychologists, psychiatrists, members of parole boards, parole officers, judges—will have a great deal of influence over Sam's ability to achieve what, for him and others, is the ultimate goal: to get out of prison and back into the community. If he emerges a better person, that is value added.

GOALS OF THE BOOK

This book is an ethnography of a prison unit for sexual offender treatment, the "Hound Pound" of my title. *Hound* is prison slang for sexual offender, and *Hound Pound* is the term that the inmates have coined for their sexual offenders unit.

The book has three basic goals. First, I want to begin to fill in a large gap in forensic treatment by providing an ethnographically rich account of the experience of treatment itself, particularly within the complex world of power relations that is a federal prison. "There is still little that addresses the culture of the therapeutic setting—the broader context in which treatment takes place—and especially the *active* participation of those undertaking treatment," write Ware, Frost, and Hoy (2010: 731). This focus on those undertaking treatment necessitates a consideration of power relations, and in this I am inspired by Desjarlais's (2005: 369) critical phenomenological perspective to engage with the "interrelated concerns and lifeworlds" of the inmates within the context of the "social, discursive, and political forces" that underpin these lifeworlds (see also Good 1994). Very little is known of the experience of treatment in part because most research on prison rehabilitation has been dominated by quantitatively oriented psychological and psychiatric perspectives, with an intense focus on issues directly relevant to public safety, such as risk to reoffend. Inmates are assessed at several stages throughout their sentences, including at the beginning and end of their treatment programs. Sometimes the instruments used involve file reviews only, with no interaction with the inmate. These tests afford very little opportunity to comprehend the experience of treatment itself and how the dynamic interaction of inmates, therapists, security personnel, and treatment paradigm works to influence these assessments and, concordantly, the individual inmate's ability to "do" the program. While my aim here does not involve an assessment of the effectiveness of this treatment program, such an assessment cannot be fully and properly undertaken without a rich understanding of how that treatment is experienced (Ware, Frost, and Hoy 2010).

I do aim here, in part, to problematize the somewhat simplistic assumption that therapeutic prisons, like prisons themselves, can be characterized by one-way power relations. I seek, as Jefferson (2003: 56) would say, to "conceptualise the complexity" of the therapeutic prison and, while emphasizing the power and control of the treatment and correctional staff, to nonetheless acknowledge the inmates' agency to engage with the staff, each other, and the program in dynamic ways. As Foucault (1982) suggests, power, in this sense, references how humans are created, shaped, and regulated as subjects and how they resist such efforts (see also Rose 1998). The ethnographic approach—combining a variation of the person-centered perspective with more traditional, group-oriented ethnography—is ideal in this situation, yet for many reasons little prison ethnography is undertaken (Wacquant 2002). Indeed, Lorna Rhodes, in "Toward an Anthropology of Prisons" (2001), was surprisingly able to cite relatively little work by anthropologists, noting that we have largely left this field to sociologists and psychologists. Perhaps my work will spark other anthropologists to go behind the walls. What goes on there affects us all.

A critical engagement with the dominant treatment paradigm, Cognitive Behavioral Therapy (CBT), is my second goal in this book. The experience of treatment for the inmates can be understood only within the context of CBT, an approach common to most sexual offender treatment programs in North America and much of the Westernized world as well as many other therapeutic contexts. While there has been research on the utility of CBT in forensic treatment, no one has approached the issue from such an experience-near perspective as I do here. I am interested in therapeutic pragmatics, that is, how a treatment theory is put into practice in context with actual therapists and inmates, and how the inmates in turn learn, accept or reject, manipulate, and otherwise engage with the therapeutic lessons derived from that theory. This kind of detailed ethnographic exploration flows naturally from broader critical engagements with the "psy" disciplines, especially those with a Foucauldian concern with relations of power (e.g., Rose 1998).

The third goal of this book, then, is to explore the impact of power relations and truth discourse on the employment of narrative in forensic treatment. Rather than simply presenting and dissecting narratives, as has become fashionable in anthropology as well as many other social science and health disciplines, I seek to examine the dynamic context in which narratives are generated, manipulated, shared, contested, and defended. In particular, I seek to examine how narrative is dynamically situated when truthfulness and accuracy become central to its validation and acceptability and when authority is invoked not only as a force for refereeing narrative delivery but also for judging its acceptability in terms of both specific details and overall theme or message. Such can be the case only in situations of power imbalance, whether structurally or more informally imposed. While the judicial process, and prisons especially, represent a severe form of structured imbalance, I will argue that this is augmented by the imposition of a scientifically based theory of treatment that, by invoking authority, defines not only what is likely to be "truthful" but also what is likely to represent acceptable verisimilitude in the absence of the necessary information with which to assess truthfulness. In more explicitly dealing with the dynamics of power and control, this work deviates somewhat from most of the narrative scholarship in anthropology.

The struggle that emerges in this form of forensic treatment, then, is between narrative as an inherently subjective process designed, in part, to generate and communicate personal meaning, and what psychologist Jerome Bruner (1986) refers to as the "paradigmatic" or "logicoscientific" mode of cognitive functioning, another mode of thinking and communicating that is fundamentally at odds with narrative but that shares its space in the daily lives of individuals. The articulated relationship between narrative and paradigmatic modes has not been explored in detail by medical or psychological anthropologists. As a result, we may have overstepped the useful bounds of narrative as an analytical framework for understanding human experience and missed the obvious role that the existence of the paradigmatic mode plays in the creation, delivery, and receptiveness of narrative.

Finally, across these three goals is an overarching theme to reconceptualize prison treatment programs as processes of "habilitation" rather than "rehabilitation." While this theme will be developed throughout the book, it is important here to at least touch on how I frame the two.

Rehabilitation is a term synonymous with prison treatment and one common element of public discourse on what to do with criminals (the other being to punish, or worse). Strictly defined, *rehabilitation* refers to a process of restoring the individual to some prior point in time, presumably a nondysfunctional period characterized by a noncriminal lifestyle, a time when life was good and prior to a descent into criminality.[2] Such a definition of rehabilitation is nonsensical for the men in my study, as there is rarely an appropriate restore point in most offenders' lives; if, for argument's sake, there were, then most certainly the stigma of being a sexual offender in the community would act to ensure that such an unproblematic return would be unlikely. Instead, contemporary prison treatment programs, including those for sexual offenders, focus on public safety, with recidivism the measure of successful rehabilitation. This means that inmate rehabilitation is clearly and specifically for the benefit of society, and short of committing another crime what a released offender does or does not do in the community is of almost invisible concern. Certainly his progress in prison treatment programs will be monitored and personal changes in attitude and cognitive functioning will be noted, but, as I will discuss later, "risk to reoffend" remains the singular most definitive measure of treatment success or failure.

Here is another way to look at rehabilitation, one that will weave throughout this book: the unarticulated assumption of treatment for sexual offenders is that risk to reoffend is best achieved through a process of *habilitation*. This is a transformative and not restorative process; the idea is to create moral individuals who emerge from prison as "fit" for society, individuals rendered safe to be among us. Habilitation is a process of attempting to create in others that which we most admire or wish to emulate morally, ethically, and socially; hence the model of morality employed in this sexual offenders program is an ideal, un-nuanced, and unambiguous one. This necessarily involves education in what is often referred to in prison programs as "prosocial behavior," delivered in the form of uncontestable and utopian social and moral truths about the nature of human sociality. The success of habilitation should be measured by the extent of sociality inculcated in the individual, his ability to live among us in a moral manner, to *be* moral, which, of course, does not in and of itself preclude committing a crime. Such an assessment is never done, of course, and defaults to recidivism are inevitable. So while in both rehabilitation and habilitation one measure of success can still be the degree to which *we* are better off, habilitation shifts attention away from so-called "criminogenic" factors, those individualized characteristics, behaviors, and attitudes that influence criminality, and toward the broader moral lessons being taught and the extent to which individuals experience them, learn them, and invoke them in prison and community contexts. This opens the door for other ways to assess treatment success than simply recidivism and allows us to begin to explore the vicissitudes of an inmate's life in prison as well as the community as a moral—or newly habilitated—individual, with all the opportunities and challenges that this entails. While evaluating treatment success per se is not a goal of the book, it is my hope that the research presented here will spur further work on life in the community among released sexual offenders who have undergone this form of treatment, to explore if and how the lessons of habilitation introduced in prison make any sense to a released sexual offender in the community, and, yes, even to determine how meeting the challenges of everyday living as a habilitated individual contributes to public safety. But first we need to understand what the experience of habilitation is like for incarcerated sexual offenders.

TRUTH DISCOURSE AND THE STRUGGLE BETWEEN NARRATIVE AND PARADIGMATIC MODES

Narrative theory has emerged over the last two decades as a major framework in psychological and medical anthropology, and the work of Jerome Bruner remains central to much of this scholarship. For many anthropologists who have engaged with this "narrative turn" (or "turns"; see Garro and Mattingly 2000), Bruner's theorizing on narrative is often the jumping-off point and, frequently in combination with phenomenological or "meaning-centered" approaches, has led to some sophisticated analyses of illness and trauma experience (e.g., Becker 1997; Becker, Beyene, and Ken 2000; Foxen 2000; Garro 1992, 1994; Kirmayer 1996; Mattingly 1998a, 1998b; Waitzkin and Magana 1997; Waitzkin and Britt 1993).

According to Bruner (1986, 2002), narrative—stories about experiences—represents a fundamental and perhaps preferred mode of cognitive functioning and a means by which individuals order their experiences, construct reality, and communicate with others. Narrative gives meaning to experience, and through narrative the speaker discloses personal forms of thought and feeling. Narrative also allows the individual to construct order from the disorder and chaos that sometimes plague our daily lives (Viney and Bousfield 1991) and to come "to terms . . . with a problematic experience" (Garro and Mattingly 2000: 28; see also Jackson 2002). A good story typically revolves around a complicating factor, an element that confounds the plot but is theoretically resolvable. In Bruner's terms, then, narrative is "about the violations of the shared ordinary, and about how such violations are resolved" (J. Bruner 2008: 36). Through narrative, these "deviations from shared ordinariness" are rendered "both conventional and manageable" (35).

We can think of criminal behavior as one kind of deviation from or violation of "shared ordinariness"—be it a dominant moral order or more specifically codified laws—that calls out for resolution. Prison programs can be seen as an attempt to enhance, educate about, or reconfirm for the offender the particular "shared ordinariness" of that dominant moral order regarding appropriate behavior, one that is underwritten by law and the system of justice and has been enacted to put him in jail. Narrative seeks resolution of such deviations by providing an avenue for the meaning of personal experience to emerge and more importantly allows the narrator to communicate that meaning in a more or less deliberate fashion. While for sexual offenders their crimes and subsequent incarceration constitute rather significant "problematic" experiences that call out for narrative rendering, within the CBT theory of forensic rehabilitation such renderings are the source of much conflict. This is because the therapeutic process in prison is dominated by truth discourse and paradigmatic-like thinking, narrative notwithstanding.

Anthropologists generally have paid little attention to the idea of a paradigmatic mode, so a few words of elaboration here are needed.[3] Bruner, in a relatively brief discussion in his groundbreaking book *Actual Minds, Possible Worlds* (1986), outlines his theory of the paradigmatic mode largely as a means to move his discussion of narrative forward. The paradigmatic mode, according to Bruner, "attempts to fulfill the ideal of a formal, mathematical system of description and explanation. It employs categorization or conceptualization and the operations by which categories are established, instantiated, idealized, and related one to the other to form a system" (12). Further, the paradigmatic "deals in general causes, and in their establishment, and makes use of procedures to assure *verifiable reference and to test for empirical truth*" (13; emphasis added). He writes:

> Each of the ways of knowing [narrative and paradigmatic], moreover, has operating principles of its own and its own criteria of well-formedness.

They differ radically in their procedures for verification. A good story and a well-formed argument [the latter being Bruner's comparable example of the paradigmatic mode] are different natural kinds. Both can be used as means for convincing another. Yet what they convince *of* is fundamentally different: arguments convince one of their truth, stories of their lifelikeness. The one verifies by eventual appeal to procedures for establishing formal and empirical proof. The other establishes not truth but verisimilitude. . . . A story (allegedly true or allegedly fictional) is judged for its goodness as a story by criteria that are of a different kind from those used to judge a logical argument as adequate or correct. (11, 12)

Several questions begin to emerge upon a review of Bruner's ideas. If narrative and paradigmatic modes are "complementary" yet "irreducible to one another," as Bruner (11) maintains, what happens if the criteria for judging a story and that for a "logical argument" conflate in such a way that the "correctness" of the narrative is centrally in play? What happens if one mode moves beyond simply being a "means for convincing" to the extent that it acts to shape the other and then evaluates the merits of the reshaped form? More specifically, what happens when narrative must play by paradigmatic rules and convince of its "truth"?

Of particular relevance to the narrative experience of Sam and the other inmates is Bruner's description of paradigmatic language as "regulated by requirements of consistency and noncontradiction" (13), two attributes rigidly required and policed throughout forensic treatment as inmates present their life stories. As I shall demonstrate, the CBT theory of sexual offender treatment is constructed upon this paradigmatic mode, and the inmates struggle with it because, as Bruner iterates, it aspires to increasing levels of abstraction and "in the end disclaims in principle any explanatory value at all where the particular is concerned" (13). In other words, the goal of treatment is the dismantling of subjective narrative meaning and its replacement, to varying degrees of success, by a CBT-compatible narrative that is, presumably, therapeutically "meaningful" for all precisely because it no longer values "the particular." This, of course, is not unique to CBT or forensic treatment, as much "modernist" therapeutics involves "the slow but inevitable replacement of the client's story with the therapist's," according to Gergen and Kaye (1992: 169). Nor is the authority of the treatment team to determine "truth" unique, as this is common in other kinds of therapeutic programs as well (Lester 2007), although critics suggest that the employment of "privilege and brute force" to settle "mnemonic disputes" is incompatible with current understandings of memory, as I shall discuss later (Wertsch 2011: 27).

In such a therapeutic context, argue Gergen and Kaye (1992: 169), "The client's story does not remain a free-standing reflection of truth, but rather, as questions are asked and answered, descriptions and explanations are reframed, and affirmation and doubt are disseminated by the therapist, the client's narrative is either destroyed or incorporated—but in any case replaced—by the professional's account." The "professional's account" represents a kind of scientific narrative, a "structured stor[y] of how things come to be as they are," that owes allegiance to the particular model of therapy in which the practitioner has trained or is implementing, in this case CBT. Such training and the knowledge underpinning it are avowedly "scientific," and therapists are trained to be either "scientist-practitioners" or technicians employing scientifically validated theories and techniques from which their authority to assess emanates. It should not be surprising that the power of science is brought to bear on the evaluation of narratives offered by patients, since, as Gergen and Kaye (1992: 169) write, "The trained professional enters the therapeutic arena with a well-developed narrative for which there is abundant support within the community of scientific peers." The inmates in my study are even provided with reviews of scientific research on sexual offending that bolster the authority of the treatment paradigm and its practitioners to evaluate and assess the inmates' lives as a whole as well as their treatment progress. So, while the idea that therapists should seek to develop "shared narratives" with their patients carries much appeal (Kirmayer 2000; Mattingly 1994), at least in my research it seems that the power imbalance favors the therapeutic approach critically described by Gergen and Kaye, an approach that is fundamentally paradigmatic in orientation.

As I shall demonstrate in this book, then, much of the treatment experience for inmates involves how they choose to respond to challenges to their personal narrative. These challenges come from two sources. First is the positivist ethos of the judicial-correctional process (Wesson 1984–85), best encapsulated in the well-worn expression "the truth, the whole truth, and nothing but the truth," communicated by justice and correctional officials and enacted throughout the judicial process, from police interrogation through trial to forensic treatment. This ethos is manifested in the creation and maintenance of an "institutional memory" (Linde 1999) about the inmate, which is considered to be far more "accurate" than the inmate's own memory.

The second challenge to personal narrative is from CBT, a set of theoretical propositions and therapeutic techniques constructed on a platform of science-based empiricism with allegiance to "best practices" models, communicated by registered or licensed therapists, and enacted in the quotidian experience of treatment and, more broadly, life on the unit. Together, truth discourse and CBT form a more or less coherent, enacted therapeutic system. This system reflects the institutional mandate to emphasize and privilege the "truth" of criminal activity as determined and reinforced through forensic avenues, be they police and court reports, judicial pronouncements, or assessments by mental health, parole, and other correctional officials. This truth is in turn interpreted through the theoretical lens of CBT, in which both the "landscape of action" (or "story grammar") and the "landscape of consciousness" (or "what those involved in the action know, think, or feel, or do not know, think, or feel") come under scrutiny (J. Bruner 1986: 14).

This search for "truth" that is philosophically fundamental to our legal system casts a long shadow over all aspects of the individual perpetrator's life as an inmate and dogs him even upon release. The "facts" of this forensic "truth" provide the only acceptable building materials for narrative construction—the *fabula*, as narratologists would call it—setting the stage for a clash between narrative and paradigmatic modes that dominates the experience of treatment and establishes the grounds for continual contestation that is, in my view, unnecessarily disruptive to the broader therapeutic goals. In some ways Bruner's work anticipates this clash even if he does not directly address the possibility, as when he notes that, in everyday discourse "we have no compunction about calling stories true or false" (1991: 5). As Sam experienced, in this treatment program the inmates, who themselves act as cotherapists but lack training in CBT, become preoccupied with this idea of the truthfulness or falseness of narrative, scrutinizing for a "lack of consistency" and "noncontradiction."

As noted, Bruner's original work in narrative suggests an inherent complementarity between narrative and paradigmatic modes, and in more recent work (J. Bruner 2002: 105) he cautions that we not "isolate narrative and bare factuality from each other," using the example of patients' stories of illness versus the "facts" on the medical chart. I take this caution seriously and suggest that the paradigmatic and narrative modes engage each other rather substantially in some contexts. But I also suggest that they are potentially more conflictual than complementary. Certainly it is necessary to reject any sense that the paradigmatic and narrative modes are simply "incommensurable," as Bruner suggests, if we are also willing to accept that legal cases (J. Bruner 2002), medical records (Mattingly 2008), and science texts more broadly (E. Bruner 1986; Gergen and Gergen 1986) can be seen as having narrative dimensions and if the paradigmatic mode can be employed to analyze narrative, and narrative to analyze the paradigmatic (Polkinghorne 1995). It should not be surprising to find that the two modes influence and contaminate each other.

I argue that the dominance of the paradigmatic mode in the form of a therapeutic model has the effect of laundering subjective meaning and explanatory value from inmate narratives, which are generally seen as problematic. Therapeutic success within this model hinges on the replacement of these narratives with ones that are more therapeutically valid. But I will demonstrate that for many inmates the paradigmatic therapeutic model employed slowly transforms inmate narratives from mechanisms for the generation of self-meaning to measures of therapeutic compliance and effectiveness. Many inmates become preoccupied first with resisting the imposition of this therapeutic narrative and then with learning it for the purpose of obtaining a successful evaluation in the treatment program. The very character of the narrative mode is challenged here: when Jerome Bruner (1990: 53–54) writes that "to make a story good, it would seem, you must make it somewhat uncertain, somehow open to variant readings, rather subject to the vagaries of intentional states, undetermined," he is describing a mode of communication that can negatively affect a sexual offender's experience of treatment, leading to failure in the program, sometimes expulsion and return to the home penitentiary, and quite possibly denial of parole. "Narrative mind reading," as Mattingly (2008: 137) defines it—"that practical capability of inferring (rightly or wrongly) the motives that precipitate and underlie the actions of another"—opens the door to such a negative experience for inmates, as they are invited to actively explore each other's motives and intentional states, and not always for purposes of assisting the narrator, as Sam discovered.

So narrative and paradigmatic modes do not simply "live side by side," as Jerome Bruner suggests (1986: 43; see also J. Bruner 2002), in a parallel but separate existence; rather, they engage and influence each other in contexts frequently rife with power relations. Bruner tends not to consider how the existence of paradigmatic knowledge—or more precisely the idea of the paradigmatic—especially bolstered by formal and informal structures of power, affects the shape and rendering of narrative (J. Bruner 2002) (and I would suggest the reverse is also true). For all his contributions to narrative theory, and his assertion that " to ignore one at the expense of the other inevitably fail[s] to capture the rich diversity of thought" (1986: 11), Bruner himself seems to truncate his discussion of the relationship of the two modes in favor of advancing his narrative theory, which of course he does superbly. In his discussion of both the inappropriateness of applying Karl Popper's criterion of falsifiability to the believability of stories and of narrative's central concern with "the vicissitudes of human intentions" (J. Bruner 1986: 16), however, Bruner does provide some direction for my analysis here. While the application to stories of a criterion similar to that of falsifiability—that a story could be shown "false"—is indeed an example of "misplaced verification" (14), I will demonstrate that this is precisely what happens in the treatment program. The "clear and definite reference and literal sense" (22) characteristic of the paradigmatic mode comes to be the standard by which the inherent ambiguity and subjectivity of narrative are judged.

Part of the problem, I shall show, is that the *fabula* of a story, its elemental materials or details and the sequence in which they "really" happened, comes to take on a heightened significance in the validation of the story because of the dominant, even hegemonic therapeutic model bolstered by the overt power structures that represent the penitentiary, including the authority of the "disciplines" (such as psychology and psychiatry) to render judgment on treatment effectiveness (Foucault 1979; Rose 1998). Attention to the "truthfulness" of these details includes consideration of both "fact" and sequence—or the "historical truth," as Donald Spence (1982a) labels it—that are empirically open to validation. This is a forensic preoccupation that begins the second an individual is apprehended by police. Indeed, the form of therapeutic intervention that inmates undergo in this treatment program invites a kind of scrutiny that is akin to what they went through in their court cases. In this nascent process forensic officials emerge and are entrenched as "authorized primary recipient[s]" and "authorized overhearers of narratives" (Ochs and Capps 1996: 35); they are positioned to judge the compatibility of inmate narratives with the "historical truth." Such a focus on the details detracts from the broader story as told, how the events are represented—the *sujet* as narratologists define it—that communicates the meaning of the story for the teller, its "narrative truth" (Spence 1982a). Narrative truth is dependent not upon fact checking but rather, as both Spence (1982a) and Jerome Bruner (1986) suggest, on its "goodness" as a story, one that convinces and, in so doing, characteristically plays with the "facts." Perfect correspondence with past events is not essential to narrative truth. Hence, while with historical truth we are engaged in the process of reconstruction, in which memory is crucial, narrative truth involves a process of construction, in which memory per se carries less importance than the broader aesthetic value of the story. The appeal to empiricism found in the idea of reconstruction reflects that found in the paradigmatic mode, and, as I noted above, Bruner (1986: 11) argues persuasively that the procedures for verification within the narrative and paradigmatic modes should, typically, "differ radically."

The therapeutic approach employed by the treatment unit that is the subject of this research, and much psychological and psychiatric treatment more generally, is ultimately all about "fixing" the individual's story, and hence the "self," through what Rose (1998: 17) refers to as "therapies of normality," that is, "the pedagogies of self-fulfillment disseminated through the mass media" that serve to shape the form and content of one individual's aims and desires. This kind of disciplining of the self-psyche appeals to the broader authority of the "psy" disciplines, as Bruner (2002: 11; see also Howard 1991; Kirmayer 2000) seems to suggest when he elaborates, "Patients must be helped to tell the *right* kinds of stories in order to get well" (emphasis added). It is the therapist's job to assess that these emergent stories are adequate, that the details are compatible with the empirically verified record, and that the meaning of the stories is compatible with the CBT therapeutic paradigm. Eventually, these "right kind of stories" may come to emulate the moralizing "institutionalized master storylines . . . that define world views of criminality, sanity, and sexuality" (Ochs and Capps 1996: 33), and as they do the inmate may be seen to be making progress. But resistance to these master storylines is inherent in the process and confounds treatment. And forensic treatment is not simply about the patient developing insight or self-actualization; it is about the patient being transformed into the "right" kind of citizen, one that is both a moral being (i.e., according to community ideal standards) capable of self-governance (conducting himself according to these standards with minimal or no supervision) (Foucault 1988; Rose 1998) and safe for the community.[4] I will show in this book that these two goals, while obviously related, are hardly equal at the end of the day, since measures of therapeutic "success" focus almost entirely on the matter of community safety.

So my aim here is to interject into the scholarly conversation the need to critically explore the interrelatedness of the narrative and paradigmatic modes within the contexts of power and to urge that this be more directly addressed in our research on narrative, because everyday life—including narrative expression—is lived within an authority-emboldened paradigmatic as well as narrative context. The paradigmatic mode—think "science" as an example—presents as a powerful, even hegemonic influence on our thoughts and behavior. It intrudes on narrative, just as narrative intrudes on the paradigmatic. The power accorded the paradigmatic in our society ensures that narrative in particular must necessarily engage with it, even if only in passive assertions by narrators that the stories they relate "really happened." Here I challenge all readers to watch for this next time you tell a story about a shared event; notice how interlocutors will challenge the details (e.g., the day of the week when the event took place, its location, who else was there, who said what), in so doing upsetting the narrative flow. Note how an error in the details can be fatal and terminate the entire narrative, as evidence of its overall lack of veracity, its "believability." Now consider how the meaning of the narrative itself can be forced into a conceptual framework emanating from the paradigmatic mode, where the assumption that a narrator will lie or exclude details is de rigueur and where meaning becomes subjected to "falsifiability" according to some externally generated standard. Imagine that you can be directed to tell and retell "your" stories of personal experience until you get them "right." Think of a context in which the audience is hardly passive or not there to be entertained but is rather entreated to be active in your story, to challenge and dispute, to poke at the details, to trip you up, to relish the premise of narratives' falsifiability. Now consider that there is an arbiter, a judge, another individual or, more broadly, a paradigm, positioned to render a verdict as to the acceptability of your story, not so much its verisimilitude anymore as its veracity along with its personal meaning, and to punish you when you get it "wrong," to literally imprison you. This is not a world of scholarly engagement and theorizing about narrative; this is narrative in context, a therapeutic pragmatic, in a real-world situation, with all its sloppiness and contradictions, all its nastiness. Welcome to Sam's Autobiography. This is therapeutic intervention, and this is life in the Hound Pound.

OUTLINE OF THE BOOK

This book, then, invokes narrative in several ways. I present the story of the experience of sexual offender treatment from the perspective of my participants, in a somewhat linear fashion from arrival at the treatment center to the end of their program and anticipation over the future. The book is also about how the inmates engage with narrative as a central element of their treatment programs. More obliquely, this book is even about the story of my experience studying their experience.

The structure of this ethnography is a little unorthodox, as I adopt a somewhat unusual approach in an effort to provide readers with a more global feel for the treatment program as experienced by the inmates. This is because so many things happen during the day, inside and outside the program, that interconnect and affect the experience of treatment for the inmate. What is happening in one group session is affected by what is happening in others; what happens in the sessions is affected by what happens outside them. The inmates, on any given day, may be involved in two or three separate kinds of programs, and the flow from one to another is not always smooth. They work in two separate cohorts as well, and incidents in one cohort spill over to affect the other. Sometimes the unit is abuzz with activity; other times nothing much seems to be happening.

In chapter 2 I explore the nature of this therapeutic prison within the context of power relations that affect both the inmates' experience of treatment and my own ability to undertake this research. I describe in greater detail the research process. Here I also introduce brief italicized vignettes, several per substantive chapter, to touch upon other elements of inmate experience that are salient. Derived from either field notes or interviews, the placement of these might sometimes seem out of sync with the surrounding chapter content. This jaggedness is intentional, and at times readers should feel that they are "out of place" in the otherwise orderly unfolding of the text. Abrupt, often unannounced changes and developments are common in the program, and this is an element of the inmates' experience. The program does not typically unfold in a seamless, orderly way, so this ethnography should not either. And being "out of place" is, in the end, the lot of the sexual offender in our communities, a point I will develop in chapter 8.

In chapter 3 I look at the issue of the nature of the "problems" for which the inmates are being treated and present a more detailed description of the Cognitive Behavioral Therapy paradigm. Chapter 4 looks at the early days of inmates on the treatment unit and the manner in which a moral, therapeutic community forms despite the challenges of the "con code."

The following three chapters reflect the three main components of the program of interest—chapter 5, on the Autobiography; chapter 6, on the Crime Cycle; and chapter 7, on the Relapse Prevention Plan. These chapters are bookended and interrupted by moral habilitation "chapterettes," detailing some of the many other programs the inmates are taking at roughly the same time that, I argue, are designed to further the development of their moral character. These little chapters, in combination with the vignettes mentioned previously, challenge the seamlessness of much ethnographic writing. Together, I hope these features will provide at least some sense of the many and varied things that are going on in this very closed community and will lessen the necessary "flattening out of experience" (Throop 2010: 241) that ensues when the complexities of lives being lived are reduced to textual presentation.

Chapter 8 examines prospective narratives, as the inmates look into their futures as sexual offenders and explore anticipated experiences both in their home penitentiaries and in the community. The case of one of my participants who was released subsequent to my research is presented, allowing us a glimpse into the kind of civil society reaction that awaits many released sexual offenders. This chapter also raises the question of the appropriateness and utility of the idealized process of moral habilitation for life in a very unruly community context.

In chapter 9 I return to some of the central themes and arguments of this book and make the case for an anthropology of therapeutic intervention that explores the experience of treatment in nonvoluntary contexts, especially where the issue of the designated beneficiary is complex, as a means to further advance our understanding of the process of healing.

The book concludes with a brief epilogue about the study participants and responds to a question many readers will have by this point, "where are they now?"

CHAPTER 2

Goin' Down with the "Hounds"

"This ain't a hospital," declares Harvey. "Hospitals are cleaner, hospitals have got more nurses and they don't have guards." But it is also not a prison in the Hollywood, Alcatraz sense, although that style still exists in North America. You know the picture: rows of barred cells rising in tiers from a central, internal courtyard, allowing for panoptic surveillance by heavily armed guards; guard towers in turn rising above high, brick prison walls overlooking exercise yards, topped by razor wire. It's not quite like that here. Except for the razor wire.

The single-story, low-slung compound that is this therapeutic prison seems to hug the landscape around it. It gives a first impression of being a set of typically nondescript government buildings, their purpose unclear. One cannot easily see the compound in its totality, how it extends far back from the main entranceway, which itself is set well back from the road. Only by moving in more closely does one notice the thick wire mesh hung between heavy iron posts. Two rows of high fencing, in fact and, yes, all topped by vicious-looking razor wire.

A green four-wheel-drive pickup truck drives slowly by. The two occupants inside look at me, expressionless, then turn their eyes back to the fence. The truck continues on its circular journey around the perimeter. As I approach the compound's entrance, a small building next to the gate, another pair of eyes appear, shrouded behind translucent, tinted glass. Reaching the first steel door, I casually pull open my coat to reveal the photo identification tag clipped to my shirt pocket, trying to project an air of nonthreatening authority, that of an individual with permission. *Buzz-click*. The pulse of electricity is followed by the sound of a metal latch giving way. I pull on the door handle and walk inside. The guard's eyes are clearer now. Without speaking, I present my identification badge for inspection and sign in. "Wallets and cell phones to lock up?" the guard asks. I do as directed, although the idea of leaving my personal identification behind and replacing it with an institutional ID always makes me uncomfortable. The guard turns his head as if to point. Dutifully, I now move to the x-ray machine and place my briefcase on the belt. I walk through the metal detector—no alarm sounds—and I reclaim my bag.

I stand at the heavy metal door for several minutes as the guard seemingly ignores my silent but obvious desire to continue my journey. Only one access point can be open at a time, I have been told; somewhere in this vast complex full of locked doors, another one must be at that moment ajar. So I wait. *Buzz-click*. I yank the door open. Twenty steps later, another barrier, this time the high steel mesh fence with a barred gate. I press the button. I wait. *Buzz-clang,* the sound of strong metal on metal. The heavy gate pops open ever so slightly; with some effort I swing it wider and step through. I pull it behind me. *CLANG!* A short outside walk now across the front of the compound, a pleasant respite from a seemingly endless set of locks. The sound of children's voices is startling in this environment. I can see two playing off to my right, in the low fenced suburban-looking yard of one of the family duplex units, where deserving inmates can earn time with their families.

The next door opens with ease; no need to request entry. This is the entranceway to both the front office area and the inmate units. But for me this unlocked door leads nowhere really, except to more locked doors. So the door following is the same old . . . *buzz-click*. This time, after I press the button on the wall by the door, I notice the small red light flashing, an indication that I am being watched by another set of eyes, these disembodied and unseen, from an office somewhere in the building that is off limits to me. This would be the security command center, where corrections officers surveil their realm on banks of monitors. I turn, look up at the ceiling camera behind me, and offer my face for silent scrutiny. *Buzz-click*. In I go, working my way down the hallway. I could go right or left, it does not matter here. The central courtyard, completely encircled by the building, stands quiet. It always seems like a lush space to me, an oasis of sorts, with grass, picnic tables and benches, some basketball hoops. A walkway rings this compound.

There is no one out yet today; at other times inmates can be seen walking and jogging. It is early morning, and everyone is still locked on their units. The two iron gates I encounter in the hallway are open to allow free passage; sometimes these too are locked, as they are when I come in on weekends.

The next door I arrive at today is like the last. Press the button, watch the light, smile at the camera. *Buzz-click.* I walk down several steps, press yet another button, and smile through the tinted glass and at the inhabitants inside the room. There are voices to my left and my right, coming from the day rooms or lounges, inmates chatting as they finish breakfast. A psychiatric nurse rises from her chair and walks over. Rotating the handle to open the door, she turns away without uttering a word. The other nurses, in their white clinical coats, are huddled in a back corner, presumably meeting about a "patient." A corrections officer—"guard" or "bull" in inmate parlance—sits at a computer. Wearing a blue short-sleeve shirt, with no gun in sight, he is positioned at the apex of the "Bubble" so that he can see in all directions. He is streaming video on his computer monitor, observing movement in some corner of the unit. He too seems to ignore me. Indeed, the nurses and the officer seem oblivious to each other, and I wonder if they even view themselves as part of the same team. I reach in a drawer, pull out a security alert device, and phone Security to report my name, the unit I am on, and the device number. As with the employees, my presence in the prison and my exact location are to be known at all times, and if I find myself in a problematic situation I am to press the button and, presumably, receive assistance within minutes. I am not fond of this device and in my previous prison research often managed to avoid using one. The rule is more rigid now, so I clip the device to my belt, careful not to press the red button, and then adjust my photo ID tag so that it remains visible. Ready for a day of research, I exit the Bubble without having said a word to any of its inhabitants. "Good morning, Jim," says a passing inmate.

This story represents a typical morning arrival at my place of research. I have worked in many prisons in Canada over the years, and this one is, by design, quite unlike those other maximum- and medium-security institutions that are designed to contain inmates and the minimum-security institutions that are designed to facilitate reintegration into the community. I am in a prison without question. But I am also in a psychiatric hospital, a center offering mental health services, forensic psychiatric evaluation, and treatment to federal-level offenders and those charged with serious crimes where mental health issues are suspected. It is the dynamic interplay and tension between these two functions—custody and caring, in some contemporary discourse—that creates the unique circumstance both for my research and for the experience of the inmates.

Canada has several of these therapeutic prisons, located in various regions of the country. Typically there are a number of distinct treatment and custodial units, including units for those with severe mental disabilities and lower cognitive functioning and for those with particularly chronic aggressive or violent behavior. Each unit has its own distinct character, reflective of the nature of the inmates housed there and their relative needs for assessment, treatment, and protection. The treatment unit where I work—hereafter simply "the unit"—is dedicated to treating sexual offenders. The inmate residents here are largely protected from the nonsexual offenders housed on other units, but at times during the day they can emerge from this protective lair to join the others for various leisure activities. Some choose not to leave the unit at all during these times, fearful of being "outed" as sexual offenders and harassed.

The unit, to quote one inmate, is "like your 'rec' [recreation] room, only with us in it." It consists of two large and mostly identical and windowless common day rooms that serve multiple functions: group treatment sessions are held here, but these areas also serve as lounges for watching television or playing games and otherwise socializing, and as eating areas. A variety of single chairs and couches generally orient toward the unit television, but these can be moved for the therapy sessions. The unit also has a kitchen with a fridge, stove, and microwave—the inmates have some independent access to food and corresponding responsibilities to maintain the facility—and an open area housing several computers. There are several interview rooms as well, glass-walled spaces facing the Bubble where private therapy sessions and group meetings with or among inmates can be held and where I do all of my interviewing. Any inmate engaged in a session in one of these interview rooms is in plain view of any others who walk by; accordingly, the inmate often maintains an ever-vigilant lookout to see just who is looking in.

Each day room is surrounded by sixteen single-person cells, or "houses," as the men refer to them. The cells are small, self-contained living units with stainless steel sinks and toilets (no seats; the "seat" is molded as part of the toilet so it cannot be used as a weapon), a narrow single bed with a thin mattress and, it seems to me, an even thinner blanket, some shelves, a desk and chair, and a small window on the outside wall that allows a fragment of daylight to intrude. Many men have a variety of electronic entertainment systems that they have purchased with their own, prison-generated funds from employment. Televisions and stereos are quite common, and during off-hours across the day units can be heard the soft cacophony of voices and music.

House doors are solid metal, with small glass windows and secured slots for placement of food trays when inmates are being confined and for handcuffing if need be (the inmate puts his hands through the slot to be handcuffed before the door is unlocked). Inmates are not allowed to cover their interior windows from the inside except for a few minutes while using the toilet or changing, or when they have declared a "time out" to cool down from some distressing event. These windows provide some degree of privacy, and one can only see in when standing right at the door, something the staff will do during "count" and for a variety of other reasons when inmate behavior requires observation. There are periods during the day, such as the twice-daily "counts," when inmates must return to their houses to be locked up. They are also locked up at night, but otherwise during the day they are more or less free to move about the day rooms as long as they do not disturb any treatment sessions. With permission they may also leave the unit altogether to go to the library, school, or gymnasium or to engage in outdoor recreational activities and daily walks in the inner courtyard.

The two day rooms are joined like wings but can be locked up independently if need be. The rooms are centered by the Bubble, a combined nursing and security station. The Bubble is constructed according to contemporary panoptic principles. Inmates must pass by it to access the opposite day room, the computers, the lunch room, the laundry, the showers, and the stairs leading to the locked door that segregates the sexual offenders unit from the rest of the institution. It is from the Bubble that all actions of the inmates in all public areas of the unit can be readily observed, directly or through the use of mirrors. The corrections officer's computer can also tell him the status of an inmate's cell door, if it is locked or unlocked; inmates can lock their own cells, but this can be overridden by the officer, who also can lock and unlock them remotely. The Bubble itself is soundproof, but the translucent, darkened glass still allows inmates to see into it. They can see staff having meetings, and they can see corrections officers playing games on their computers. The only exceptions to this translucency are a small office in the back and the staff washroom.

So, while the inmates are being observed, they can also observe the staff. This often leads to a great deal of discussion among the men when they see staff members huddled together, and inmates freely speculate what, or who, is being discussed. Treatment staff meetings are perhaps the most intriguing. These are usually held at three o'clock each day, following the afternoon group treatment session, and involve discussions about various inmates. Inmate files are visible and much writing ensues. The men often insist that they can tell who is being discussed because a staff member will occasionally turn and look out toward that person. A certain degree of paranoia seems to develop, and quite a stir can erupt over the matter as the inmates debate this issue of who is the subject. One inmate once told me that he was sitting in a very specific seat in the day room because he believed that it was the only one staff could not see clearly, and he was tired of being watched and discussed.

There are three access points to the Bubble for inmates. The first is through the cracks around the entrance door, into which they often insert request forms and other notes. These small slips of paper hang precariously between door and jamb, falling to the floor when someone opens the door, and occasionally falling regardless, to lie at the foot of the door. The second access point is the two "meds" windows, long and narrow, that open into each day lounge. The men are responsible for obtaining their own medications by coming up to one of these windows at the appropriate times and knocking on it. There is barely enough room for a hand to reach out from inside, with a small cup holding pills or liquid medicine, which must be consumed on the spot under the watchful eye of a staff member. Some obtain doses of prescription medicines for psychoses or depression, but more frequently over-the-counter pain and cold medicines are dispensed. The meds window is also used by staff members to summon an inmate who is in the day room by calling out rather than emerging through the door of the Bubble. The men are attentive to this and will turn to listen in an attempt to determine who is being called and why. Occasionally an inmate will go to the window or door and knock with a request, and this tactic is sometimes successful. But this is not, strictly speaking, an appropriate means to make contact for nonurgent matters, and staff will sometimes complain about being bothered too much, especially if it is by the same individual over and over. Inmates are never to enter the Bubble, and such an attempt would be met with force.

There was a "lockdown" today before the afternoon session got started. The security alarm rang, and the corrections officer hollered, "Lockdown" out the door of the Bubble. Somewhere in this complex institution there has been a threat to security. We will never know the details for sure, but rumors will likely soon fly. None of us—me included—can move off the unit. No phone calls in or out. No idea how long the situation will last. I am literally locked in with the inmates. During these times I sense in small measure what it must be like to be them, to lack the ability to move about at will, speak with whom I wish, and go home when I want. For the moment, I am under the complete control of the corrections officers.

Field notes

CARCERAL-THERAPEUTIC TENSIONS

The conjoining of the prison and the psychiatric hospital or asylum has an interesting history in the modern era, and the tension between custodial and rehabilitative or, more properly, therapeutic or habilitative agendas of the criminal justice system endures (Rhodes 2000).[1] The modern prison, following Foucault (1979), has been built upon a platform of disciplinary punishment, in which various professionals such as judges, parole boards, psychologists, and psychiatrists play a significant and increasing role in determining the fitness of the accused/criminal to remain in, or rejoin, society.[2] The mental health aspect of criminality, whether addiction issues related to the commission of the crime or more substantive clinical conditions that affect issues of reason and perceptions of reality, has loomed large in debates over increasing incarceration rates, particularly in an era of declining institutional and community-based options for the mentally ill. The security or custodial mandate in therapeutic prisons is to maintain control of the individual inmate, thereby protecting other inmates, staff members, and, more emphatically, the community. This stands in tension with the "care" mandate of treatment staff, and the two mandates do not coexist easily (Genders and Player 1995). Added into the mix are the inmates themselves, who can be seen to engage in both resistance and self-regulatory practices that Rose (1998: 77) has referred to as "reflexive hermeneutics."

As I noted in chapter 1, "power" in this research must necessarily be conceived of as multifaceted and beyond the simple domain of singular social or political entities, and in this sense the role of the inmates in the construction, maintenance, and utilization of power is every bit as dynamic as that of the professionals. Resistance to power structures is certainly evident, but such resistance is not just unidirectional toward the jailers and involves a variety of different regulatory regimes. As I shall argue here, while inmates do not occupy a "professional" class per se, the treatment paradigm with which they are engaged allows, even encourages, them to occupy a kind of intervener class in which they are imbued with the quasi-authority to sanction, disrupt, and refute the assessment of institutional or public "fitness" of individual inmates. That inmates are the best judge of each other's psyches and motives is a core element of the therapeutic paradigm; as one inmate explained it to me, "You can't bullshit a bullshitter." As we shall see, the inmates live within a web of self-generated power relations as part of their maintenance of a "moral community" (to be discussed further in chapter 4). Further, the inmates join with the staff to function as an integrated mechanism of surveillance. So, as Jefferson (2003: 67) notes, prison staff "do not have a monopoly on power" in the therapeutic prison, and like the inmates they are "caught up in power relations" that see them form therapeutic and carceral alliances with their charges.

Such a complex situation betrays the ongoing tensions between the custodial and treatment mandates that pervade the institution where this research was undertaken and affect the daily work and experiences of all, including me. This tension is most evident in ongoing discussions over the status of the inmates themselves. To create an alternative environment that would facilitate the therapeutic mandate, most inmates in this psychiatric facility—and all on the sexual offenders unit—are officially referred to as "patients." Over the course of my research I found the juxtaposition of such therapeutic rhetoric with obvious signs and symbols of the carceral mandate puzzling and sometimes ludicrous. The inmates themselves tended to share my confusion.

"My primary [nurse] has said to me, 'This is a hospital and you guys are patients,'" Billy tells me in an interview one day. Billy, serving three years for a variety of offenses committed concurrently, including sexual assault, is a heavily muscled Aboriginal man with a baby face. He explains further. "I said, 'Well, as far as I'm concerned it's a jail and we're inmates. You guys have the keys to the door, you lock us in when you need to. You tell us when to go to bed, you tell us when to eat, you tell us when to go to programming.' I says, 'The moment you tell me what to do,' you know, 'and take away my freedom, that's jail. Don't sugarcoat it,'" he continues, relating as if talking to a therapist, "'and don't tell me just because you wear a white smock . . . and you say you're a facilitator. But you're actually also an authority figure here as well.' I say, 'I can see why you guys say it's a hospital because you're trying to make people more relaxed, to be more forthcoming with themselves and stuff like that, it's understandable. But to me this place is a jail,' I says. 'You can take away the bars, you can put a door up, and whatever. You could design it any way to make it look like a hospital and whatever. But it's still a jail.'"

This sentiment is shared by many inmates. Jerry explains to me that "I feel like both [an inmate and a patient] really because like, technically, I am in a psychiatric center that is run like a hospital so, 'patient.' But that's to the treatment staff, right? To them," he adds, gesturing toward the officer in the Bubble, "I'm just an inmate."

I would not frame this issue as an either/or one. Rather, my research demonstrates clearly that the two statuses, patient and inmate, are fluid and are contextually invoked and manipulated by everyone on the inside in a flexible manner. The inmates become adept as well in playing off the custody and treatment mandates of the institution to seek an advantage, an example of what Goffman (1961) referred to as "secondary adjustments." Self-identity within the institution vis-à-vis the institution, for the inmates, is not fixed or unidimensional. "I feel like a patient," explains Justin, serving his second sentence for sexual assault on a young adult female, "although I know I'm a federal inmate."

Even though they are officially referred to as "patients," then, I have chosen to refer to my research participants as "inmates" in this book because my research suggests that the custody function of the institution, and by extension the authorial regime of the treatment program, remains paramount. This may be controversial to some in the correctional system, no doubt, and especially those engaged directly in treatment programs. My goal is not to subvert their intentions. But the inmates are clearly under the control of the corrections officers (logically, of course, because this *is* a prison) as well as the therapeutic staff, and although all the inmates have "volunteered" to come to the institution for advanced treatment and can quit if they wish, they are well aware that success in the program has an important impact on parole hearings and judicial pronouncements of their fitness to return to society; even those who are some distance from being allowed out hope to achieve a change in their security status and possible relocation to a more favorable, less strict prison environment. This represents a form of therapeutic intervention that works in tandem with disciplinary punishment.

Indeed, over much of the eight or so months that they are on the unit, the inmates struggle with the "patient" identity and have a difficult time relinquishing the "con" attitude of the penitentiary in order to engage therapeutically (Cordilia 1983). Many are not successful in this and are expelled for inappropriate or "treatment-interfering" behavior, such as "muscling" or intimidating other inmates. Others are only partially able or willing to engage with the "patient" identity, turning it on during formal treatment sessions but, behind the scenes, engaging in the interpersonal power relations that are central to everyday life in prisons. One of the most challenging tasks of the treatment team is to help inmates transition from "inmate" to "patient" so that they can be open to the demands and approaches of the treatment program. But when they do "buy in" to the treatment paradigm and participate in the therapeutic work—for instance, when they employ narrative to tell their stories and contextually position their lives—they open themselves up for a critical reinterpretation of those lives. Central to this reinterpretation is the paramount role that official records and judicial or clinical pronouncements play, these being the stuff of the custodial or, in Foucault's terms, disciplinary mandate. Buying in to the treatment paradigm, for many, becomes an instrumental means to a particular end, and their genuineness in this process is, as well, subject to professional evaluation.

One might think that successful treatment of offenders would be difficult to achieve in such a prison environment, especially one rife with fear and suspicion. Despite a pervasive therapeutic discourse of "trust," I came to learn that no one trusts anyone else in any way. In all field research situations, anthropologists must deal with the so-called gatekeepers, individuals—some official, many not—who seem to have influence over our access to others, the ability to permit our research to ensue and, by corollary, to have us removed from our research sites. In prison, the gatekeepers are literal. Corrections officers, as they must, control all physical movement and have complete control over every individual who ventures through that first gate. It may be a hospital, but matters of treatment are subservient to matters of security. While the institution also has a research agenda, and a corresponding university affiliation, research seems like a distant concern. It is not surprising that so little ethnographic research has been done in such institutions (Wacquant 2002; Waldram 2009a).

So it is called a hospital, but its paramount regulatory mode is still that of a prison; its mandate—what distinguishes it from other penitentiaries—is a concentrated focus on various forms of psychological and psychiatric assessment and treatment, but its modus operandi is layered, with the therapeutic existing alongside of and often subordinate to the custodial; the men are referred to as "patients" but are treated much like, and mostly see themselves as, "inmates." Such contradictions are not lost on them.

Jurisdictional issues clash in various ways. The security personnel are under pressure to ensure everyone's safety inside the institution. They are successful when there are no breaches of security, when none of the inmates is harmed or escapes to cause harm. They appear, at least to me and the inmates, to care little about rehabilitation. The forensic treatment personnel, in contrast, are under pressure to successfully treat the inmates so that they can potentially be released to the public. But, as I shall discuss, success in the treatment program does not necessarily mean that the inmate will be seen as less of a risk in the community, and this judgment is a separate process, a task that ultimately falls to members of various professions who administer and evaluate many of the tests used to predict the likelihood of violent behavior and recidivism once the released individual is among us and who may do so without ever meeting the inmate. In my limited interactions with them, the corrections officers tended to discount the possibilities of rehabilitation and often warned me not to be duped by the "bullshit" characteristic of such "experienced liars." Psychologists and other members of the treatment staff, in turn, are under great pressure to demonstrate the success of the program, to show that sexual offenders can be rehabilitated and made safe. There is much skepticism among the public about this, fueled by occasional reports in the media about high-risk sexual offenders released into the community, and in times of fiscal restraint any treatment approach must prove its effectiveness if it is to stave off budget cuts, even when that treatment is widely accepted by a strong professional discipline like psychology, is successfully employed in many other contexts, and is relatively cost-effective, as is the case with CBT. All take their responsibilities seriously, and the consequences of misjudging, for both security and therapeutic personnel, can be terrifying.

This afternoon at the end of the group session one of the therapists announces that the rocks in the fish tank will have to be removed because an inmate on another unit in the institution has used one as a weapon. The men are not happy about this because they feel that they are being punished for someone else's transgression on a different unit. A couple of men go over and reluctantly start to scoop out the stones while the

*conversation continues. A few men begin to detail all the items in the
lounge within eyesight that they could use to make weapons. The dictate
to remove the stones seems silly to them.*

Field notes

THE SYNOPTICS OF RESEARCH IN THE PANOPTICON

"You are being watched here more," explains Stan, comparing the unit
to the penitentiary. Stan is thirty and handsome, an Aboriginal man
raised in a non-Aboriginal adoptive home. He has several adult sexual
assaults on his record, but his current sentence involved a female juvenile in her early teens. "They make a report on you almost every hour
when they walk around." "How does that make you feel?" I ask. "You
feel like you are in a fish tank here," he replies, "because they watch
you. They watch your behaviors for the next eight months in here."
Stan pauses, but then adds, "So I watch them back."

The panoptic simulation of the modern prison is actually much less
rigid than one might think. In prison, everyone watches everyone else
in some way or another; a "compulsory visibility" (Foucault 1979:
187) works both, or better said, all, ways, as both panoptic and synoptic "mechanisms of power" are invoked. Not surprisingly, suspicion
is rife. The inmates are most certainly watched, including when they
are with me, and many were initially wary of my presence on the unit.
They watch me while I watch them. They watch me talk to security
and treatment staff. They watch me undertake individual interviews
in the "private" glassed interview rooms. They watch my behavior in
group therapy sessions. They watch me talking to other inmates. They
always seem to know what I am up to. They even find out when I have
traveled to other units to meet with inmates who have been removed
from the program, either temporarily for conduct or personal safety
reasons, or to await the corrections bus to transfer them back to their
home institutions as a result of the commission of fatal infractions. And
they are acutely aware that the corrections officers are "watching" me,
often joking about my security device and threatening to push my alarm
button "to see what would happen."

So one might think this is a context in which participant observation would definitely not work. Allen Feldman (1991: 12) would seem
to concur in this assessment, arguing that in a "culture of surveillance,
participant observation is . . . a form of complicity with those who
surveil." But a reserved response to my presence existed only in the early

stages of research, such as on the very first day I arrived on the unit and, under a careful gaze of several inmates, walked up to a small group and simply introduced myself. Observation was "resisted," as Rhodes (2001: 72–73) suggests, but only initially. Perseverance paid off, and my sheer exoticism as someone who did not fit any existing category of "outsider" proved irresistibly intriguing to many. I appreciate that a prison-hospital is not the same as the other institutions that perhaps Rhodes and Feldman had in mind here. But it is still a penitentiary. It houses inmates primarily with medium- and maximum-security designations, freshly plucked from other penitentiaries and dropped into this new and unfamiliar (to most) kind of prison. I have undertaken research in many penitentiaries and correctional facilities, and while this one definitely looks and feels different, as the inmates suggest it is still a penitentiary to them.

What I had proposed to do in this research was to undertake an ethnographic study of the sexual offenders unit in order to comprehend their experiences as federal inmates undergoing "high-intensity" treatment and as pariahs even within the twisted normality of prison culture. While I agree with Rhodes's (2001: 76) assessment that "fundamentally . . . no outsider/observer can 'participate' in the situation of the prisoner," I am not certain that this is unique to research in prisons; indeed, I think this is true of all ethnographic research, as we try to approximate the experience of another, something that cannot ever be fully accomplished. And I write this ethnography in part to dispel such stereotypes on the nature of the prison and its inhabitants, the existence of rigid thinking that characterizes this form of research in this kind of place with these kinds of people as invalid, essentially impossible, or so restrictively circumscribed that little meaningful data can be acquired. Such research does have complications, however.

Despite multiple levels of institutional approval, my research approach confused the corrections officials with whom I briefly interacted daily. The corrections officers, in charge of security, are made nervous by activities that fall outside the normal routine of the prison, and in my case they seemed concerned about my methods. They were particularly wary of what appeared to them to be an unnecessary amount of loitering in nonprogram contexts, that is, participant observation! They—and the psychiatric nurses as well—grasped that interviewing per se was "research," and they were not overly concerned by my use of semistructured, recorded interviewing and the long hours I often spent with an inmate in an interview room. But what on earth was I doing watching football on a Sunday with the inmates, or playing cards or baseball, or just chatting? What secrets were we sharing, what plans were we hatching? What lies was I being fed? Why, when I was not actively "researching," was I not somewhere else—in my research office, just like the psychologists, for instance, who would arrive on the unit with paper and pencils, whisk a patient away to the interview room, and then disappear themselves upon completion of the task?

Over a period of eighteen months I spent a great deal of time on the unit, much of it outside programming. More than one inmate jokingly suggested that I "take a room!"—a suggestion that of course I never took seriously. Virtually all aspects of group programming were open to me, but not sessions involving one or two therapists and a single inmate. All inmates who consented were available for interviewing. A few declined, though they often then proceeded to discuss the issues of my research "off the record" and tell me their life stories anyway. And even the most initially intransigent and often vocal critics of my research usually came around and offered to sit for interviews.

One day, for instance, during a group session, I was passed a note by Alfred, an early thirties Aboriginal male with a succession of sexual assaults on women in his past. "I will give you opportunity to interview me tomorrow after noon providing I do not have program," the note said. Alfred had always been flippant toward me, once saying that he was "90 percent certain" he would not consent to an interview. I had given up asking but remained cordial despite his attitude. Even today when he sneezed and I, sitting beside him, said, "Bless you," he responded sarcastically by asking, "Are you a priest? Only a priest can bless someone." As he related, during the break in the group session he asked himself, "Why get interviewed?" and he answered himself with "Why not?" It would help him to have to look into his life again, he determined, suggesting that the interview might contain some therapeutic benefit.

Throughout the research, several other inmates suggested that they had gained a great deal from the interviews, especially because of the supportive environment I provided to talk unchallenged about their lives, which contrasted sharply with the highly conflictual nature of the group sessions. As inmates came to know me and grow more comfortable with my presence, my research seemed to take on a kind of adjunct therapeutic role for many. While I resisted offering opinions or advice—and officially was not allowed to do so in group sessions—this was not always possible. It seemed rather rude too, and unethical, to expect inmates to privately share their stories with me and then, if they asked for my feedback, hide behind by role as a researcher to say nothing. Ethnography, we are often reminded, is enabled through the establishment and maintenance of personal relationships between the ethnographer and research participants, and while these are rarely fully reciprocal they nevertheless remain important to our craft (e.g., Gay y Blasco and Wardle 2007).

I was not required to obtain the permission of the inmates to be on the unit, but I did post signs explaining who I was and why I was there, and I made an effort to personally explain the research to all of them. However, I needed their permission to sit in on group therapy sessions and, of course, to interview them. Over the eighteen months I was able to join four cohorts of roughly fourteen to sixteen inmates each (this number varied, and there was attrition) as they started the eight-month program. Thirty-five of them—almost all those I asked—agreed to sit for recorded interviews, sometimes over multiple sessions, and at different times during their program. The first interviews, however, were always undertaken within a month of their arrival on the unit, before they had gotten very far in the treatment program. I did not use any particular criteria for selecting inmates for interviews and made an effort to ask as many as I could manage given my other commitments. In some cases I might have already heard an individual present his Autobiography before I had a chance to interview him, but for most my first knowledge of their life and crimes came in the interview. This was a surprise to many, who were accustomed to meeting with and being interviewed by officials who had already read their case files and, in the views of the inmates, had already formed opinions of the inmates and formulated the "correct" answers to the questions they would raise. So when I commenced our first sessions by saying, "I know nothing about you at all, other than that you are on this particular unit," I was opening a narrative door that they had rarely if ever encountered in their criminal careers.

My approach to interviewing was influenced by person-centered approaches (Levy and Hollan 1998) in that my interest was in learning how each individual experienced both life on the unit and the treatment program, rather than attempting to generate a more abstract rendering of the unit and the program itself as a type of village. However, the fact that I cannot present extensive biographical detail about individuals— for reasons of legality and confidentiality—renders this a somewhat different kind of person-centered approach. My opening question during the intake interviews set the tone and often led to an hour or more of continuous narration without a comment by me. "I would like you to tell me the story of your life, beginning wherever you feel you want, but ending up with us talking here today," I would begin. Then to clarify: "In other words, please tell me your life story in a way that you think would help me to understand why you are in this program today." I refer to this as a directed narrative technique, in which I provide a potential shape to the narrative rather than leaving it completely open-ended, as would be the case with a question such as "Tell me the story of your life." This encourages some degree of focus on the topic of interest—the experience of sexual offender treatment—while still leaving the narrative open and the narrator in control. It also engages, from the outset, the rather obvious fact that we both know the inmate has been convicted of a sexual offense and this in some way reflects the reason I am doing this work. While I never asked the inmates directly to relate their sexual crimes, most included them in their narratives.

In almost every case, this one question took up the entire first session of the "intake" interviews. Additional open-ended questions about more specific aspects of the program, often anticipatory as the inmate was typically at a fairly early stage, were the subject of a second and sometimes third session. "Exit" interviews, generally undertaken at the completion of an inmate's program and just prior to his departure from the institution, allowed the inmate to look back on specific aspects of the program as well as to look into the future, providing a prospective narrative. "I would like you to tell me how you think your life is going to unfold from this day forward," I would ask. As is typically the case with ethnographic interviewing, these open-ended questions provided a framework rather than a firm plan for collecting the data, and they typically opened access to other issues that I pursued vigorously on a case-by-case basis. Participant observation and casual conversation between intake and exit interviews allowed me to trace the experiences of the inmates as they moved through the program.

All interviews were tape-recorded. Somewhat surprisingly, the inmates seemed quite accepting of this. After each interview the tapes were removed from the institution and never returned. My university Research Ethics Board insisted that I offer each inmate an opportunity to review and approve his transcripts, despite my protests that to bring the transcripts into the prison would be risky, as they could easily be stolen or seized by security staff. Most inmates recognized this risk and waived their right to see the transcripts, and the few who did review them never asked for a single change. No individual associated with the institution, the police, the courts, and so on ever saw the transcripts. Thankfully, the various officials in the prison, including the treatment staff, honored our understanding that they not ask me to inform on the inmates.

All inmates that I interviewed gave me permission to access their offender management files, the sometimes massive paper and electronic dossiers that contained police, court, and prison reports as well as reports and evaluations from the unit staff. My security clearance actually gave me greater access to information on an offender than he had access to himself. While inmates can request to see what is in their files, and some do, the stripped-down versions that they typically receive are heavily censored for security reasons and are sometimes mere shadows of the actual files available to me. Most seemed resigned to the fact that, while their files invariably contained "lies" about them, there was nothing they could really do to correct these official documents. Never once did an inmate ask me to reveal what I had found in his files.

In each instance, I did not examine inmate files until near the completion of the inmate's program, and in the case of electronic files often not until sometime after he had left for his parent institution or, less frequently, the community. This was a deliberate decision on my part, and I saw no reason to "fact-check" or to engage with discrepancies between inmate reports and the file records (cf. Bourgeois and Schonberg 2009: 12). The "truth" of these files, it became clear, was interesting contested ground, an area in which the paradigmatic and narrative modes clashed, and hence was worthy of attentive study. This not only helped me avoid the bias that would no doubt have developed from reading the "official" reports before hearing the inmates' own narratives but also helped to ensure that I would not be perceived as a member of the treatment staff, or worse, the broader correctional or judicial system, a likely event if I had used the files to challenge the inmates' stories. This also meant that I, like the inmates, was unaware of the specific sexual crimes and other offenses of which the individuals had been convicted until they were related in group therapy, a strategy that better positioned me to approximate the inmates' own experiences. My insistence that the specifics of the crimes were not an issue in my research strategically placed me in a different "outsider" space than other outsiders that they encountered.

My participation in group treatment sessions was governed by the rule—invoked by the unit's treatment director—that I observe only and not actively participate. I was quite comfortable with this and each day would settle into my regular chair in the horseshoe-shaped "circle" at the commencement of a session. I was in the circle, but not *of* the circle. Indeed it was at the inmates' insistence that I occupied a spot alongside them and the staff, rather than hanging back and observing from a more distant vantage point. I was not allowed to take notes or record events, although it was understood that I would be making mental notes and detailing events after the fact. Physically speaking, I hardly blended in, however, as the inmates arrived each day wearing their institutional-issue drab green slacks and jackets over white T-shirts, with most staff wearing white clinical smocks over street clothes. I tended toward comfortable outfits, along the lines that the inmates themselves would wear after programs ended each day and on weekends: jeans, cotton shirt. One day, running from a meeting elsewhere, I arrived wearing this same outfit plus a blazer and was soundly mocked by several inmates for "dressing up."

Over time, however, in each cohort, the nonparticipation rule did loosen up to some extent. I never became one of them, obviously, but I did become more active as a kind of useful third party. For instance, during role-playing exercises I was sometimes asked by inmates and treatment personnel alike to participate when there was an odd number of men that day. More significantly, in several instances I was invited—always by inmates—to take a more active role in the therapeutic aspect of the group sessions. Alfred, for instance, whom I discussed above and who enjoyed subtly subverting the rules, surprised me one day by asking, in group, what I thought of his presentation. I replied that the arrangement that allowed me to attend group sessions included a rule against me offering such commentary. I was not to act as a therapist. Several other inmates agreed that my silence was appropriate. Alfred, not one to give in easily, then asked if I would meet with him outside group. Caught, with everyone watching, I realized that dancing my way out of this would be awkward. "I am always happy to meet with guys," I said. We did meet, and, while emphasizing that I was not a therapist, I told him what I thought of his presentation. He accepted my feedback, adding that he did not want me to be a therapist—"I don't need more of those"—but saw me as a "normal person," by which I took to mean someone not involved in a therapeutic or correctional relationship with him.

As I have explained, the inmates were understandably suspicious of me at first; in such a closed environment the arrival of anyone new creates intense interest, of course. Unlike Goffman (1961), whose work in a psychiatric hospital involved his going "undercover" as a recreation specialist working in the institution, I presented as openly and honestly as possible as a university faculty member and researcher. As such, my presence, for them, was qualitatively different from what they normally experienced in prison. As with the corrections officers, I represented to the inmates somewhat of a puzzle, an individual who did not act according to known scripts. I was not a psychiatric nurse or social worker, not a guard, not a psychologist or psychiatrist, not a parole or police officer. At the beginning there were suggestions that I was some kind of judicial spy, maybe an undercover police officer, and several inmates worked hard to deduce exactly what kind of power relationship must exist between them and me. But I was able to convince most of my real role by bringing in some of the Aboriginal Elders I had worked with before in prison research who could vouch for me, and by showing inmates my previous book on prison treatment programs (Waldram 1997), as well as pages from my university website (they do not have access to the Internet). With each new cohort arrival, it was still necessary to explain my work and wait patiently for the suspicions to dissolve. In such cases, the senior cohort of men were my best advocates, as they responded favorably to questions by the new arrivals about who I was and what I was doing.

Although I had all the necessary approvals, I was still watched carefully by both security and treatment staff. That I seemed to have a cavalier attitude toward some of the rules of prison governance simply confirmed in the minds of some that I was up to no good. In reality, I was often unaware of these rules. My prison orientation session had focused more on security aspects typically relevant to outsiders: do not bring anything in or out for the inmates, do not do them any favors, do not give them anything, of course do not bring in any drugs (a lesson that included being exposed to a drug-sniffing dog). I was shown a variety of crafted weapons, rather ingenious inventions, to demonstrate how inmates could creatively disrupt the security of the institution with everyday, seemingly harmless objects. But other aspects of life on the units were left largely unexplained, in part I think because the orientation did not envision the kind of space I would actually occupy in the institution, and as a result I learned more about rules from the inmates than from staff. I think that my anomalous status worked to set me so far outside the bounds of the known categories that I was free largely to find my own way, fairly easy to do since my security status opened almost all institutional doors without direct question.

Occasionally my lack of knowledge of proper policies and procedures created problems, though. For instance, several times I was observed entering an inmate's cell, usually to talk confidentially about some matter or concern. While the cell doors were never closed, such an act represented a direct threat to the corrections officers' responsibility to protect me (Liebling 1999). The officers were clearly not amused when they would arrive at the cell door, four strong, within minutes of my entry. During an interview in one of the designated interview rooms—with a wall of glass that ensured complete observation by those in the Bubble—I was interrupted by a corrections officer who pointed out that I was to keep myself between the inmate and the door, with me closest to the door, a reference to the possible need for a quick escape. This was rather awkward, of course, since the inmate was sitting there as I was so instructed, but his chuckling as we switched places assured me there were no hard feelings between us. Needless to say, it is very difficult to build and maintain trust with research participants when you must abide by rules and regulations that suggest that they are not trustworthy. Another time I was observed talking about martial arts with an inmate. Suddenly, there was a "phone call" for me in the Bubble. The unit officer handed me the phone, told me to pretend to talk to someone—recall that I would have been visible to the inmates on the outside—and while looking away from me gave me a stern lecture about the ill-advisability of talking to inmates about the martial arts. Shocked at the whole intrigue of the situation, I speechlessly failed to defend myself or explain that he had misunderstood our conversation. I was most definitely not teaching the inmate any techniques. But one word from this officer and my access to the institution would be terminated, so I kept quiet. The ruse was noticed by several inmates, however, who questioned me about it later. Like Clifford Geertz's (1973) experience running from a police raid in Bali, contravening prison rules and being chastised by security staff served to establish the trust between researcher and participant that cameras and personal security devices potentially thwarted. The obvious suspicions of staff members toward me reinforced in the minds of the inmates that I was not part of the system. I could get in trouble too.

My ability to work within the prison environment was restricted to some extent by the nature of the institution, of course. It was necessary for me to fit my activities into a variety of schedules determined by the corrections and therapeutic mandates, and these schedules could change on a moment's notice without warning. My access to the inmates was relatively open, however; I was able to meet with them whenever they were not otherwise involved in programs or working at prison jobs. Evenings and weekends were particularly available, but also some times during the workday when there were no sessions and inmates were available to sit for an hour or more.

I did not have formal access to the treatment personnel for research purposes. They were not interviewed for this research, a condition of permission to do the work by decree of the unit treatment director. This is not an unusual situation in institutional research, where the higher up you go in the bureaucracy the less accessible people become. Goffman (1961), for instance, in his study of a mental institution that spawned the development of his "total institution" model, appears to have undertaken no formal interviews whatsoever, and his methods (and interpretations) overall have been the subject of much criticism (see Weinstein 1982, for example). Rhodes (2004), in contrast, "talked with" prison staff members and interviewed forty staff volunteers. Both Goffman and Rhodes employed extensive observational data. In comparison to both, I would say that I was able to collect a substantial body of interview data, as Goffman did not do, and I was able to have much greater sustained contact with the inmates than Rhodes. Importantly, within this particular institution where there is a research mandate, historically only the inmates have ever been seen as the subjects of research. In general, the circumscribed nature of my research can be seen as a reflection of a broader institutional culture and existing power structures of the prison system. There are those who are to be observed, studied, managed, and manipulated (inmates) and those who do the observing, studying, managing, and manipulating (staff), a reflection of the existence of a firm, long-standing, and avowedly one-way research tradition, cultivated over the years by psychologists and psychiatrists and their respective scholarly gazes on inmates. Nonetheless, it was never my intent to interview the treatment team members as part of this research, and I do not see their exclusion from my work as a particularly meaningful limitation.

This is an ethnography of inmate experience in a *prison* treatment program, and as such I could not be oblivious to the power dynamics at work. To be seen fraternizing with the staff would have jeopardized my rapport with the inmates, who might conclude that I was some sort of covert operative or else sympathetic to staff concerns and perspectives (I was, of course, but could not let on). While I did speak with treatment staff informally on an occasional basis, these encounters tended to be brief and off the record, and as my research unfolded I came to appreciate the need to avoid being observed in detailed conversation with individual staff members. Like Goffman (1961), I avoided social contact with the therapeutic staff, even off-unit, such as in the cafeteria. Of course, also like Goffman, I overheard staff conversations about inmates, but unlike Goffman I did not record these in my field notes, nor do I relate these comments in this ethnography. My work was predicated on gaining the confidence of the inmates to share their experiences with me; this would not have been possible had I been seen to engage significantly with the staff. Inmates often asked me if I spoke with the staff about them or shared information from our interviews and discussions; I could honestly answer "no," and this was important to them. The inmates repeatedly reminded me that they did not want me to be a part of the treatment team, that they saw me as an unbiased outsider who could better represent their views. Indeed, the fact that staff members were largely oblivious to my presence was just as crucial to the work. Like the inmates I received very little information about events and schedules, and like the inmates I often arrived for a therapy session only to learn it had just been changed. There were times when all the inmates and I sat in the treatment lounges wondering aloud what was going on, where the therapists were, and what we were doing that day. Being in the dark, as the inmates frequently are, about matters of programming and governance on the unit simply reinforced that I was *not* a staff member. This was not a limitation of the research; indeed, since my goal was to be as "experience-near" as possible to the situation the inmates were in, being treated somewhat like an inmate was an advantage. My effort to attain ethnographic empathy is a strength of this work.

As noted above, however, I did have access to the files on every inmate in my study, and this included the interim and final reports written by the treatment staff. I read these latter files in particular with great care and so gained very detailed knowledge of the perspectives of treatment staff members on particular inmates, how they made their assessments, and how judgments were ultimately rendered concerning the inmates' progress in the program. However, the problem from the point of view of this ethnography is that I cannot use any of this material, not directly anyway, as these are legally protected documents. Hence I am able to speak in general terms about what a treatment team member may have thought, but without the specifics. So in no way can this ethnography be said to reflect the views of treatment staff. Nevertheless, the treatment staff members are clearly visible throughout this book, and their presence in the various group sessions looms large as they work to communicate and put into practice the theory of the treatment program with an offender population, its therapeutic pragmatic.[3]

> *Franklin was called to Admissions and Discharge today. He thought this was about some of his personal effects, which had yet to arrive, but it was a ruse. He was really taken for a surprise drug test. He is quite angry about this. Someone must have "snitched," he assumes. He explains that it took him a long time because he had just gone to the bathroom, and he didn't have any urine. He adds that he also has a shy bladder and has difficulty urinating in front of others. The correctional officer watches you carefully, he explains, looking directly at your penis the whole time in case you try something. "Quite degrading," declares Franklin. "I wonder if there are any gays among the guards."*
>
> *Field notes*

• • •

Prisons, as we know, are complex, secretive, and somewhat dangerous institutions of hyper-regulation and, as such, difficult places to undertake ethnographic research. As I have suggested here, however, precisely at the intersections of regulatory regimes seams are created that open space for just such a mode of inquiry. This is especially true of therapeutic prisons, where the custody and treatment mandates exhibit more tension than harmony and where the anomalous status of the ethnographer allows a certain cloak of regulatory invisibility. Falling outside the power relations of institutional governance, including the power to assess fitness, and falling outside the power relations conferred by forensic fiat, through the creation of an "inmate" category, I found my comfort zone. I simply did not fit any preexisting category recognizable by inmates and staff alike, and this allowed me to associate with my key reference group—inmates—without too much retribution from others. But since it was clear to all that I was not an inmate, I was able to escape the relations of power that pervade that status. I came to be seen as a nonjudgmental, even sympathetic ear by inmates—a characteristic role of the ethnographer—and they responded by taking me under their wing, telling me "like it is," and talking and talking. While some have warned against getting "too close" to prison inmates (e.g., Thomas 1993), it seems to me such a position is an ethnographic non sequitur.

Prisons are places of both panoptic and synoptic surveillance. This is especially true of the therapeutic prison and the unit where this research takes place. The conflict between regulatory regimes is but one, albeit dominant, theme that emerges from this research. With everybody watching everybody, with unclarity as to who is friendly and who is not, with the categories of "therapist" and "inmate" deliberately breaking down in treatment, and with staff members acting alternately as corrections officers, nurses, and confidantes, the inmates in particular emerge as, if not "professionals," then at least confederates in a process to enact disciplinary punishment. This regulatory rat's nest foreshadows the inherent conflict found within the treatment paradigm itself that I shall detail here: the conflict between the paradigmatic mode, bolstered by the regulatory regime that supports and reproduces the power and authority of the "professionals" to dictate what constitutes "truth" and appropriate treatment, as well as inmates' fitness to reenter the community, and the narrative mode, which leads inmates into thinking that they are agentive beings whose subjectivity is valued and whose subjective honesty will be rewarded. The first step in this process of narrative disenfranchisement is to convince inmates that publicly relating their story is a key step in their treatment. But what, exactly, are they being treated for?

CHAPTER 3

Disordered Sex

"So what are you in for?"

I am certain no one really asks that in prison. Another Hollywood figment, I suspect, because it is such a dangerous question, both the asking and the answering. This is not to say there is not an intense interest among inmates to know about each other's crimes. However, they are much more likely to speak of "doing my own time," meaning minding one's business and not other people's. This keeps one relatively safe. But the nature of inmates' offenses remains fuel for much speculation, even more so when it comes to sexual crimes. Generally, sexual offenders keep pretty quiet about the nature of their crimes, especially so if they are housed in "general population" with all the other inmates with various criminal backgrounds. So, in the words of my mythical inmate, what *are* they "in" for?

This is a far more complex question than one might suspect. The inmates are both "in" prison for the commission of crimes, and "in" an accredited hospital for treatment of medical, psychiatric, and especially behavioral issues that are assumed to underscore that criminal activity. I will approach this issue from several angles, beginning with a brief overview of my participants' criminality, followed by a discussion of Cognitive Behavioral Therapy (CBT), the dominant therapeutic paradigm on the unit. Treatment teleology—a characteristic of the "psy" disciplines generally (Rose 1998)—is evident in that the formulation of an inmate's "problem" is intimately tied to the potentialities for treatment as defined by CBT. In other words, the treatment program must necessarily be based upon the idea, first, that inmates have diagnosable "problems" and second, that these problems can be successfully treated; this in turn shapes the kinds of "problems" they are deemed to have and how efficacy is conceptualized and measured.

CRIMINAL DEMOGRAPHICS

Figures on the proportion of sexual offenders incarcerated in federal institutions in Canada have varied between 15 percent and 25 percent over the past fifteen years. The most recent comprehensive published data for Canada suggest that in 1995 some 4,545 sexual offenders were under federal jurisdiction (which would include those on parole), a number that constituted about 20 percent of the total federal offender population (Motiuk and Belcourt 1996). Of these, estimates placed the number of sexual offenders in federal institutions at 3,245, or about 24 percent of the incarcerated population. Approximately 20 percent of these were housed in maximum-security institutions, with 68 percent in medium-security and 12 percent in minimum-security institutions. As noted previously, the therapeutic prison where this research was undertaken is classified as a "multisecurity" institution, in that inmates across all three security levels are present.

In 1983, Canada changed its Criminal Code to remove references to specific sexual acts in its conceptualization of sexual assault. Terms such as *rape* and *indecent assault* were eliminated. This was done in part because of the perceived stigma that the criminal charge labels had for the victim, labels that clearly identified the specifics of the trauma and assault experienced. Indeed, currently there is no actual definition of *sexual assault* in the Criminal Code; instead the code now conceptualizes sexual assault as assaultive in nature, that is, an act of violence, rather than sexual in nature, and recognizes three levels of seriousness expressed as "sexual assault," "aggravated sexual assault" (involving injury), and "sexual assault with a weapon, threats to a third party or causing bodily harm" (Chase 1983; Gunn and Linden 1997). Other changes to the legislation removed spousal immunity, disqualified evidence about the victims' background, changed rules concerning consent that altered the ability of the perpetrator to easily argue that the victim willfully gave consent to sexual activity, and reduced the ability of the perpetrator to argue that he or she believed that the victim was of the age of majority (sixteen years) to consent to sexual activity unless he or she could show that "all reasonable steps" had been taken to determine the age.

There are also separate offenses that pertain to those under the age of sixteen. These include "sexual interference," involving physical contact to the body of the victim for a sexual purpose; "invitation to sexual touching," in which an underage person is invited to touch the body of the perpetrator or another underage individual for a sexual purpose; and "sexual exploitation," an extension of the first two in which the perpetrator is in a position of authority or trust. Further, a variety of other offenses deemed to be of a sexual nature exist, such as exposure and public nudity.

In Canada, a sentence of two years or more usually results in incarceration in a federal institution (sentences up to two years less a day typically involve provincial correctional facilities). Sentencing on sexual offenses varies according to the severity of the offense and whether there are repeat offenses on the individual's record. Sexual assault nets a sentence up to ten years; sexual assault with a weapon ranges from five to fourteen years; and the penalty for aggravated sexual assault ranges from five years up to "life" (defined as twenty-five years before parole eligibility). Penalties for sexual interference, invitation to sexual touching, and sexual exploitation involve prison terms of between forty-five days and ten years. Actual sentence lengths, of course, differ from those called for under the Criminal Code, as the courts have considerable latitude. The most recent aggregate data that I have found indicate that the average sentence length for all sexual offenders is typically less than maximum penalties allow. In a review of data in 1995 (Motiuk and Belcourt 1996), the average sentence length of the sex offender institutional population (that is, individuals incarcerated at the time of the review) was four years and eight months, much lower than the average for all incarcerated federal offenders of six years and six months. The data also show that 50 percent of the sexual offenders had committed a sexual assault, 21 percent a mixed offense (a combination of sexual offense types), and 15 percent a pedophile offense, with the remainder a variety of less common offenses such as incest and exhibitionism.

There are several means by which an incarcerated federal inmate can be released from prison. The first, of course, ensues when the sentence expires. The second is to successfully obtain parole. Day parole can be granted after one-sixth of the sentence has been completed and full parole after one-third. A third means to gain release involves a statutory requirement that inmates be released at the two-thirds mark of their sentence if they have not otherwise received parole. However there is also a legal provision that allows the courts to detain such an individual until sentence completion if he or she is believed to be a serious threat to public safety; failure to successfully complete a sexual offender treatment program is one criterion that is considered in these deliberations. Inmates refer to this as being "gated," as in the gate to the outside world being shut on them. Further, a small minority of offenders with extensive records of violence may be judicially declared "dangerous offenders" and detained indeterminately regardless of their actual sentence. Paroled and released inmates may be placed under a recognizance order, with specific restrictions placed on their activities. In the case of sexual offenders, such restrictions typically would include avoidance of certain locales, such as schoolyards, and certain individuals, such as former victims or individuals under the age of sixteen; a ban on firearms possession; and a requirement to report one's status as a sexual offender to potential romantic partners, employers, and even neighbors. Convicted sexual offenders are recorded in a "National Sexual Offender" registry, a database available only to police and justice officials that keeps track of the whereabouts of released individuals to facilitate police investigations. Some provinces maintain websites alerting the public to the release of sexual offenders, and various public notification polices may also be invoked to inform community members when a released sexual offender is likely to be in their area. The community experiences of released sexual offenders will be discussed later in this book.

The inmates, not surprisingly, do not generally like the implications of the current Criminal Code and community notification provisions. From their perspective, for example, the current statute aggregates too many different sexual and violent acts and so blurs the distinction among, say, date rape, statutory sexual assault involving a teenager who "consented," sexual assault that may have involved stalking, and sexual assault on a child or infant—all distinctions that are crucial to the hierarchy established in penitentiaries, on the unit, and in many ways in the community as a whole. There were times during the research when the language denoting more specific sexual acts was encouraged or demanded by the staff, which led to considerable confusion. (I should add that terms such as *rape* remain common as descriptors even in official publications emanating from the Correctional Service of Canada.) Sometimes it was not sufficient for an inmate to say that he "sexually assaulted" his victim, and the term *rape* in particular was used with some frequency.

For legal and ethical reasons I must be somewhat vague about the nature of the crimes committed by the inmates I interviewed, as well as their sentence lengths, which, in some cases, could identify them. Actual sentences being served among my participants range from twenty-seven months to "life." Needless to say, almost all understand that they will be released into the community at the expiration of their sentences, if not sooner as a result of statutory release provisions or parole. Most of my participants have previous adult criminal convictions and very often juvenile records as well, typically involving an escalation from mischief-type offenses and petty crimes to more serious offenses involving violence or threats of violence. Not all offenses on many inmates' records are sexual crimes, then—drug-related convictions, assault, breaking and entering, and other property crimes are common—and several of my participants are serving combined sentences for sexual and other offenses. Those serving "life" sentences were convicted of murder, again not necessarily involving the sexual assault victim. A few participants, however, have no prior offenses at all, and in these cases their sexual crimes typically involved sexual relations with underage teenagers or children.

Despite the vagueness of the Criminal Code, in the treatment program specific criminal acts of a sexual nature are discussed openly in great detail. A wide variety of criminal actions are represented among my participants, from touching for sexual purposes and exposure to penetration orally, vaginally, and anally. The degree of physical force employed also varies, from none (usually with children or teenagers) to forms of kidnapping and forcible confinement with restraint. For roughly half of my thirty-five participants, their victims were women; the victims in the other cases were underage teenagers and children of both genders. Only a few crimes targeting adult victims involved assault against complete strangers, sex trade workers being the most common, and fewer still involved calculated planning (evidenced by, for instance, the purchase of duct tape or the scouting of likely residences in advance), the stereotypical modus operandi in much public perception. The rest involved assaults directed toward spouses, ex-spouses, girlfriends, and other acquaintances, and children known and often related to the offender. While the adult-targeted offenses, with a few exceptions, tended to be more or less spontaneous acts, typically involving the influence of alcohol and/or drugs, the crimes involving children and underage teenagers were sometimes spontaneous but also sometimes the product of "grooming," gaining the victim's trust and thereby positioning the offender to commit the crime. Premeditation was therefore more common among those who offended against children than it was for those whose victims were women. Sam's case, presented in the opening chapter of this book, is fairly typical of the kinds of crimes committed by many men in this research: opportunistic, involving someone known to the offender, and committed while under the influence of alcohol or drugs.

At any given point during the research period, roughly half of all program inmates were "Aboriginal"; the others were mostly "white," in local parlance, or "Caucasian" according to the racial categorization of inmates as documented in their files. These demographics are not reflective of national trends, where in Canada as a whole we find that almost 18 percent of federal sexual offenders are Aboriginal and 75 percent are Caucasian (Motiuk and Belcourt 1996). These skewed numbers reflect the regional dynamic at work in terms of the location of the therapeutic hospital at the center of this research, a region where Aboriginal offenders more broadly are disproportionately incarcerated. Of the thirty-five men that I interviewed, fifteen identify as Aboriginal. I have chosen not to undertake this ethnography as a study comparing Aboriginals to non-Aboriginals or "whites," however, because to do so would detract from my broader goals. I found Aboriginality to play a minor role in program participation generally, and treatment staff made few efforts to search for or accommodate any perceived cultural differences. Similarly, Aboriginal inmates rarely made Aboriginality an issue in the program, and all were fluent in English and literate (although all inmates varied in their level of literacy and a few were functionally illiterate). A comparative study, then, would create a false dichotomy and add nothing insightful to the aims of this ethnography. I have undertaken a great deal of research on Aboriginal men in prison, exploring the implications of cultural difference for treatment experience (Waldram 1993, 1994, 1997), and have otherwise engaged with the complex issues of contemporary Aboriginality (Waldram 2004; Waldram, Herring, and Young 2006), and I feel that I am well positioned to render this observation. In this ethnography, I will engage with issues of Aboriginality and Aboriginal experience where warranted as an integral part of my person-centered approach.

Paul met with the psychiatrist today. The doctor told him he seemed "agitated" and wanted to put him on medication. Ironically, this made Paul angry. "Look at me," he explains he said to the psychiatrist. "Look where

I am, and what I have done. You'd be agitated too if you were in here!
It's normal to react like this. If I was all calm, that would be abnormal!"
However, he has agreed to take the medication anyway. "It's hard to say
'no' to these people."

Interview with Paul

THE DISORDERLY DIAGNOSES OF SEXUAL OFFENDING

The interplay of criminality and "illness" creates profound problems
for forensic professionals called upon to rehabilitate inmates. Obviously there is a sentiment that criminality represents a "deviant" or
"abnormal" behavior pattern and, in our modern era, one that calls for
rehabilitation and not just punishment (although some would argue that
"the therapeutic has become a mode of state punishment," as Haney
[2010: 117] does). More pragmatically, the regulatory environment governing the therapeutic prison demands that inmate "patients" have some
kind of diagnosable condition to be admitted. But there is a conundrum:
sexual offenses are crimes, not psychological disorders or sicknesses.

The *Diagnostic and Statistical Manual of Mental Disorders (DSM),*
published by the American Psychiatric Association (2000)—the bible
of the mental health professions—handles the issue of sexual offending
only peripherally. The main reference is to the "paraphilias": "recurrent,
intense, sexually arousing fantasies, sexual urges, or behaviors" (566)
that may involve the suffering or humiliation of the victim, including
children and other nonconsenting individuals. It is noted briefly that
these thoughts and behaviors *may* involve the commission of crimes and
subsequent incarceration, but such is not necessary for a diagnosis to be
rendered. Indeed, it is the content of the fantasies or sexual urges that is
relevant to the making of a diagnosis, in combination with evidence that
these cause distress or impairment for the patient (Lehne 2009), none
of which represent criminal activity. While a variety of paraphilias are
detailed, of direct relevance to the criminal circumstances of my research
participants are exhibitionism (exposing of genitals), pedophilia (sexual
focus on prepubescent children), and sexual sadism (inflicting humiliation or suffering), which could apply to several of the men I interviewed.
These disorders are believed to be "chronic and life-long," a judgment
that pervades even inmate experiences of treatment, as I shall show.

The paraphilias, therefore, represent psychological states and, less so,
behaviors, and not crimes per se. Further, the diagnosis probably covers
only a minority of the sexual crimes for which men are imprisoned, and
few of those in my research. These crimes, it seems, are likely to involve

more or less spontaneous acts perpetrated on victims known to the offender. An inmate who, in a drunken state, seizes an opportunity to violate a child sexually is not necessarily diagnosable as a pedophile, for instance, because such a diagnosis requires that the act be the product of a recurrent preoccupation with and sexual arousal by children. Physical violence perpetrated on an ex-spouse or girlfriend might be an expression of anger toward the individual but not necessarily the product of a more general preoccupation with inflicting suffering or humiliation.

Hence it must be emphasized that the commission of a sexual crime is not necessarily evidence of a sexual disorder as understood by the American Psychiatric Association and that a diagnosis of a sexual disorder is not evidence of a crime. Sexual assaults are frequently "socially patterned and not the idiosyncratic acts of mentally disordered individuals," note Monahan, Marolla, and Bromley (2005: 311). Within psychological anthropology, this social patterning could be considered the product of certain cultural schemas harbored by individuals but derived from broader, shared experiences (Strauss and Quinn 1997). A good example would be mainstream, ubiquitous patriarchal gender attitudes, which seem relevant at least to our understanding of the sexual assault on adult victims. Power and control are central to dominant schemas (Busch, Hotaling, and Monto 2002), and forced sexual acts may not be expressions of sexuality or sexual drives at all. Busch, Hotaling, and Monto (2002: 1107–8), for instance, in a study of male customers of prostituted women, found that while most men did not in fact find sexual violence attractive or believe that sex workers enjoyed their work, they nevertheless exhibited common "structures of beliefs and attitudes that parallel feminist theories of violence against women." And criminologists Langton and Marshall (2000: 171) argue that "attempts to differentiate rapists' attitudes toward women from those of comparison groups of non-offending males have been inconclusive."

Such attitudes regarding women in particular may be astonishingly (for some, at least) prevalent. A Canadian judge in a 2011 sexual assault trial concluded—in what could easily be described as a cognitive distortion—that "sex was in the air," made comments about the clothing that the adult female victim and her friend were wearing ("tube tops, no bras, and high heels"), and noted that they had on "plenty of makeup," according to a news report on the case (Winnipeg Free Press 2011). Describing the perpetrator as a "clumsy Don Juan," the judge suggested that the victim shared some of the "moral blameworthiness" because of the "inviting circumstances" of her interaction with the perpetrator. The judge gave the perpetrator a two-year conditional sentence that allowed him to avoid prison time. In a similar vein, a Toronto police constable recently told a class of law students that "women should avoid dressing like sluts in order not to be victimized" (Millar 2011). Of course neither the judge nor the police constable committed a sexual assault, and an issue for forensic treatment, then, would be to understand why and in what contexts some individuals, such as my participants, act in response to such cultural schemas in criminal ways while others do not. Such acts may or may not be linked to a diagnosable *DSM* sexual disorder, and few of my participants were so diagnosed. But the prevalence of these "cognitive distortions" transcends the offender population and creates some degree of confusion for the inmates in treatment when they are told that these views of women are erroneous and deviant, even when held by judges and police officers.

That cognitive distortions regarding women are pervasive is not to say that there is no evidence for psychiatric or psychological disorder of some type among sexual offenders, or some neuropsychological impairment. Raymond et al. (1999) present research that suggests that the majority of sexual offenders have *some* kind of mental disorder that falls under Axis 1 of the *DSM*, including mood and anxiety disorders (see also Kafka and Hennen 2002). Other research suggests that sexual offenders may exhibit lower self-esteem, increased loneliness, decreased empathy, and disordered emotional attachment (Fisher, Beech, and Browne 1999; Lyn and Burton 2004). And a study by Myla Young, Jerald Justice, and Philip Edberg (2010) suggests that sexual offenders may have greater psychoneurological impairment in comparison to nonsexual offenders. All of these studies have significant methodological limitations, however, and have often sampled very specific subpopulations (e.g., pedophiles) that make generalization difficult. And the actual connection between these disorders and the commission of sexual crimes remains unclear.

Nonetheless, the degree to which a psychiatric diagnosis is important in treating sexual offenders appears less than one might expect. There is a tendency to refrain from "hard" diagnoses, characteristic of the *DSM* approach, in favor of more "soft" diagnoses involving an even more subjective application of therapeutic models in assessment (Lester 2007: 382). Bambonyé (1996), in a review of the existence of mental disorders among Canadian incarcerated sexual offenders, highlighted how the *DSM* has been underutilized in assessments. While some 65 percent of the inmates in her study had some mention of a psychiatric diagnosis in their files, compared to 30 percent for nonsexual offenders, many of these were not *DSM* diagnoses but rather descriptive labels, such as "primitive personality." When such doubtful diagnoses were eliminated, the research showed no difference in mental disorder diagnoses between sexual and nonsexual offenders, an observation that also held for the existence of psychopathy. Further, of the sexual offenders given a diagnosis, only 12.5 percent had a diagnosis "directly related to the nature of their sexual offence." Generally speaking, "The results indicate that sex offenders do not report more psychosexual disorders than non-sex offenders." The psychological and psychiatric picture for sexual offenders, then, is anything but clear.

So, to be eligible for treatment in this institution, some diagnosis other than a psychosexual disorder is typically needed. Indeed, according to the *DSM*, personality disorders are also frequent in such cases, as are symptoms of depression and expressions of guilt and shame. It is these, it seems, that allow for the kinds of diagnoses and treatment that can cover the broader range of sexually offending behavior found among inmates in our prisons. Hans Toch (1998) suggests that criminal acts per se easily invoke the *DSM* classification of antisocial personality disorder. This certainly resonates with what I heard from several forensic psychologists in the institution. Indeed, antisocial personality disorder, as one psychologist explained to me, is such a broad catchall category that it is easy to apply to anyone in prison. "A shorthand recall for the diagnosis" of antisocial personality disorder, confirms Luhrmann (2000: 115), "is that the . . . patient is a male criminal." Perhaps surprisingly, though, research suggests that sexual offenders are less likely than other types of offenders to endorse antisocial or criminal attitudes (O'Shaughnessy 2009), so even this diagnosis is not clear-cut.

According to the *DSM*, antisocial personality disorder "is a pattern of disregard for, and violation of, the rights of others" (685). Simply put, a propensity to commit crimes, one *DSM*-identified sign of such a disorder, is a handle to the diagnosis, and the diagnosis in turn opens the door to treatment. Demonstrating "an enduring pattern of inner experience and behavior that deviates markedly from the expectations of the individual's culture," the pattern of antisocial personality disorder is "manifested in two (or more) of the following areas," which, as we shall see, are the focus of treatment on the unit:

(1) cognition (i.e., ways of perceiving and interpreting self, other people, and events)
(2) affectivity (i.e., the range, intensity, lability, and appropriateness of emotional response)

(3) interpersonal functioning

(4) impulse control (American Psychiatric Association 2000: 689)

More concretely, such individuals may be seen to lie, be irritable and aggressive, rationalize or minimize the harmful consequences of their actions, show little remorse, and demonstrate a lack of empathy. Individuals, and especially criminals, with antisocial personality disorder are sometimes labeled, and even diagnosed, as psychopaths, an extreme variant characterized by a "lack of empathy, inflated self-appraisal, and superficial charm" (703). Several inmates in my research were so labeled, especially by other inmates, though not necessarily diagnosed.[1] Antisocial personality disorder is also often associated with a substance-related disorder, particularly the abuse of alcohol and drugs.

So while a sexual offender in a therapeutic prison may or may not have a sexual disorder diagnosis, he or she is almost certainly diagnosable with an antisocial personality disorder, often with a substance-related disorder in tow. The tussle between the *DSM*'s Axis I and Axis II that Rhodes (2000) describes in her study of supermax inmates, the distinction between the "mad"—those with clinical disorders—and the "bad"—those with personality disorders—is not visible in my research. These are mostly "Axis II" men.[2] But how does one treat this kind of "badness"?

Several of us are playing cards in the day room. Ethan explains that he is on the unit for sexual crimes he has committed some ten years ago. His current offense was a "regular" assault. He has done his time for the previous sexual assaults and wonders why he has to attend the treatment program. Franklin begins chiding him, saying that if he didn't have a sexual problem he would be in another unit in the institution, for anger management. Ethan agrees that he has an anger problem but not a problem with sexual deviancy. Franklin continues to berate him, however, saying he hates it when Ethan "takes the victim stance." Ethan laughs, a little nervously, and admits that he doesn't expect to make it through the entire program. [He doesn't].

Field notes

THE COGNITIVE BEHAVIORAL PARADIGM FOR SEXUAL OFFENDER TREATMENT

The response of forensic psychology in recent decades has been to recast inmate problems as cognitive deficits, as problems in values and attitudes, personal agency, self-control, and even morality, all wrapped in a discourse that emphasizes freedom of choice to act, or not act, in a criminal manner. In a sense, then, there actually is no "badness," no character essence, only bad behavior fueled by cognitive and affective deficits and, perhaps, moral deficits as well (with the possible exclusion of psychopaths; see note 1). The domain of the moral is one that centers on choice, Robbins (2004) suggests, and "One of the reasons you dislike them [criminals]," according to Luhrmann (2000: 115), "is an inexpungable sense that they are morally at fault because they could choose to be different." While accepting the role of choice, the inmates do not generally buy into the moral angle, at least not at first, clearly distinguishing actions from essence (Waldram 2009b). "I see myself as not a bad person, but I just made a very bad choice," explains Andrew, convicted of a statutory offense against a teenage girl.

The treatment approach concentrates on this idea of choice and aims to offer an explanation for "bad choices," behaviors and associated thought patterns that lead to criminal actions, and a plan for avoiding them in the future. But moral issues are difficult to dodge, and a considerable amount of energy is also spent trying to instill a different moral sensibility, suggesting often rather explicitly that the inmates are indeed morally deficient. Crimes are obvious breaches of the moral order, so this is perhaps not surprising. As such, the program's approach reflects Nikolas Rose's (1998: 156) definition of "therapeutics" as "a heterogeneous array of techniques of subjectification through which human beings are urged and incited to become ethical beings, to define and regulate themselves according to moral codes, to establish precepts for conducting or judging their lives, to reject or accept moral goals." Since the inmates are seen as potentially fully agentive in their actions, treatment targets "dynamic" factors that intersect with agency in the sense that they are factors over which the inmate is theoretically perceived to have potential control and that can therefore be altered through therapy. Morality can be seen as a "dynamic" factor: in the treatment model one is taught how to be moral, or more moral, as the case may be. This is in contrast to "static" factors such as demographic and criminal facts that can be gleaned from official records and that are logically not amenable to alteration. The inmates generally are frustrated by the use of static factors in any way, because by definition no amount of treatment can alter the factors, and therefore the inmate's ability to demonstrate positive change or treatment success is circumscribed. This, in turn, leads to some conflict in the treatment program, as I shall discuss starting in chapter 5.

The engagement with dynamic factors is done primarily through the therapeutic paradigm known as Cognitive Behavioral Therapy (CBT), a very common psychotherapeutic approach (with many variants) often used in many different institutional and clinical contexts for a wide variety of disorders, yet uniquely enacted in this prison program. CBT owes its genesis to the work of psychologists Albert Ellis and Aaron Beck (Ellis 1989; Beck and Weishaar 1989), who argue that the way each person thinks is reflected in cognitive representations or schemas concerning their understanding of the world and that these influence their behavior. Further, psychological or emotional disturbances, including deficiencies in moral reasoning, can emerge from inaccurate or maladaptive modes of thought that are linked to these schemas. Such maladaptive behaviors and emotions are essentially learned reactions to stressful situations. These disturbances in turn manifest themselves in inappropriate or antisocial behaviors. Cognitive representations are the products of sociocultural processes and are therefore learned, so in theory they can be unlearned and replaced with representations that are more prosocial, reflective of contemporary mores and codes of behavior. CBT proponents argue that people can consciously adopt or invoke "reason" as a characteristic element of their thinking and that they can be trained to uncover and correct faulty information processing and modify dysfunctional beliefs and assumptions that maintain maladaptive behaviors and emotions. CBT therefore stresses the link between cognition and behavior and demonstrates an advance over straightforward Pavlovian or aversion approaches to behavioral remediation for sexual offenders (Marshall and Eccles 1993).

The basic principle of CBT of relevance here is that some individuals engage in "thinking errors" or "cognitive distortions." Cognitive distortions are conceptualized as simplistic, reactive, and primal ways of thinking that serve to distort the subjective interpretation of external stimuli and information, such as might be the case in our interactions with others. Cognitive distortions can also affect the interpretation of internal stimuli, such as bodily sensations. Cognitive distortions are considered to be frequently self-serving, allowing the individual to achieve self-centered goals while discounting negative self-interpretations of behavior even in the face of disconfirmatory evidence (Harris 1991).

The idea of cognitive distortions entered into the psychological treatment of sexual offenders in the 1970s as a means to assist them to recognize their patterns of distorted thinking and related dysfunctional or antisocial behaviors, viewed as an essential first step in their rehabilitation (Marshall, Anderson, and Fernandez 1999; Ward et al. 1997). In particular, emphasis is placed on cognitive distortions that facilitate minimization, justification, and denial, which are believed to allow the offender to victimize without the guilt or moral restraints experienced by others (Abel, Becker, and Cunningham-Rathner 1984; Auburn and Lea 2003; Fox 1999; Mann 2004). Well-known yet false cognitive distortions include the perceptions that women secretly want to be sexually taken by force; that style of dress—for example, wearing a short skirt—indicates sexual availability and willingness; that women are socialized to initially respond with "no" to sexual overtures when they really mean "yes"; that children can behave "seductively"; and that a man, once aroused, must obtain sexual relief.

Accordingly, then, an offender may deny an assault entirely, or deny responsibility by shifting blame onto someone else (often the victim), onto a personal state (such as intoxication), or onto past personal experience (such as childhood sexual abuse). He may minimize the impact of his offense by arguing that the victim was not really harmed, perhaps because she "really wanted it." He may justify the offense by suggesting that she dressed provocatively or acted seductively. He may indicate that he was emotionally upset or intoxicated at the time and that the assault therefore was out of character. The assault may have occurred spontaneously, he may suggest, and not as a premeditated act. He may even argue that the victim "deserved" the assault as punishment because of her negative behavior toward him or that he had a "right" to sex because he had become aroused in her presence. Despite acts of a sexual nature, he may deny that a "sexual" assault was committed while admitting to physical assault, in an effort to minimize and eschew the "sexual offender" label. Suggesting that the victim, whether an adult or child, consented to the sexual activity is also seen as a form of denial. Overall, the effect of these cognitive distortions is said to reduce judgments of the harm experienced by the victim and therefore the culpability of the offender (Marshall, Anderson, and Fernandez 1999). More broadly, these cognitive distortions are deemed to act to preserve the offender's positive sense of self in the face of harmful, often violent, antisocial actions. In all, the CBT model emphasizes the implications of erroneous thinking believed to lead to sexual assault by stressing the singular agency of the perpetrator, the idea that he alone is morally and legally responsible for his behavior with no excuses; it renders the commission of a sexual crime as the product of a conscious decision by the offender (McCulloch and Kelly 2007).

Psychological research on the existence of cognitive distortions among offenders has been primarily psychometric in orientation (Auburn 2005), with offenders in research offices responding to lists of hypothetical statements describing appropriate and inappropriate sexual attitudes, activities, and justifications. The question of how such distortions are invoked in the commission of actual crimes, in "giving permission" in CBT-speak, is really the crucial question, yet the answer is unclear. In the treatment program, therapeutic pragmatics dictate an intense focus on identifying, rooting out, and challenging cognitive distortions as they emerge through the contemporary narrative processes of relating distant past events and surmised cognitive and affective states; how evidence of cognitive distortions related in such a here-and-now carceral-therapeutic context can explain a past criminal act is problematic from my view. Beginning in the next chapter I will demonstrate that what are conceived of as cognitive distortions tend to emerge as the product of a synergistic and intersubjective process involving the imposition of the therapeutic paradigm within the prison context, the presence of other offenders who are also being evaluated, and session management by CBT-trained therapists (who do the evaluation).

My analysis will suggest that the focus on cognitive distortions is possibly misplaced and may act to subvert other, more tangible therapeutic goals. In this I am guided by the assertion of Auburn and Lea (2003: 295; see also Maruna and Mann 2006) that "cognitive distortions do not have a status as cognitive entities but are analysts' categories abstracted from sequences of talk in which culturally available narrative forms and rhetorical devices are deployed to manage responsibility and blame for the occasion at hand." My research demonstrates how instances of the CBT-defined categories of cognitive distortions can indeed be identified in such "sequences of talk"—narrative in particular, as I shall demonstrate—if one is so inclined, but are these psychotherapeutically meaningful when excised from that narrative context? Largely lacking in conceptualizations of CBT is an understanding of the normative, interpretive, and characteristically imprecise role of narrative in communication. CBT's inability to discern the cultural processes that work to shape the particular crime genre to be related and shape the broader autobiographical story to fit the CBT paradigm is also an issue. In the treatment program, offenders are required to speak not in abstract terms about attitudes toward others but with direct reference, with specific details, to their sexual assaults and, as importantly, to their thoughts and emotions at the time of the commission of their crimes. This is often done as part of a singular exercise alternately and contradictorily referred to as an "autobiography" and a "disclosure." As I will argue, these are fundamentally different processes, and the confusion between them creates the conditions for considerable conflict in the treatment program. It is in this arena that the paradigmatic mode upon which CBT is constructed clashes with the narrative mode expressive of personal experience.

Also unacknowledged within the CBT paradigm is that cognitive distortions are culturally patterned and variably distributed, laden with cultural and personal meanings that are "ordinary," as Jerome Bruner (2008) would suggest, learned over a lifetime and shared by many noncriminal people in the "local social world" of the offender (Kleinman 1995); the judge and the police officer referred to earlier are evidence of this. Yet within CBT cognitive distortions are viewed as the "property" of individuals without direct reference to their shared nature within the broader social and cultural milieu (Auburn and Lea 2003). As I shall demonstrate in chapter 5, the form of disclosure encouraged by CBT deliberately decontextualizes offenses and serves to derail autobiographical explanations for offending behavior in preparation for the rebuilding of personal narrative (Waldram 2008). In effect, then, CBT thwarts the resolution of violations of the "shared ordinary" (J. Bruner 2008), in part by focusing so much on instrumental concerns. Cognitive distortions may emerge as artifacts of psychological theorizing that may have little resonance for lives lived. "The idea of cognitive distortions," writes Auburn (2005: 700), "provides a means for the technical specification of an abnormality that has been identified by the courts or other institutional body and the means for specifying and measuring one of the arenas of change required of the individual." In other words, cognitive distortions are said to exist because they represent the kind of dynamic factors that are measurable, theoretically compatible with CBT, and hence treatable, creating a therapeutic teleology. As Tanya Luhrmann (2000: 83) puts it in her study of American psychiatry, "What one learns to do affects the way one sees."

Despite my critical tone, however, I must stress that there certainly is evidence that CBT is efficacious to varying degrees for many psychological and behavioral disorders (Butler et al. 2006), depending on the criteria used to define and measure efficacy.[3] In forensics, recidivism is often the main measure of efficacy, and in comparison with nontreatment cohorts, CBT (often in conjunction with relapse prevention programs, described later in this book) has proven—though not conclusively by any means (see Marques et al. 1994)—to reduce levels of recidivism among sexual offenders (Lösel and Schmucker 2005; Hanson et al. 2002; Olver, Wong, and Nicholaichuk 2009). So some elements of either CBT or the broader therapeutic process may be having a positive impact, especially if increased public safety is the goal, as opposed to fostering positive psychosocial change in the offender. But can recidivism rates *and* the experience of treatment be improved further? Are there additional ways in which the inmate can benefit? It is my contention that these are, in fact, related issues, and I focus my work here on the latter.

> *Hank is leaving in a few days, involuntarily discharged back to his home institution. He is all packed, as his effects will leave at a separate time. He is angry because he believes that the treatment and correctional staff have written "lies" about him in his files. As an example, he says that when he gave his Autobiography and talked about his early life, he described it as normal, happy, and functional, with no problems or issues. He was not believed by the treatment staff. He adds that other men have confided in him that they sometimes made up stories about troubled childhoods to satisfy the therapists. But Hank rejected this advice. The refusal of the therapists to believe him, and his refusal to cop to a situation he did not think appropriate, conspired to contribute to his early exit from the program, he believes.*
>
> *Field notes*

THERAPEUTIC PRAGMATICS

"There's still some good left in there somewhere," David explains one day. We are sitting in the interview room, working our way through our second interview session in the days before he will leave for his home penitentiary. David is a thin, tall, and very articulate Aboriginal man in his late thirties, serving a four-year sentence for sexual assault; he has several prior convictions for sexual assault as well and has done time in the penitentiary before. "Sure, I had bad behaviors, but that doesn't mean I'm a bad person all around," David continues. "Trying to get that through [to me] is a rough thing to do for me." He looks out the window as he finishes his thought. "You know, I always think the worst of myself, that this is what I've done and this is what I'll always be. Trying to change that little by little is a tough job. A tough daily job."

That "tough daily job" is orchestrated by a dedicated therapeutic staff consisting of psychiatric nurses and social workers, directed and supported by psychologists and psychiatrists, with the ever-present corrections officers in a less therapeutically visible role. Most aspects of the daily functioning of the unit, including the conducting of the group therapy sessions, fall to the nurses and social workers. Their office is in the Bubble, and as a result they have the most direct and sustained contact with the inmates. The psychologists and psychiatrists who are assigned to the unit are located elsewhere in the institution and make only occasional forays into the Hound Pound to meet with inmates or undertake assessments. Only rarely do they sit in on group therapy sessions. It is much more difficult, then, for the inmates to develop meaningful relations with the psychologists and psychiatrists, in contrast with the on-site staff, who are ever present.

As David suggests, offenders are conceptualized as individuals who have made problematic choices based on erroneous thinking, particularly in the form of a sexual offense or behaviors leading up to it, rather than as inherently deviant, bad, or evil individuals who *are* sexual offenders. This is crucial to the project of rehabilitation, as an essentialist perspective would deny that possibility and fuel much public perception that sexual offenders should be locked up and the key thrown away (Waldram 2009b). "It is the problematic behaviours that need to be changed, not the whole person," according to forensic experts (Marshall, Anderson, and Fernandez 1999: 44), although, as my analysis demonstrates, these "problematic behaviors" are so complex, diverse, and embedded that the thrust of the program, to the inmates, in fact seems to be about changing the "whole person." As these behaviors are seen to be the product of cognitive distortions, much of the treatment program is aimed are recasting how offenders think about themselves and others, including notions of individual rights and empathy. Invariably, for offenders this means both publicly accepting the official facts of the sexual crimes and accepting the treatment paradigm's interpretation of those facts within the context of a life lived. It means accepting the authoritative basis of the therapeutic pragmatic, in which treatment staff working with a theoretical model are positioned to assess the accuracy and acceptability of one's personal narrative, one's recounting of thoughts and feelings, and to reconstruct these in ways that are more compatible with the theory. Many inmates struggle with this.

The treatment program lasts roughly eight months and runs five days a week, morning and afternoon, with some private evening homework as well. It is categorized as a "high-intensity" program, and as such the inmate's full-time job while on the unit is undergoing treatment, engaging in extensive group work and individual activities. Behavioral and verbal techniques are employed to examine the patient's beliefs, challenge dysfunctional ones, and provide skills and model experiences that promote more adaptive cognitive processing and prosocial behavior (Beck and Weishaar 1989). Through a group therapy approach, other individuals, including inmate peers, are positioned as intentionally active players in the treatment. Marshall, Anderson, and Fernandez (1999:35) explain that "when the offenders challenge each other, they often illustrate their point with their own experience which not only helps the person being challenged, but also the challenger." But the dominance of a group approach to treatment is not simply about therapeutic efficacy; it is about therapeutic efficiency, as large numbers of men can be treated simultaneously with relatively few staff resources (Marshall and Williams 2000).

Invoked is a form of "therapeutic community" (De Leon et al. 2000; Lees, Manning, and Rawlings 1999; Lockwood et al. 1997; Luhrmann 2000; Shuker and Sullivan 2010; Ware, Frost, and Hoy 2010), "a social order that applies its entire organization to therapeutic outcomes" in the context of group-oriented treatment (Ware, Frost, and Hoy 2010). The therapeutic community approach is common in forensic programs, including for sexual offenders, throughout Europe and North America and typically involves the creation of a residential or in-patient treatment unit in which daily life itself is expected to conform to therapeutic principles. Residents of such programs typically take on responsibilities for the management of social and administrative tasks involved in running the community and engage in democratic processes as a group to make decisions, air grievances, and seek collective resolutions. As the concept is learned and enacted by the inmates in this program, the therapeutic community serves also as a moral community and finds its basic guidelines of operation, its language, if you will, in the CBT model that they are learning. Inmates are expected to challenge their own long-standing beliefs, values, and attitudes and to do so with the active assistance of others. It is anticipated that inmates, by participating in the treatment program of others, will gain greater insight into their own issues. Lessons learned in the treatment context are to be acted upon in the daily activities and interactions of life on and off the unit; inmates are expected to "work the program." Treatment is something to be lived every waking moment, and inmates are acutely aware that their behavior is under scrutiny at all times. Surveillance and assessment are twin "mechanisms of power" in the therapeutic prison (Jefferson 2003: 64), and both are the domain not only of the professionally trained treatment staff and corrections officers but also of the inmates themselves, who are brought into the "reflexive hermeneutic" (Rose 1998: 157) process as a parallel mechanism of surveillance and power.

In addition, inmates are expected to role-model ideal behaviors. For instance, there are always two separate cohorts of up to sixteen inmates in the program, a "junior" group and a "senior" group, chronologically separated by about four months or half the program. The senior group is expected to demonstrate appropriate unit and treatment behavior and to assist in the penitentiary deprogramming of new arrivals in preparation for their own treatment programs.

There are three central, and inherently performative, components to the sexual offender treatment program. All three are done in presentation to the group of staff and inmates and form the core of my analysis in this ethnography. Done in sequence, they are the Autobiography, the Crime Cycle, and the Relapse Prevention Plan. The Autobiography, as I shall discuss in more detail in the next chapter, does not actually involve a free rendering of a life story by a narrator, and in the case of these sexual offenders their sexual crimes are expected to occupy a central place within the story. The Crime Cycle looks more specifically at the context in which specific crimes were committed, in an effort to identify when one is "cycling," or engaging in the kinds of behaviors that tend to lead to the commission of offenses. The Relapse Prevention Plan helps the inmate identify the triggers for his criminal activity and the strategies he might employ to prevent reoffending. Because of the sequential nature of these three steps, the therapeutic community develops a memory: what is said in earlier performances carries forward to subsequent ones, as the group's collective and individual oral recall knowledge of the inmate's story builds. This establishes moving benchmarks in which newer versions or interpretations of crimes and lifestyle are compared to previously related ones.

Along the way, inmates participate in a variety of psychoeducational programs involving what I refer to as moral habilitation. There are units on cognitive skills, values and attitudes, empathy, anger management, assertiveness, and relationships (these will be the subject of the chapterettes). Inmates are expected to do "homework" exercises throughout, and this work is often submitted to the staff for review. Journals are to be kept as well, where the inmate records his thoughts and feelings as the program unfolds. Piece by piece a kind of treatment manual is assembled, as photocopied sheets on the various aspects of the program are disseminated as needed, allowing the men to incrementally gain the big picture of the treatment theory. There are also a variety of other programs available to the inmates that are often operated in conjunction with inmates from other units, such as Alcoholics and Narcotics Anonymous, and spiritual programs operated by the institutional chaplain and Aboriginal elders. Some inmates also attend school or employment within the institution as time permits.

The synoptic nature of the institution pervades the modus operandi of the treatment program. Inmates are expected to share intimate details of their lives, including details of a sexual nature, with the other inmates and staff through the group therapy performances and educational sessions. They are reminded that full openness and disclosure is essential to their treatment and that what is disclosed in treatment is confidential and not to be communicated outside the group or the session. But what they say is often recorded in notebooks by treatment staff members and is the subject of further analyses during staff meetings. Some inmates even believe that the treatment rooms are bugged and that the corrections officers listen to their conversations with the psychiatric nurses. Information is an extremely valuable commodity inside prison. And none of the patients seriously believes the group sessions are confidential given the nature of the other participants. Further, inmates are rather loose with the "what is said in group stays in group" mantra and often engage each other outside of the sessions over matters that arise there.

While the "con code" of incarceration calls for the inmates to protect their secrets and to resist or manipulate prison personnel—hiding the details of their past, especially as sexual offenders, is essential to their personal safety the con code also calls for the punishment of individuals whose offenses are disreputable. Men are often surprised to see an acquaintance, even a friend, from the penitentiary when they arrive on the unit, being unaware until then of the individual's history of sexual offending. Still, it is usually not until the moment of disclosure in the group that the exact nature of those crimes is revealed. Disclosure in a treatment session could lead to new charges, it is believed, and perhaps a beating or worse, as regulatory regimes of judicial process and con code crash one into another. The moral ranking of sexual offenses, with offenses against children at the very bottom, is as much in play on the unit as it is in the broader penitentiary system. Stories abound of security or treatment staff releasing conviction information about inmates to other inmates. This could not be confirmed, of course, but that is irrelevant to the point inmates are making with such suspicions and allegations. Getting inmates to buy into the treatment program, therefore, is a tall order.

At the completion of the program, very few inmates are released into the community. It seems that coordinating the availability of a treatment space with inmates' sentence schedules is difficult, and it is almost impossible for an inmate to be able to attend the program in the latter months of a sentence. This surprises me, given the importance of recidivism as a measure of overall program effectiveness, and is a source of much concern among the inmates. Available evidence suggests that inmates released directly into the community from prison therapeutic treatment programs have lower recidivism rates than those who are returned to the penitentiaries for a time before release (Ware, Frost, and Hoy 2010). Yet most inmates in my study were actually returned to their home institutions, where the lessons learned on the unit are not easily invoked. Some will subsequently be released on parole or reclassified to a lower level of security and transferred accordingly, but this can take months, even years.

"Success" in the program is determined by the therapeutic staff, the forensic nurses and social workers who deliver the program, in consultation with the unit's designated psychologists and psychiatrists. It is their heavy responsibility to render judgment as to the extent, and sincerity, of an inmate's engagement with the program and observable changes in thought patterns and behaviors, including those exhibited in nonprogram contexts as observed by therapeutic and corrections personnel. The stakes are high for the inmate: a successful evaluation can lead to a reduction in security level and subsequent transfer to a facility with better comforts and more freedoms; it can have an impact on parole decisions as it is employed as one factor in assessments of risk to reoffend; and, for some, it can also represent a positive affirmation of a sincere effort to change and become a more prosocial person. But a successful evaluation may have no effect at all, much to the consternation of the inmates. Further, simple completion of the program—attending all sessions and completing all assignments—does not necessarily return a successful evaluation, and sometimes such inmates are offered the opportunity to continue for several months more or return at another time to try again. There are no guarantees.

Treatment staff produce extensive and detailed reports on all aspects of the inmate's experience on the unit, carefully documenting performance in group and individual therapy sessions as well as behavior on the unit more generally, and noting areas in which positive change has been seen and others where more work is needed. There are detailed descriptions of performance in the three narrative events I explore in detail in this book, participation in the psychoeducational sessions, and the results of phallometric testing if applicable (more on this later). It is clear from reading the reports that the staff observe carefully and record much in their notes, reinforcing the inmates' views that they are indeed under constant observation.

Part of the responsibility of the treatment team as well is to assess the risk of recidivism, which they do through both qualitative description of the inmate's treatment progress and the application of a risk assessment instrument. An instrument known as the Static 99 assessment tool remains the most prominent in North American forensic psychology to assess risk to reoffend of sexual offenders (Vincent, Maney, and Hart 2009). This is a ten-item tool that can be completed entirely through file review without a need to interview the inmate, and it does not include any items that relate directly to treatment. Most of my participants, however, were measured pre- and post-treatment by the newer and less-used Violence Risk Scale—Sexual Offender Version (VRS-SO) (Wong et al. 2003; Olver et al. 2007). This instrument combines seven static factors adapted from the Static 99 with seventeen dynamic factors, many of which are potentially responsive to treatment, and is seen as an improvement because the Static 99 appears to lose its predictive accuracy when individuals undergo treatment (Olver and Wong 2010). The twenty-four factors are weighted equally in the summative process to determine the overall risk-to-reoffend score. Examples of static factors are age at the time of release, age at first sexual offense, sex offender type (incest, adult victims, child molester, mixed offender), prior sexual offenses, number and nature of the victims (unrelated, strangers, gender), and number of previous convictions, all factors over which the inmate has no direct control (Wong et al. 2003). The seventeen dynamic factors include sexual compulsivity, cognitive distortions, emotional control, interpersonal aggression, insight, impulsivity, and treatment compliance and are scored from both file review and offender interviews (Olver and Wong 2010). The latter is conducted using a detailed, semistructured instrument. Within this interview, being "successful" or not in the treatment program is specifically scored in one scale item of the seventeen, "treatment compliance"; however, many questions in the interview also probe areas that are targeted in the treatment program. For instance, the interview asks questions of a factual nature, such as the existence of prior charges for sexual offenses and the inmate's views of the specifics of the criminal charges, which can be checked against the official record in the inmate's files. Further, the inmates are asked a variety of questions that could indicate cognitive distortions, including recourse to justification, minimization, and denial, and sexual deviance, and are asked as well to recall "thoughts and feelings" before, during, and after the commission of the crime, all of which feature centrally in the treatment program and create much conflict and controversy for the inmates. Each inmate treatment report presents the initial risk-to-reoffend score at the commencement of treatment (expressed qualitatively, as in "high risk to reoffend") and is also used to identify those items on the scale that require particular attention in treatment. The risk score at the end of treatment is also recorded on the inmate's final report.

The stakes are high for the treatment staff, psychologists, and psychiatrists who engage the inmates and offer their expertise on treatment progress and risk to reoffend, and everyone is cognizant of high-profile cases where released inmates reoffended, sometimes horribly. Indeed, one of my participants was awarded a "successful completion" at the end of his program and yet, a few years later, was charged with the murder of a female acquaintance. The inmates I worked with uniformly condemn such acts, as they detract from any positive attention the treatment program receives from the public and, in their eyes, threatens its very existence. Forensic psychologists express the same worries. Indeed, they seem to be under intense pressure to produce evidence that their program works—there are both financial concerns and a fearful public to contend with—all the while harboring in the back of their minds the fear that one of their positively evaluated charges will reoffend. Since I was not allowed to officially interview treatment staff members, I am not in a position to communicate in greater detail the stresses they experience working with and evaluating the offenders, but I am certain there are many.

"My Autobiography was hard, but . . . I was struggling with it. I was trying to remember some parts that was happy, you know, for me, and there was none. It was all negative. And you know, it was just like I was telling on myself. Because I was told from a small child, you don't tell anybody about our family problems, you know. 'Keep it in the family.' And even like if our brothers and sisters told on each other like, for hurting, you know, rough playing like, because that's how we knew how to play was rough, and if we told, well, "He hurt me," or "Mom, he hurt me," kind of thing, you know, we'd get in heck for that, you know? Like, "Oh, you're ratting on your brother," kind of thing. So you don't do that *kind of thing. So that stuck. So doing that I was just like, oh! I was telling on myself. And then I thought I was betraying the family because I was talking about this stuff too, and that was hard."*

Interview with Andrew

"DO YOU THINK YOU HAVE A PROBLEM?"

Early on in treatment, the inmates are given a basic overview of the treatment process and the cognitive behavioral model. If this is their first time in a treatment program, even a small amount of this information can seem baffling. Even those who have been engaged with programs in their home institutions, where programming is likely only part time and less intense, will struggle with the CBT concepts. "Thinking errors" do not represent an easily comprehensible explanation for their behavior. While agreeing to treatment, they typically arrive on the unit nervous and uncertain about what awaits them. The professional judgment of forensic specialists, as we have seen, is that these individuals suffer from "cognitive distortions" that seem to have a loose relationship with a *DSM* diagnosis of antisocial personality disorder and/or substance-related disorder. It is in the days after their arrival that I engage them with "intake" interviews, endeavoring to explore how they view their own "problems" and prospects for treatment. Then, months later and just prior to their transfer out of the institution at the completion of their programs, I talk to them again about this issue.

Generally, the "problems" identified by the inmates for which they believe they need treatment are dominated by alcohol or substance abuse, and to a lesser extent issues of anger management, depression, and self-esteem. A few men express their "problems" in language compatible with the program, describing issues of morality, emotions, attitudes toward women, lack of empathy or caring, the cycle of violence, and assertiveness. Sexual deviancy, pedophilia, and other mental illness issues are rarely raised, and almost all inmates reject any idea that they suffer from a mental illness. They are willing to be "bad," more likely to admit to "bad" behaviors, but uniformly reject the idea that they are "sick" (Waldram 2009b). The expressions "cognitive distortion" or "thinking errors," or the basic elements of this concept, are rare in the intake interviews when inmates frame their "problems" but, not surprisingly, somewhat more common in the exit interviews.

Ralph was convicted on counts related to sexual assault on children and for having a large collection of pornographic images of children on his computer. Over several years he worked in capacities that allowed him to get close to and gain the confidence of children and their parents, demonstrating the "grooming" behavior characteristic of these types of offenses. A small Caucasian man, he seems to me to be an individual who is socially awkward, prone to saying inappropriate things to other inmates. He believes this to be an expression of his "assertiveness," something that he has learned from a psychologist back in the penitentiary is a problem for him, but it does not seem to be tempered by a sense of propriety, a sense that there are situations in which one should keep one's own counsel. He does not seem well liked on the unit—he is a misfit, if you will. His offenses, well known even early on because of his propensity to announce them at will, do not make his situation any better. On intake, he expresses his "problem" as essentially one of morality. "Yes," he admits to my question, "[I have a problem] because I don't know what's right and what's wrong. So I'm here to get a basis for what's right and what's wrong, and how to implement that into my lifestyle, which up until now has been destructive." Looking away toward the glass wall of the interview room, he adds, "I've had nothing but a destructive lifestyle."

When I interview Ralph seven months later, his explanation of his "problem" is more reflective of the program. "I had major cognitive distortions, major sexual deviant fantasies," he tells me. "My sexual preference was totally wrong." Couching his pedophilia in terms of a "preference" is perhaps an expression of the individualistic agency that is at the heart of the program; to suggest it was a compulsion or the expression of a biologically driven libidinous attraction would be to deny that agency. Yet he seemingly accepts the predominant psychological wisdom pertaining to the paraphilias generally, that these are lifelong conditions, when he concludes, "Yeah, I had a lot of problems, and I still have a lot of problems that I am dealing with and will still be dealing with even when I hit the streets."

Cure, then, is not a word heard on the unit or in treatment, and it exists as a separate concept clearly distinct from that of program "success." It is the sense of the finality of the process that is rejected. The inmates uniformly decline to speak of being cured when they relate their problems. Sam even rejects the term *changed,* preferring to use *changing.* David, an Aboriginal man whom we met briefly earlier in this chapter, was raised mostly in the city and has a long record of alcohol- and substance abuse–related crimes dating back to when he was young, surviving on the streets. He has been to the unit before and was expelled for "treatment-interfering" behavior, which he explains meant, in his case, a refusal to take the program seriously and do the necessary work. He has also been in several other prison treatment programs, and as result the way he initially constructs his "problem" reflects the creep of program language. "I'm a sex offender," he declares matter-of-factly to me during our intake interview, no apparent denial in sight. "And what they're dealing with here is trying to help me understand why I do the things I do. You know, it's from crime cycles through relapse prevention techniques, through telling my life story, understanding what significant parts of my life attribute to my offending."

During the exit interview, as he reflects on his "problem" after eight months of full-time treatment, he again utilizes the language of the program but in more formal terms and now is willing to confront the matter of a "cure." "Well, if you look at cognitive therapy, I need that," he begins, looking away from me as he watches the activity in the day room through the glass wall. "I still got distortions that have to be worked out. I'm a sex offender. I've got sexual behaviors that have hurt people. And I think those are two of the major, major problems that I have right now, you know, is my way of thinking. I think I've got a lot of the understanding feelings part, I think it just needs to be practiced, needs work, needs time."

Returning his gaze to me, he continues:

> You know, I've been this way for many, many years, and to change, just all of a sudden change, it's not going to happen. I've still got fears of being vulnerable, being open to, you know, being hurt. I don't like that. But I think it is a step in the right direction, although, it will . . . be a while before I can actually change, before there's a big change, I guess. You know, I can make the small changes, I can do the small things right now, but as for making leaps and bounds, I don't think I've done that, you know.

"So what you're saying is that your problems have been treated?" I ask. "I don't say 'treated,'" he replies:

> "Treated" sounds like they're done. I think they're *in* treatment. I think they're in the works, you know? And I think there's still a lot of work to do. It's like climbing a hill and . . . and I'm at the bottom of the hill right now. I'm trying to work my way up. Sometimes I'll stumble back, sometimes I'll go forward. It's not . . . it's not easy. It's not going to be done. It's going to be years down the road . . . If I can keep going the way I'm going I'll still be struggling up that hill, you know. But at least I'm making progress. It's not like I'm staying in the same place that I've always been. I am sure I moved beyond that point but I think I still have lots of work ahead of me. You know, practicing it daily . . . and trying to get comfortable with the new feelings, you know, trying to get comfortable with being open. There's

a fear there, but hey, sometimes it feels better, you know? It feels like I don't want to hurt people, and I don't want to hurt myself. But then I get back into that comfort zone where I just don't care . . . And I go there, you know, it's a safe place for me.

Oren hates prison, he tells me while we are sitting in the day room, watching television. "It makes you dysfunctional," he notes, then describes how drugs are readily available, and how one can learn dozens of ways to make weapons and kill people so no one will know. Gangs are always recruiting in prisons, he adds. Expressing what would surely be considered a cognitive distortion, he concludes: "We come in as sex offenders, but we go out as criminals."

Field notes

• • •

As they grapple with learning and "working" the program, the inmates are faced with the realization that complete rehabilitation is unlikely. There is no "cure" for what ails them. Initially, they tend to frame their "problems" in terms of immediate factors, alcohol or substance abuse, bad attitudes toward women, anger, and so on. These problems are almost always of long standing; these men demonstrate troubled lives usually reaching back into childhood. Treatment, to them, is not about being returned to a better, previously "happy" life because, as David notes, for many their "safe" place is a pathological one in which behavioral problems are normative. In many ways they seek new ground, not a return to the old. Some actively seek moral habilitation; others just want out of prison.

Over the course of treatment, they begin to learn about the broader psychological framework in which their problems are embedded. They struggle with the concepts of cognitive distortions and thinking errors and incrementally deduce the basics of CBT. New ideas and ways of discussing their problems enter into their discourse. But while the impact of the program is discursively evident—after eight months there *should* be some evidence that they have at least paid attention to what they were supposed to be learning—this does not speak to the broader issue of psychological and behavioral change. Learning the language, ultimately, is the easy part, and employing it in the service of nontherapeutic goals—such as to obtain a positive evaluation for parole purposes— while appearing to be engaged in treatment creates a tangled web of intentionality that falls to the treatment staff to sort out.

What happens in between the two points introduced in this chapter, between inmates' arrival on the unit and their discharge? Their experience of treatment, I argue, is as important if not more so in understanding the program impact as is the specific content of the psychological and educational information. *How* they receive this information, and in what ways they choose to give it serious consideration and act upon it, are shaped by the power relations extant in the therapeutic prison, by the dynamic created on a quotidian basis at the point where prison inmates of a particularly stigmatized ilk encounter the theoretical framework of CBT (and, less explicitly, the *DSM*) and therapeutically enacted by authoritative treatment professionals—or, in other terms, where the subjective interpretation of a life lived—narrative—collides with a more powerful, authoritative, objective paradigmatic interpretation of that same life. This is the forensic black hole, an area hitherto largely beyond the reach of research. And this is where we journey now.

CHAPTER 4

Moral Citizenship

Local social worlds, according to Arthur Kleinman (1992, 1997, 1999a, 1999b), are not so much a matter of place as they are of morally imbued relationships and networks, and such worlds of experience create the conditions for the genesis and perpetuation of moral life. An inevitable product of human sociality is the formation of "moral communities," not so much in the sense Durkheim (1912/1965) defined them, with the focus on religion, but more broadly in the production of values and codes of behavior, alongside notions of transgression and punishment. Yet this approach to the idea of moral living suggests both a kind of agency and a freedom of association that are not reflective of the circumstances of this ethnography. Prisons—forms of "unintentional" communities as much as "total institutions" (Goffman 1961)—do not consist of individuals voluntarily assembled to pursue common goals, generating, promoting, and enforcing moral codes that respect both individual and collective pursuit of the good life. Citizenship here, to borrow from Aihwa Ong (1996: 737), reflects "a cultural process of 'subject-ification,' in the Foucauldian sense of self-making and being-made by power relations that produce consent through schemes of surveillance, discipline, control, and administration." These communities—and they are indeed "moral" communities despite the popular discourse on the nature of sexual offenders—consist of an involuntary citizenry, anchored to place, that rails against both its membership status and those who employ power to define their citizenship and circumscribe their rights. While these "citizens" must work to survive on a daily basis, they can do so only through the development and maintenance of a moral code relevant to their unique social world, one that emerges within the context of, and often in reaction to, a more powerful moral code backed by the force of law.

Life on the unit, then, is not just about the formation, maintenance, and enforcement of a therapeutic community centered on the group therapy sessions. It is also about community in the broader sense of having to live together, in a confined space, for up to eight months and not only get along but also assist each other in both programmatic aspects and daily living. The boundary between therapeutic and non-therapeutic realms of daily experience blurs but does not disappear. The treatment personnel expect the inmates to take the lessons of therapy and put them into practice in all social contexts of life on the unit. These lessons—derived from the broader CBT and therapeutic community paradigms—both create the conditions for and force the development and maintenance of a moral community. The very structure of the unit, its physical layout, which ensures the viability of both panoptic and syn-optic surveillance, encourages the inmates to be active in self-regulation and self-governance, or "policing" as one inmate described it, to put the program into action, because they are being monitored even during their most relaxed, nonprogram moments (cf. McCorkel 1998). Inmates learn that program-related and prosocial behaviors should be visible to those who surveil if one is to be successful in their program.

But other moral regimes coexist, most notably the "con code" of prison behavior that plays out in both therapeutic and especially non-therapeutic contexts (Cordilia 1983). In contrast to the code of the therapeutic community, elements of the con code that the men bring with them from the penitentiaries should remain hidden from staff, as these represent behavior patterns that are "treatment interfering" and punishable, but they rarely disappear. And, simply put, living in such a restricted space for such a long period of time, under such stressful conditions, creates problems. Inmates get on each other's nerves, and this plays out in all aspects of the program.

Ernest spoke bluntly about this. "Fucking right," he replied, in response to my question about daily life on the unit. "Yeah, you start to get sick of their little habits. You see a guy slurping on his coffee and you just yell, 'Hey man, fuck! You're fucking annoying!' You tell him that." Ernest stops momentarily, and switches into program mode to clarify. "But, what I have been taught here so far, I don't say that to people. I just look at them, you know, stare at them like that until they stop." Returning to his general theme, he concludes. "You hear the same jokes, the same humor, and you get sick of it after a while, yeah, for sure."

The ethos of the therapeutic community and that of the con code merge with that being taught in the treatment sessions in tense and fragile ways, then, to create the unique foundations of this new moral community. The unit's therapeutically based rules "shake one out of the everydayness of being moral," as Zigon (2007: 133) might suggest, by challenging the moral rules of the penitentiary. This challenge represents a "moral breakdown" that characterizes much life on the unit, in which the inmates "need to consciously consider or reason about what one must do" in given situations (Zigon 2007: 133), a reasoning that cuts across these various moral codes. A tenuous harmony does seem to develop, however, representing a balance of moral codes in which con code values and attitudes are more or less kept out of official program activities but loom larger in the daily life of the unit, sometimes as quiet, under-the-breath moments and other times as overt conflict, "muscling" and fighting. Of course this bifurcation is hardly rigid, and moral boundary transgressions happen all the time. Some men struggle to fully embrace the therapeutic moral order and often find themselves removed from the program. And every four months (more or less), this tenuous harmony is disturbed by the arrival of a new cohort, as the con code once again intrudes directly into and overtly challenges the therapeutic community.

Leon complains to me one day about this. A Caucasian, Leon has just turned thirty and is serving two and a half years for a sexual assault on a sex trade worker, committed after he picked her up but forced sex after refusing to pay in advance for the sexual services. This type of crime, I learn, is common among the men in the Hound Pound and reflects an overall negative, even dehumanizing, attitude toward sex trade workers as a whole. This is Leon's first conviction for sexual assault, although he has been known to police for frequenting young women in the sex trade and offering drugs in return for sex. "In the last little bit [a new inmate cohort] there's a couple of kids, I guess, that they're out there doing stuff and it gets irritating," Leon explains. "You get twenty-four people living in an area that's confined, you know, it gets on you after a while, right? You know, where you let things slide on the street, but in here it seems to accumulate until the point of an explosion, and then it seems to, you know, cool down for a while."

As Leon intimates, the lessons of the past must be relearned, new inmate citizens must be socialized and moralized, and disruptions caused by new arrivals must be managed. While the staggered nature of the cohorts helps to ensure the viability of the moral community across cohort generations, this moral community undergoes a continual process of dismantling and reformation that creates points of tension and distress. A significant portion of an inmate's experience of treatment is devoted to reconciling differing moral worlds—CBT therapeutic regimen, con code, therapeutic community, the world "outside"—in an effort to remain in the program, avoid conflict, strategically position oneself within the unit power hierarchy, benefit from the program, or obtain a positive evaluation. This represents life beyond the formal treatment sessions as much as it does what happens in them. It plays out during meals, in evenings and on weekends, and during recreational periods. It is an integral part of life in the Hound Pound.

> Today during a Relationships session the issue of consent is discussed. Several men who had been convicted of statutory offenses regarding underage partners seem perplexed about how one is to be certain that a potential sex partner is of legal age. Meeting women in bars is particularly vexing to the men. One man stresses that, if they are in a bar, they must be "legal." A nurse replies that this is a thinking error, because underage people get into bars all the time. "Well, how are we supposed to know their age?" another inquires. "If we ask them, they would probably lie." "True," admits the therapist. "Ask them for ID," she continues. "What?" several men exclaim. "You can't ask women in a bar for ID! That's not how it works! No one does that!" The nurse does not back down, however, adding that the only way one can be absolutely certain is by checking ID. "But it could be fake," adds another inmate. "They could have used a fake ID to get into the bar. Then what?" The nurse, now a little perplexed, simply responds, 'it's your responsibility to make sure she is legal." This is not well accepted by the men. For the rest of the day this is the topic of much conversation on the unit.
>
> Field notes

"WATERHEADS"

The bus pulls in to the gate, a big, iron-clad highway bus with no windows. The sunlight reflects mirrorlike off the side the way it does on those roundish aluminum trailers one sees throughout tourist country. But these are not tourists. The passengers of record on this bus are prison inmates, new arrivals or "fish" being brought to the institution, most from the "gladiator pits," as one of my participants describes the penitentiaries. Their places on the bus will be taken by those who have completed their programming, or been kicked out, as the bus continues on its circuit from penitentiary to penitentiary. I am never able to see inside it, but I hear many stories from the inmates about the difficult conditions of prisoner transport. The bus is essentially a moving fortress, with the men shackled to their seats, carefully watched by armed guards. No smoking allowed, maybe the most punishing aspect on trips lasting eight or more hours.

As the big iron gate closes, the bus swings around toward the admitting department, where the men will be processed and their personal effects recorded. Most of their possessions will arrive separately, and it will often take several weeks before their televisions, stereos, and non-institutional clothing arrive. These, too, will go through the admitting process, being inspected and enumerated, before being delivered to the inmate's house. Men complain bitterly about these delays, which they interpret as deliberate correctional harassment.

The inmates are given a basic orientation to the institution and its rules before being transferred to their respective treatment units. On the sexual offenders unit, the appearance of "fish" is always the cause for much tension and conflict. A new cohort arrives in dribs and drabs often over several weeks, and the new men find themselves with little to do until their program gets under way. Members of the senior cohort watch warily as the arrivals cross the day room, holding small boxes of institutionally issued personal items (such as towels and blankets) tightly in front of them as their eyes dart about the unfamiliar terrain. The newcomers are sensitive to their vulnerability. Will they be recognized? Will they recognize another inmate? Escorted by corrections officers, they are likely to be locked in their houses right away for a period of "decompression," or else to voluntarily confine themselves. The whole scenario can be shocking and destabilizing.

"I had no idea what I was walking into," explains Ryan. Ryan is a short, somewhat paunchy Caucasian man, with thinning dark hair, in prison for a sexual assault involving a sex trade worker. He suffers from poor health despite being in his early forties and over the course of his program is taken several times to hospital. "All I knew was that it was a treatment program," he continues. "And when I walked in here and down those stairs, I seen all those people. Holy man! I just went to my cell and basically put the wall up and closed the door. I barricaded myself. And when I came out, I was very nasty. Like, 'What are you looking at? Don't look at me like that!' Yeah, it was a frightening and scary experience." A friendly face here, a grumpy one there, an old nemesis in the corner, a mate from the pen who, until now, had kept his history of sexual offending hidden. The surprise is often mutual.

"Yeah, it does cause disruptions," explains Oren of the new arrivals. Oren offended against his stepson and freely refers to himself as a "pedophile." Caucasian, he is now in his late thirties. His crime makes him particularly vulnerable to those freshly arrived. "We've got some guys that have been here waiting [for the cohort to fully assemble], well, by the time we leave it will be three months, sitting doing nothing, you know. They have nothing to do, so they cause problems. Boredom causes problems." Compounding this is that, while two day rooms on the unit are used for group sessions, the inmates from the two cohorts are sprinkled throughout both rather than having a cohort assigned to one room, with their cells in the same area. This means that, when a group session is on, those from the other cohort can be rather disruptive. They are expected to stay in their houses once a session starts or, if they are elsewhere at the time, to wait in the other day room until the session breaks. They do not always do this. "What I have noticed right now is a lot of the guys that have come in are young," continues Oren. "They are in their twenties, very immature; they like to cause the shit, just to have fun. That is their way of having fun. So it disturbs the groups. There is no respect for the groups that are in session. They will come in to your group to go to their room or whatever. It's very disturbing."

"We are a couple of months ahead of them," explains Ryan. "We are like the teacher. They're the student. And that's how it was with the other group [the senior group that just departed]. I just pass it on, what I learned from the other group, because they were three or four months ahead of us, and that's how they did it." His group now has the added responsibility of helping the new inmates adjust to life on the unit, a very different way of being incarcerated than most have experienced up until that time. It will not be easy.

"They're testy," is how Clifford characterizes the new arrivals one day. Clifford is a midtwenties Aboriginal man with an extensive criminal past, including three convictions for sexual assault starting when he was only age thirteen. He is in prison this time for yet another sexual assault, this one quite violent and committed during a home break-in. Physically and sexually abused as a child, he spent his adult years in a whirlwind of drugs, alcohol, and crime. He and his treatment group are roughly at the halfway mark when he speaks with me about new arrivals, and his group is about to transition from the junior to senior status. The group ahead of them has been transferred out, and the all too few days of low density and relative calm are about to change. "They bring the so-called 'pen' attitude," Clifford explains. "They have the attitude of 'I don't care, I don't want to be here. I'm only here because I have to.'"

Harvey is blunter than Clifford. "They're like fucking animals, you know," he complains to me. Harvey is doing five and half years. Drunk, and on a day pass from a residential correctional program, Harvey broke into an apartment and, using a knife, violently assaulted the adult female resident. Harvey is Aboriginal, in his midtwenties.

Describing a kitchen scenario, Harvey continues to characterize the newcomers. "They are . . ." He paused, and made a sweeping gesture with both hands, exasperation in his voice, "Fuck, bread all over, butter, ice is gone. The eggs are all gone. Like they give us portions of eggs and bacon and ham and whatnot, right? And by eight o'clock in the morning that shit's all gone, right? It's like you tell them, 'Hey, can you clean up?' You know? 'Can you wash the dishes or your frying pan or whatever you used? Can you clean it up?' 'Well, why should I?' Right? 'Well, you know, we do live in a clean environment, you know.' Or else they'll take things without even asking. And then you hear their negativity, you hear all the name-calling. What a bunch of waterheads."

As I indicated earlier in this book, the transition from "inmate" to "patient" is not managed easily, and many men never really fully accomplish it despite the best efforts of staff. The hold of the penitentiary is strong, and the inmates do not easily absorb the new way of doing things. New arrivals can be confounding. "It's very frustrating," says David, a member of the senior cohort. "You're already at the point where you've done a little bit of change, and you understand that these behaviors [by the new inmates] aren't acceptable. You follow the rules. And you get these new guys come in and they don't know diddly squat." David motions with his hands as if opening a book. "They knew the rules that they went by in the institution, then they come here and it's a totally different set of rules. And you see these behaviors and it's frustrating." "How do you handle that?" I ask. "What do I do?" David reflects for a moment and then mimics a conversation with a newcomer. "Well, some of them I'll tell them, 'Hey, you're not allowed to do that.' 'Well, what are you, a guard?' 'No, it's just part of the rules.' And you get frustrated, and you get mad. Sometimes I just tell them off. But it can be frustrating. It's a struggle, something that we have to deal with on a daily basis till they get through their head that this is a totally different institution. The rules are not the same."

Ralph also contrasted the unit with the penitentiary:

The prison mentality is that you don't say a damn thing, you don't talk. You fight back. And the program mentality is, we are here to do the program, we don't fight back. Whereas the prison mentality is you fight back. Here we stand up for our rights to a point, but if it's going to be detrimental to the program, then we don't. And the new guys coming in are just starting to learn this, that they don't get their way. Because this is a hospital, and the staff does not buckle down like they do in an institution. So, yeah, the stress levels go up, the anxiety levels go up, and the chances of walls going up happen quite regularly. There's a lot of name-calling, there's a lot of backstabbing in a lot of ways. It only happens when a new group comes in.

"They always get this big macho attitude right away," adds Perry. Perry is in his early forties, an Aboriginal man now on his fifth federal sentence, this time for physically assaulting his ex-wife and several other offenses. Perry was in the sexual offenders program because of prior convictions for sexual assault involving two young preteen and teenage girls, one of whom was assaulted many times over a period of more than a year. An inmate who has a sexual offense in his past will still be considered "untreated" if he does not attend the program, regardless of his current offense. This is not a status conducive to positive parole assessments. "Because they think they know the rules and the regulations and policies and all that," Perry continues, "they think they know it really well. Well, they carry this big aggressive attitude and it's all like, 'C'mon, get a grip! They're going to kick you out with that.' You know, they don't get it."

Andrew, whom we met briefly in the last chapter, is in his later thirties, a Caucasian man with thin blond hair and boyish looks. He is serving his first federal sentence, convicted of sexually assaulting his teen stepdaughter over a period of several years, actions that at the time he considered consensual despite her age. He has clearly bought into the therapeutic community concept. "We are responsible for policing ourselves," he explains during an interview, speaking about the social and organizational life on the unit. "They [staff] don't make the decisions for us, they don't tell us what to do. And if things get out of hand, they don't butt in and fix it for us. It's entirely up to us. If we want to remain part of society and be responsible for looking out for the community, we have to run our own community in here."

Andrew's interpretation of unit governance is, of course, somewhat illusory, as all actions are carefully overseen and only those that are compatible with unit rules are unchallenged by staff. Treatment staff certainly does "butt in" to manage problematic situations and can take this apparent power away from any and all inmates at a moment's notice. Crisis meetings, called "process groups," occur with some frequency, called by the staff to deal with disruptions on the unit. Lockdowns are the most dramatic form of sudden group disempowerment, with the inmates confined to their cells. But Andrew's description does speak to the fervor with which some inmates embrace the highly circumscribed collective agency—an expression of citizenship—that they are permitted to manage their daily affairs while on the unit, a significant change from the penitentiary.

Bookending the program, however, it seems that any advances made over the eight months in adjusting to the new form of governance and daily life on the unit, as well as the exigencies of the program itself, must, by necessity, quickly give way as their programs come to an end and they prepare to return to the penitentiary. This again demarcates a change in their citizenship status. Perry compares the two moments in the inmate's experience. "The first day when the guys come in, they're either afraid to face themselves or just, you know, just the con mentality. Then, at the end, guys are putting back on that con mask because they are going back to the pen and all that. They lapse back into their old behavior of when they first came here. To protect themselves when they go back to the pen." Sometimes that "old behavior" includes such things as gambling, loan sharking, and muscling for favors, which, when they occur near the end of a cohort's program (when they are supposed to know better), often result in harsh penalties not only for the culprits but sometimes for the whole cohort. Recreation periods can be canceled, for instance, computer privileges revoked, and all games removed for long periods of time. In this way the staff continually reinforce the mutual responsibility that all have for the self-governance of the program. The problem for the men, of course, is that "tattling" or "ratting" at any time during the program is against the con code, and to report such offenses to the unit staff is seen to be just as heinous here as it is back in the penitentiary. But ratting and, perhaps more frequently, accusations of ratting, do still occur and undermine the stability of cohorts. Cell searches, especially for drugs, often lead to accusations of inmate ratting, for instance.

The unit is in an ongoing state of flux, therefore, constantly reconstituting itself. It is a dynamic community-in-the-making whose citizenry changes rapidly and can, over the span of a year, be completely replaced. Inmates are bound together by a common thread, a citizenship based on certain acts deemed criminal by the state. The senior-junior system works well to ensure a degree of continuity in living experience on the unit and to integrate the new citizens, with the recently arrived hotheads either brought under control by the wise elders or punished individually and collectively, with penalties including possible expulsion. Yet it seems that everyone is either in the process of learning how to be a moral citizen within the context of the unit and its dominant treatment ethos or preparing to set all this aside to return to a place where this newly acquired morality and associated skills such as assertiveness may get you killed. For a sexual offender, citizenship—whether on the unit, back in the penitentiary, or in the community—is by necessity "flexible" (cf. Ong 1999).

> *There is a coffee party today for the men in the senior group who have finished their programs and are awaiting transfer. It is like a graduation ceremony of sorts, although the inmates must fund the event themselves. A fund-raising drive has been ongoing for the past few weeks in an effort to raise sufficient funds for the coffee, cake, and ice cream. Correctional rules prevent me from contributing. They will attend with some members of their treatment team who are not otherwise busy. The members of the junior cohort will not participate. The mood among the members of the senior cohort is mixed: happy to be done a very demanding program but apprehensive about the future. All of them are heading back to the penitentiary.*

> *Field notes*

"SHIT RUNS DOWNHILL"

"Waiting," sighs Ralph. He is responding to my somewhat gratuitous question, "Whatcha' doin'?" He is watching the television in the day room but appears to be paying little attention to what is on the screen. I have noticed on many occasions that he always seems to be sitting there, on his usual couch and in the exact same spot. This time his face is expressionless, uninspired. But his response suggests that he has more to say.

"It's been a month of doing nothing," Ralph laments. He has complained of this often, and loudly, to anyone who passed by, and an anthropologist is a perfect audience for this complaint. His cohort has started to assemble, but it is a slow process, and he is frustrated. He had begun a treatment program back in the penitentiary and is anxious to keep the momentum going. The break is not helpful. But it is unclear when his program will begin, and his repeated requests to the treatment staff that he be given something to do are, in his eyes, being ignored. So there is lots of time to watch and learn from the members of the senior cohort, "Getting to hear what all the inmates say." Then, changing voices to mimic another inmate: "Well, don't say this, don't say this, don't say this, don't say this."

"What concerned you the most when you arrived here?" I ask. Ralph mulls the question over, and then repeats it: "What was I concerned about when I first arrived?" Then: "What are they going to use against me? How are they going to use this against me?" "Who's 'they'?" I ponder. "Staff, other inmates," Ralph replies. He flicks his head to motion across the day room toward a small group of inmates playing a board game. "Somebody's going to come up behind me and shank me even though they are in here for more or less the same reason.[1] Maybe not the exact same reason but still a sex offense case. That was my big concern." Then, betraying a sense of vulnerability, he adds, "Plus, would anybody . . . yeah, would anybody like me once they found out what I was in for."

Unless they have been to the unit before, inmates tend to be very anxious upon arrival, and it takes a while for them to grow comfortable enough to engage in the program. "Well, when I first arrived here," explains Jerry, "I was kind of edgy, kind of cautious, you know, like I didn't know what I was getting myself into. But I knew I was here for treatment." When I interviewed him, Jerry, an Aboriginal man in his midthirties, was in the midst of a five- year sentence for a particularly violent sexual assault on two female acquaintances. "The other people thought that I was a troublemaker. I guess just the way I talked I guess, you know, I guess the way I express myself." His correctional record certainly bears this out. "The first month was very, very boring. It was slow and I wanted to go back to the . . . institution where I came from."

Leon, like Jerry and Ralph, was also forced to wait a long while before the program started. "When I came here there was nothing for me to do, so I found it very boring. Pacing and everything else. When we started our like, introductory stuff, you know, when the program started, I guess I was afraid, you know, like, of opening up. Didn't know the people. So the lack of trust there. So I always had my guard up. So from there I . . . started to . . . you know, take a chance and just talk, open up a little bit, share a little bit about myself, letting them know who I was, you know, what my charge was."

Ryan also had a rough start. While on the unit he is at times quite studious, quietly focused on learning what is required of him, the violent nature of his offense suggests he is quick to anger. "I met one of the facilitators here," Ryan begins, "and within the first two hours I was swearing at them, calling them filthy names, foul language. 'When's the bus coming? I want to get on the bus!' I just didn't care. I cared about me and that was it. Didn't care about the rest of the world. Didn't even care about my family, friends. I had no intentions of changing, no intentions. I was so used to living that lifestyle of controlling people, manipulating people, hurting people, verbally aggressive." He then grows reflective and, looking back to when he first arrived, his voice hushes and he speaks admiringly of the staff. "They didn't give up on me here. They kept on saying, 'You really want to go on that bus, we can have it arranged.' But they didn't give me the ticket. They had faith in me."

Like many, Ernest withdrew in the beginning, unsure of the others on the unit and what was being asked of him. Ernest is an Aboriginal man in his midtwenties, with a strong build and a square jaw. He is famously sarcastic on the unit, and a little hotheaded. During his program he has been frequently involved in altercations with other inmates. Trouble seems to follow Ernest, or else he follows trouble. He is serving his first federal time, a five-year sentence for the sexual assault of a female acquaintance that he committed while intoxicated at a house party. His stay on the unit is characterized by his extreme reluctance to discuss the details of the crime. Ernest tells me about his early days.

"Okay, well, when I got off the bus, I was a little scared," he explains. "I wasn't sure what to expect. Actually, I was sure. I thought for sure that I would have problems because of what I was doing time for. That's sexual assault, eh? And I knew it would be obvious, you know, everybody would know what I was in for because I am on a sex offenders unit. So I thought maybe I would be doing most of my time in my cell and I would be just coming out for programs." But the pull of the moral community forming around him was irresistible. "And it wasn't like that," he continues, "because a lot of people that are here right now need this program too, and they have got too much to lose, so they don't want to fuck up just to fuck up, you know. So, then I caught on to that, and I knew that right away because I talked to these therapists and psychologists, psychiatrists. First two or three months, I didn't go outside because I was paranoid, but after a while you just start going out there and start talking to different people."

It is not easy, then, for the men to assemble in the cohort and form any kind of community, let alone a therapeutic one. Since they are largely strangers to each other, the suspicious demeanor needed for survival in the penitentiary makes any chance of bonding quickly rather remote. There is no "crewing up" against the staff either, because the inmates have yet to trust each other. Despite the signs of an obvious, significant power imbalance, there is no "us against them" mentality; rather, it is "every man for himself," better known in prison as "doing your own time." This attitude does break down somewhat as the inmates come to realize the effect that the behavior of others can have on their own goals for seeking treatment. This is where the self-policing perhaps becomes most visible. After one group session, for instance, in which an inmate admitted to a record of extensive violence, including during previous stays on the unit, one of his peers announced to all that he was "psycho," a threat to everyone, and should not be here. Another time, after describing one inmate's Autobiography as "bullshit," an inmate told me that "men like him don't belong here. He refuses to admit what he's done."

The inmates themselves are attuned to violations of the moral order by others and may even demand punishment. Leon explains this in some detail: "Certain of these people should never have come here, whether it is in their correctional plan or not," he tells me one day in the interview room:

> They don't have the right mentality to be here, you know what I mean? There's no reason that twenty-four grown adults shouldn't be getting along, period, right? So, if you have people that are selfish, I don't think they should be here. I don't think people with the wrong attitude should be here, or should be allowed in here, you know? Keep them locked up until they come in with the right attitude, and if you ain't coming in with the right attitude, then stay there. It's your choice, you know, but I don't think other people should come in here and screw up other people's programs.

Even conceding that, by definition, the inmates have problematic behaviors is not a sufficient excuse for Leon. "I know it's a high-intensity program. Still, you know, there's a lot of people in here that, I don't know, their attitudes I guess are . . ." he pauses as if for effect, "a few of them need smacks, it is the only way that I can describe it, because they don't seem to respect authority." Further, Leon finds it problematic when the skills they are learning in their programs do not have an impact on these others:

> They don't respect assertiveness, because you try out a lot of this stuff that you learn in here, eh. And if somebody looks at you and after you tell them politely, "Hey, listen, you know, because you cannot be taking

everybody else's breakfast in the morning, just take your own." And it continually happens. Well, something has to be done, you know, like there's something that has got to be done about it. You can go to all the meetings you want and you can go to all the, I guess, assertiveness [sessions] you can, but sometimes some of these people the only thing that they understand is a big shock to the beak and that's it. And then they seem to understand that, you know?

Having spent years hiding their offenses in the penitentiary, or else fighting off jailhouse predators and those who detest them because their offenses are known, the inmates now face a kind of exposure they have learned to dread. It takes some time for the unit to become a safe place for them. "It's scary, not knowing who to trust, and even the guys I knew, not knowing how much they were going to spread ahead of me [about my crimes] before I disclosed," says Ralph. The apprehension that one's offenses are the worst imaginable is pervasive, and many others share Ralph's fear. But some have less interest in parsing the differences in individual crimes, finding some comfort in being surrounded by peers. "The first two weeks were hell," explains Ernest. "After a while I started getting used to it. I didn't have to hide anymore. In the pen, you have to hide what you're in for. But here, you don't because everyone is equal again, eh."

Well, not quite. "Shit runs downhill, and we are at the bottom," explains Alvin, describing how the prison hierarchy transfers to the unit along with the inmates. Alvin, Caucasian, is one of the senior citizens on the unit, doing a life sentences for the sexual assault and murder of a young girl. It seems odd to find a lifer in the program, since while in Canada a "life" sentence does not necessarily mean the inmate will never be released, in Alvin's case he certainly seems reconciled to being inside for many years to come. A change of scenery was certainly a factor in his decision to volunteer for the program, and the unit is known back in the penitentiary as a place where the rules are a little more relaxed. As well, crimes against children are uniformly disparaged in the penitentiary, and the treatment unit, while not immune to the hierarchy of crimes characteristic of the penitentiary, was thought by Alvin to also be a little more relaxed on this score. As Goffman (1963) describes in his famous work on stigma, the "discreditable" live a life partially hidden from view, keeping elements of their identities secret for fear of the persecution that might follow. But some of the "discreditable" become more discredited than others when these secrets are made public. Alvin, Ralph, and others like them have much to fear indeed, including from inmates like Ernest, it turns out, who never hides his contempt for those who have offended against children. Ernest's offense is much more "acceptable" than Ralph's because it involved an adult female, the expression—albeit criminal—of a "normal" sexual attraction, according to him. "Everybody is looking for a pecking order," notes Leon. "Nobody wants to be the worst, you know."

Hence the ranking of sexual and related offenses is nuanced and serves as raw material in the ongoing construction of a moral community. And some inmates are quite blunt about all this. Take Franklin, for instance, a midthirties man of mixed Caucasian and Aboriginal heritage with a record of alcohol and drug abuse combined with sexual assaults. A large man, Franklin carries himself on the unit as someone to be reckoned with. "Some of the guys I have no problem with," he explains. "I have trouble listening to the pedophiles disclose. Actually, I think they should be in different groups. I think there should be rapists in one group and pedophiles in the other group. I have a hard time when I am sitting in the kitchen making something and a pedophile says something. I don't really talk to him. I want to choke him when I hear a guy is trying to have sex with a six-year-old girl. It flashes me right back to being eleven years old and being sexually abused by a pedophile. Like that one guy there, I don't think he should ever get out of jail. Forty-five, fifty victims? I don't think he should be out of jail. I think he's done. I think he has had his chance. Too bad, you don't deserve another. And then he bitches that he can't get visits with his kids. I want to run over there and choke him and say, 'Didn't you see what you were doing?'"

Knowing whom to trust and whom to be wary of is another key to survival in the penitentiary; distrust of other inmates is elemental in the con code. Yet trust is central to the operation of the program and life on the unit; the men are expected to disclose everything and yet keep it all confidential. And trusting the staff is also somewhat of a stumbling block for new arrivals, who have grown accustomed to viewing anyone linked to corrections with suspicion; hence the demeanor of new inmates tends to be more combative than constructive. The "bulls" must be opposed, that is the con code, unless they can be manipulated. But the nurses are the source of much bewilderment at first, as they occupy a somewhat anomalous position within corrections as individuals who present as caring and not simply custodial. And all staff members on the unit, including the corrections officers, behave differently than in the penitentiary, as they try to create a more relaxed, therapeutic atmosphere despite surroundings that never fail to demarcate this space as a prison. Many find this disconcerting at first.

"Oh, I had a big thing, me against them," says Rick, "where it was me against the staff. Because for the time that I've been inside, I've always had a strong hatred towards [correctional] staff. From the stuff that I've seen." Rick, according to his records, has a strong hatred toward a lot of people. He is in his early thirties, a Caucasian with a long record of violent offenses, and is currently doing nine years for several counts of sexual assault involving a weapon. "And so it was a big, big shock when I got here," he continues, "in the way the staff, you know, intervened with the inmates and that, and got in playing cards with them, playing games and that stuff with them. So that was strange for me. Made me suspicious and worried because I didn't know what they were trying to do. I got to learn to trust them. Because in the pen you don't talk to staff at all."

As Rick suggests, the unit represents such a shift in modus operandi for the inmates that they struggle at first, and many never fully adapt. Comparison with the penitentiaries dominates their thinking, as they employ old schemas to interpret new circumstances and these fall short. Leon's views echoed those of Rick's. "Out here [on the unit] you see them," Leon explains of the staff. "The staff will come out, they'll have chats with you, you know, they'll sit and play cards, play games, and they'll watch TV with you. You don't have that in the pen at all. Staff [there] don't come out of the office unless they're doing counts."

Eddie, a Caucasian, is the oldest member of his cohort, entering his sixties. He is in prison for a variety of statutory offenses involving underage teenagers for whom he provided shelter, sustenance, and drugs. He was somewhat shocked at the demeanor of the staff when he first arrived. "Well, day one you . . . you arrive here, right? And the nurses are treating you so nice, yeah! Like people are treating you nice! Like you're a person! You know what I mean? In [the penitentiary] they don't treat you like a person, you're just a number." Even the corrections officers seem different, although many men remain particularly wary of them, an old and well-learned response to those with the greatest visible power over them.

The prison informal (and illegal) economy works this way. An inmate borrows something, perhaps a "bale" or package of tobacco, and promises to repay at a higher rate, perhaps two bales, when he is paid from his prison work. Some men accumulate debts this way, and this can lead to problems when they cannot repay. This happened on the unit this week, and one man with high debts complained to the treatment staff that he was being intimidated because he could not repay. The treatment staff reacted by shutting down the entire treatment program for a week. The program schedule was removed from the bulletin boards, and everyone was in the dark as to when the program might start up again. An inmate explained to me that this form of prison economy is seen as "treatment interfering." It is hard to discern if shutting down the program is meant as punishment or a demonstration of control by the staff. Certainly the degree of boredom accelerates with each passing day.

Field notes

CONTRACTING MORALITY

When inmates are first incarcerated in a federal penitentiary, they undergo a comprehensive intake assessment, at which time their "criminogenic needs" are identified and a treatment plan addressing these is developed. Typically, for a sexual offender, one criminogenic need is to undertake specialized sexual offender treatment, either in the penitentiary or at the treatment unit. Sexual offenders are also assessed for their risk to reoffend and then classified as to the level of "intensity" of treatment that they need. "High-intensity" treatment, which is what the unit offers, is recommended for those with the greatest recidivism risk. But these also tend to be inmates who have had difficulties in their home penitentiaries and have not managed well in the less intense treatment programs. They must actually apply to attend the unit's program, and they are screened by the unit staff to determine their suitability and motivation as well as need for treatment. All of these various assessments can lead to an invitation to transfer to the unit and the offer of a contract to cement the deal.

One afternoon, as I am talking with Andrew, Hank appears holding a piece of paper. Hank is a skittish man, small and thin. Ever since he arrived a few weeks ago he has seemed awkward and uncomfortable on the unit. "I don't belong here," I overhear him mutter one day, to no one in particular. In group sessions he never speaks a word. He is nearing his fifties but looks much younger. Hank, Caucasian, is serving his second federal sentence, this time for multiple counts of sexual assault involving preteens known to him; his prior convictions also include sexual assault on children. He waits patiently while Andrew and I chat, but since I can tell he obviously wants to talk to me I bring my conversation with Andrew to a close and turn to Hank as Andrew leaves for his house. Hank quietly asks if we can talk in one of the interview rooms.

Once there, he explains that he wants to ask me a question, because I am "neutral." The piece of paper twists in his hands as he elaborates. "It said on the handout that you don't work for the prison."[2] I can, therefore, give him an unbiased opinion, he has concluded. He unfolds the now crumpled treatment contract on the table, and smoothes it out. We read it over together, silently.

The contract stipulates that he is agreeing to undergo treatment for "sexually aggressive behavior." This expression appears twice in the contract, and Hank explains that he has a serious problem with this. He does not have sexually aggressive behavior, he insists to me. He points out that he is in fact innocent of his current charges, one of the few men I encounter who denies in totality the charges of which he has been convicted. He asks me if I have encountered anybody else with the same issue with the contract. "Not yet," I reply, but clarify that some men have expressed disagreement with certain aspects of the official record on their offenses. "What would happen if I refuse to sign?" "Well," I say, "in my experience on the unit so far what's likely to happen is that they will explain to you that you do indeed have sexually aggressive behavior. They will say you're in denial regarding this and that you will learn this truth in treatment." I do not want to suggest that he will be threatened with expulsion, although I know this is likely. A look of great concern crosses his face. He believes that signing the form will be an admission of guilt, and he is adamant that he has not done these crimes. He wonders aloud if he will be able to stay in the program. "Unlikely," I respond reluctantly, "unless you sign the form." As we leave the interview room he adds that he is going to contact his lawyer to determine the implications of this signature.

Treatment contracts are common in many forms of individual and group therapy in the community. For the inmates and staff on the unit, the treatment contract represents many things. First and foremost, it represents informed consent to undergo treatment. It outlines the basic areas of the treatment program and identifies potential risks, such as stress, embarrassment, and strong emotional reactions such as anxiety and depression. It explains that there may be some risk to the relationship the offender has with his family. The offender also consents to a fairly wide sharing of information accumulated during treatment, including with the courts and other correctional bodies that may have an impact upon his sentence. Assessment and monitoring procedures are noted, including ongoing psychological evaluation.

The contract also lays out a code of conduct for the inmate, the building blocks for the formation of a moral community by fiat. In addition to agreeing to be "honest" and assuming "full responsibility" for his offenses and behavior, the inmate agrees to attend all sessions, be prompt, respect the confidentiality of other inmates, refrain from alcohol and drugs (including agreeing to submit to testing), avoid contact with "sexually stimulating materials," and refrain from verbally threatening or assaultive behavior.

While the offender retains the right to refuse to participate in any aspect of the treatment, this is paired with a suggestion that to do so may result in the termination of treatment and, implicitly, a return to the penitentiary. Indeed, any violation of the terms of the contract may be seen as grounds for termination. Further, the contract acknowledges that not only do the treatment staff members have the authority to determine the compliance of the inmate with the contract and terminate an inmate's program for contract violations, but they can also do so for behaviors not stipulated in the contract that they nevertheless find problematic. The contract leaves no question as to who is in charge.

As in Hank's case, most of the concerns that inmates have about the contract pertain to the required admission of guilt regardless of any plea they may have entered during trial. They tend also to be perturbed about agreeing that their offenses can be characterized as "sexually aggressive." The contractual language regarding offenses is simple and un-nuanced, intentionally so since a foundational element of CBT would interpret nuances as cognitive distortions. But many inmates do not view their crimes as un-nuanced at all, and therefore a blanket admission of culpability is often resisted. The options of signing such an admission or being removed from the program, and the implications of expulsion, are made clear. The relationship between the treatment program and various officials in the correctional and justice system, including parole officers, is explicit. If you fail in the program, important people with power over your freedom will know.

Hank gave in. "I did sign it just to stay in the program," explains Hank in a later interview. "I read it to my friends and my family on the phone and they told me not to sign it. But I was told that if I didn't sign it I would be sent back to the institution without the program. I talked to my primary [nurse], and I was told that I had to sign it to stay in the program because I need the program to get parole. Because . . . if I refuse the program it's obvious what's going to happen. I'm not getting parole."

There are often other concerns as well, about conditions attached to the contract that are specific to the inmate. One morning as I am sitting in the day room after a group session had been suddenly canceled, Oren plops down beside me. He is part of the new cohort, along with Hank, that has recently arrived and is grappling with the contract. "Has anyone else in your research expressed concern about signing these?" he asks. By now, a few have, including Hank, so I reply in the affirmative. Oren then informs me that the clinical director is telling him he must forget all about his family if he is to remain in the program. Oren, the reader will recall, offended against his stepson. Yet he is upset that he will not be allowed to have any contact with his family or anyone related to the offense, and he does not accept the judgment of the treatment staff that family visits will not be in his best interests at this time. It has been suggested to him that his wife is being irresponsible as well by allowing him to see the children while he is in the penitentiary and by continuing to have contact with him. He does not want to sign the contract as a result, because this would be agreeing to cut his ties with his family. "I don't want to erase them from my life."

The authority of the treatment staff to dictate and enforce the terms of the contracts is absolute, and this fact is made clear to the inmates. There is no room for negotiation, and the contracts follow a template fairly closely. "I feel it's a very forced contract," Oren tells me. "They're telling on one hand if you want treatment you're going to agree to everything we say whether you like it or not. But," he continues, pointing out what he sees as an incongruity in this approach, "on the other hand they teach us in groups that consent has to be without any punishment or coercion or force or anything like that, and that's exactly what they do, to get you to sign this contract."

Not all inmates have concerns about these contracts, as Hank and Oren and several others did. Some inmates desperately want to get into the program, but not necessarily for therapeutic reasons. "No problems," with the contract, explains Gabe, an early sixties Caucasian and self-styled "hippie" doing a life sentence for the murder of his victim, a crime he too denies. Sweeping his long hair back and gesturing a signature, he continues. "I told them, 'You point me, I'll go.'" Why he would want to attend such a program as this puzzles me at first, given that he is not likely to leave prison for many, many years if at all. Likewise I wonder why he was accepted into the program. It becomes clear to me in our interview that for Gabe the treatment program constitutes a "time-out" from the penitentiary, his likely home for the majority of the rest of his life. So he does not really care what he signs. He just needs to get out of the penitentiary for a while.

A change of venue is also important for John. John is a Caucasian in his late forties, with a long criminal history involving breaking and entering and robberies. He considers himself a "professional thief," telling me once in an interview, and with pride, that he only ever stole from rich businesses and never from people's homes. Wiry but tough looking, he also has several sexual assault convictions, including one involving a minor. John describes for me an extremely difficult penitentiary experience. "No concerns," he explains, about signing the treatment contract. "I was too concerned with getting out of a very volatile situation, where the inmates are let out three, four at a time in a very high-security structured area. High security for the staff, not the inmate," he clarifies, looking me square in the eyes to be certain I understand. "Let them out to fight," he continues gravely, "let them out to squirt each other with piss and shit, feces, and urine. Light fires. I was in one of the worst prisons in Canada before I came here. It was just," he pauses, searching for the right word, ". . . a nightmare. So I would have done backflips to get out of there. I would have done just about anything they asked to get out of that. So that's all I was concerned with. I didn't want to catch any diseases." His hand motions across his face as he clarifies. "I'm disease free, and I still have all my teeth. And I can deal with the scars, the physical scars and the emotional scars that I've received in the last twenty-two months [in prison]. I think I can overcome all of that. But I felt that . . . that it was still a high-risk situation and it was just a matter of time before I contracted hep C from a fight, or worse, AIDS, or tuberculosis from all the piss and shit being flung everywhere. So I would have done anything to get out of that."

Curtis, on the other hand, has a different motive for attending. Curtis has a history of sexual assault and drug offenses. An Aboriginal man in his forties, short and paunchy, he is serving his first federal sentence of five years, this one for sexual assault on his ex-common-law wife. Like many in his cohort, he committed his offense while seriously intoxicated. "I am here to do treatment and I want to get this behind me," he explains. "I need this program and I have been waiting for two years to come here. They finally accepted me." Curtis has been frustrated by his thwarted efforts to attend. "When I first came in [to prison], when I got sentenced, they told me, 'Oh, you have got to go to [treatment].'" But actually getting in was problematic. "They keep on bumping me, bumping me, bumping me," he explains. "I should have been here about a year ago. I should have been here, but I kept on getting bumped. 'Someone else took your spot, somebody else took your spot.'" "Did you have any problems signing the contract?" I ask. "Nope," Curtis replies without thinking. "Parole." He smiles.

Some inmates, of course, are willing to sign the contract because they have come to realize that they do have problems. But unless they have been on the unit before, this realization is likely to come incrementally, in which case their signature on the contract becomes a leap of faith. Ernest notes that, at the outset, "I didn't want to sign it. I wanted to leave, eh? It was my first day. Yeah, I wanted to ditch this place. I wasn't comfortable, eh, opening up, when everyone is opening up. I didn't sign my thing for a while." Ernest was worried, as many men are, that his offense was the "worst possible" and that it would be embarrassing to relate and would open him up to abuse from others. "I finally did sign it," he continues, "when I started hearing the problems that the other guys were having." A glimmer of moral light creeps in as he speaks to the idea of the therapeutic community. "I started relating, you know what I mean? And I started to see that a lot of these guys here too, they are here for help." Then, turning on the program language, he criticizes those who are failing to make the moral grade (unlike him, as he obviously believes):

> A lot of them are still, you know, in heavy denial, eh. "Oh, I was drunk," "Oh, I was blacked out." I could have said that to you during my life story, eh, but I knew what I was doing [in the commission of the crime], you know what I mean? I knew it. I took advantage of the situation. Shouldn't have. Lot of guys they will tell you, "I black out around fifty times a year and I can't remember nothing." Stupid, because I have had blackouts too but I never act like that, you know what I mean? You only do things that you have thought of before.

This kind of resistance to treatment is often seen as problematic by those who, like Ernest, see themselves as sincere in their desire to change for the better.

While inmates sometimes explain that they were "told" to sign the contracts, overt coercion does not seem to occur. But the inmates are well aware of the implications of *not* attending the program. These weigh heavily on their minds, so that some become frustrated and angry when their application to the program is rejected or when they are required to wait several years before they can be accommodated. And once they are admitted, the contract serves as such a strong vehicle for conformity to the rules that inmates can be—and are—expelled for violations, for "treatment-interfering" behavior. The attrition in the four cohorts I studied was striking. In one, the group was down to fewer than half its starting number by the time my exit interviews were concluded. Another group was whittled down to just six. Of the thirty-five men with whom I conducted intake interviews, only twenty-six remained to the end of their programs. Rumors that a particular inmate was about to be expelled often circulated about the unit. In the interests of security the inmate was often not told of the decision until just shortly before he was removed and then was usually taken to a different area of the institution to minimize any disruption he might cause on the unit. He would then ship out on the next bus. During my research one inmate quickly barricaded himself in the kitchen of the unit after getting the news, forcing the correctional officers in full protective gear—the "Darth Vaders"—to extract him. The specter of individuals being removed, occasionally by force, looms large over the daily life of the unit. The consequences for violating the contract can be significant.

Recent forensic research suggests that voluntariness is a significant factor in understanding the outcome of treatment programs. Court-mandated treatment, for example, is considerably more problematic and less successful (i.e., in reducing recidivism or program attrition) than treatment programs for imprisoned offenders that are "voluntary" (Parhar et al. 2008). Yet even in my study, where inmates must "volunteer" for treatment by signing a contract, the carceral setting and its attendant power structures dramatically affect the agency of inmates to agree to participate in treatment and to resist the power and authority of the therapists; indeed, one can ask if "voluntary" treatment in such a context is an oxymoron. To see these inmates as fully agentive in this matter would be to ignore the obvious power imbalance. And power imbalance is the essence of therapeutic intervention.

Four men are sitting at a table playing cards in the lounge. The TV is on in the background, playing a music video channel. One of the players—physically the largest on the unit at the moment—gets up and walks over to the TV and turns up the volume quite loud. Saying nothing, he returns to the table. There are two other men sitting near the TV playing chess. After a few seconds, one of them stands up and turns the TV back down. The first man shouts, "Hey!" at the second, gets up out of his seat, and again walks over and turns the TV volume up. He then carries the TV

remote with him back to the card table. When the song that is playing
ends, he turns the TV down. Nothing else is said amongst the two groups.

Field notes

. . .

The key to understanding local moral worlds, according to Arthur Kleinman (1992, 1995) is to ascertain what is "at stake" for their citizens, that is, "what we most fear, what we most aspire to, what we are most threatened by, what we most desire to cross over to for safety, and what we jointly take to be the purpose, or the ultimate meaning, of our living and dying" (1992: 129). A great deal is "at stake" for inmates in this program. To refuse to attend the program results in their being categorized as "untreated," and this has serious parole consequences. Their very presence on the unit itself is risky; they "out" themselves as sexual offenders from the moment they arrive and are seen by inmates from other units during joint recreational periods. It does not take much to deduce their unit designation and hence their crimes. When they return to the penitentiary following treatment, their status as a sexual offender may now be exposed and their personal safety jeopardized. To be removed from or fail the program maintains their "untreated" designation, and they may wait years before they are able to return to try again. Few seem to come into the program focused only on rehabilitation. Most want out of prison altogether and, barring that, a reduction in their security level and placement in a better, more comfortable institution when the program is done. This is no secret to the therapeutic staff members, who, despite disparaging comments on their intelligence by some inmates, are quite seasoned at reading inmate motives. Simply put, for the inmates what is "at stake" is their future, but not necessarily the one that is envisioned by the correctional and justice systems.

Clearly what can be seen to emerge and be recreated is not simply a therapeutic community—and how "therapeutic" it is will be a matter for subsequent discussion—but also a moral community in the secular sense of the formation and maintenance of a community of people centered on sets of values and practices alongside notions of transgression and punishment. Some, no doubt, may have difficulty thinking of a room full of sexual offenders as representing a "moral community," but not doing so would reduce the complexities of human experience to the level of an uninformed and reactionary public discourse. Further, in no way is the formation of either a therapeutic or moral community an easy, seamless process, and of course it is never complete. The juxtaposition of the carceral with the therapeutic ensures that there are many competing and contradictory values and interests, many tensions that play out each and every day, from the group therapy session to the kitchen. While I would not suggest that inmates view the program as a zero-sum game—it is possible for all to receive a successful evaluation—the therapeutic community paradigm in particular lends itself to a kind of competitiveness in which the challenges one inmate makes to another are not simply about helping him, but are also, and perhaps mostly, about advancing one's own position vis-à-vis program staff. The sense that any given individual can ruin the program for others ensures that the emerging collective morality is always tinged with self-interest.

Hence the creation of a moral community is not smooth, and its citizenry remains volatile and constantly in a state of flux. Several moral worlds collide on the unit. The first is represented by the terms of the contract and, more broadly, the prison and hospital regulatory regimes and the therapeutic paradigm pragmatically enacted by the treatment team. The second is embodied in the notion of the "con code," complete with its own values, practices, and codes for behavior appropriate to survival in the "gladiator pits" of the penitentiary. The third moral world is that created intersubjectively by individual inmates, acting with and on each other as they form a tentative cohort—a therapeutic community—and move together through the program, and as they struggle to invoke the moral ethos of therapy through the interpretive lens of disciplinary punishment characteristic of the penitentiary. By the time newly arrived inmates make their first tentative steps in their program by offering their Autobiographies, they have begun to witness and experience the conflict between the therapeutic and penitentiary moral codes; the conflict between the narrative and paradigmatic modes awaits.

"Stinkin' Thinkin'"

I use the term *moral habilitation* to refer to the process by which individuals are morally remade in the image of certain ideals regarding appropriate social and ethical conduct so that they become "fit" to be among us. Being moral, notes Zigon (2007: 133), is a largely "unreflective state" that is shattered when breaches of the moral order occur, thereby requiring more conscious deliberation and reflection. Moral habilitation in my case, then, is a response to "moral breakdown" indicated by the commission of sexual crimes, a response that requires the inmates to "consciously consider or reason" not only about their past actions but also about the new, prosocial life that is said to await them if they are successful in treatment.

The first psychoeducational group program that the men experience after orientation that kick-starts the process of moral habilitation is "Cognitive Strategies." "Cog" Strategies, as they typically refer to it, represents an introduction to the basic philosophy of CBT, "an approach to helping participants change their behavior by correcting their errors in thinking" (Treatment Manual).[1] This includes an examination of "how thoughts and feelings determine behaviour." According to the Treatment Manual, "Participants develop an awareness of how perceptions, self talk and distorted thinking influence their offending behaviour, and begin to change their distorted thinking patterns. . . . [They] learn how their thoughts can influence their emotions, and determine behaviour in a concrete fashion. They also learn how to challenge their thinking and replace their irrational thoughts with positive self-talk" (33). Put more colloquially in a handout, the men go through a three-step process of cognitive therapy: first, "Identify the distorted thinking (stinkin' thinkin') that is connected to the problem behaviour"; second, "Challenge the distorted thoughts (stinkin' thinkin')"; and finally, "Practice using alternative coping thoughts and/or positive self talk." Throughout the module, they cover such topics as "black and white thinking" (or "right and wrong thinking, when someone is unable to see a middle ground"), "cognitive theory of low self-esteem," the difference between "healthy" and "unhealthy" fantasy and how to control fantasies, definitions of shame and guilt, goal setting, "behavioral interventions to challenge and change your distorted thoughts," and "how to think rationally." The lessons include "general myths" of sexuality, such as that "all physical contact must lead to sex," "a man's penis should be large," "a man should always be aggressive," and "masturbation is an inferior form of sexuality." Separate "cognitive distortions" and "myths" related to sexual offenses against children are also covered, such as "If a child/adolescent flirts with an adult, it means that he or she wants to have sex with the adult." These lessons are frequently firmly grounded in a contextualized model of morality. For instance, another "myth" they discuss is that "in many cultures, sex with children/adolescents is accepted. It is our puritanical backgrounds that prevent sex between children and adults." In response to this myth, the inmates are told, "You are not living in another society, but one in which sex with children is not tolerated. If you choose to live in this society, you must deal with the rules and laws that govern it." Specific cognitive distortions, especially forms of minimization, justification, and denial, are detailed as "SOB," or "Sex Offender Bull," and include "She asked for it," "I was drunk," "It just happened," and "She's a bitch and deserved it." The men examine a long list of these and check off what "bull" they have used in the past and what they still use today.

There is a great deal more to Cognitive Strategies than I have detailed here, of course, but this will provide a flavor of what the men experience. The sum total of these, I argue, is to establish a baseline for "prosocial" moral, behavior. The inmates are told explicitly that the lessons learned here are to be carried forward into subsequent programs and that the treatment staff will watch carefully for evidence of this.

"I didn't know that word, *cognitive,* until I came here," explains Curtis. "Never heard it. Didn't know what it meant. Didn't know none of this." As the foundation is laid for the overall program during

Cognitive Strategies, those inmates who have never had similar treatment are required to learn a whole new language, as Curtis suggests,
a whole new way of looking at their lives and appreciating their dys-
functionality. "Like, the homework was hard for me," admits Eddie,
"because you know my brain don't want to work. And spelling was
hard for me." Justin agrees. "The kind of education I've got is only
grade 6," he explains. "And they're using big words!" Justin routinely
brings his dictionary to Cognitive Strategies and can be seen constantly
looking up words. He was called on this several times while I was in
attendance and was encouraged by the treatment staff to listen and
to search his dictionary after the session. "I just have to ask plenty of
questions in group," Justin continues, "like how I can understand that
in an easier word." "I kind of felt, I guess, dumb," adds Jerry. "They'd
give me questions but I didn't know how to do the answers. And I'd
get mad, and I'd wrinkle the paper up, and I'd go ask for another sheet.
It was a struggle for me."

The handouts that the inmates receive do make a substantive effort
to explain things simply, in recognition of the varied educational and
experiential backgrounds of the inmates. Franklin often complained
bitterly to me that the program was "dumbed down" as a result and
that it was so simple he could teach it. This may have been more the
exception, however, as most men seemed to struggle with the work
despite efforts to keep it simple.

Offered either conjointly or immediately following Cognitive Strategies is "Values, Attitudes and Beliefs," "designed primarily to present
information regarding how attitudes and beliefs are formed and how
they relate to offending behaviour" (Treatment Manual, 34). In this
unit, "participants are encouraged to challenge their present antisocial attitudes and appreciate the need for change" (p34). These values
and beliefs are "automatic thoughts and attitudes that have developed
over a lifetime," the inmates are told in handouts, and are "influenced
strongly by past experiences as well as vicarious experiences (learning
from watching others or through another's personal experience)." More
specifically, they are told clearly that the "focus will be on moral values
and issues." "It is because of our moral values and beliefs and the way
we *behave* as a result of them, that we are where we are at this point
in our life." "The group is not intended to *make* you change your value
system—no one can do that. It is intended to make you think and have
you examine whether or not the values you hold are ones you want
to keep." Of course, keeping the wrong values would be antithetical to

progress in the program, and the inmates are given many examples of both wrong and correct ways to think about values and relationships.

The instructional component here includes lessons on "belief systems that support violence against women," including the role of religious beliefs and the media. It is in this unit that gender stereotypes are directly challenged, including how men and women are characterized (e.g., "Men are dominant over women"). The manner in which values and attitudes—often driven by cognitive distortions—"affect automatic thoughts and lead to behaviors" is also explored, establishing the link between what is learned in Cognitive Strategies with the Values, Attitudes, and Beliefs psychoeducational module.

> *Reggie is almost seventy years old and seems to have been in prison "forever." Several men are talking among themselves about how long he will last in the program. "He could go at any minute," predicts one. Reggie seems to agree. He cannot read or write, he tells me, and since much of the program requires these skills he feels he is in trouble. Several men have offered to help him and have recently talked him out of quitting, at least until he has given the program a good try. But reading and writing are not the only issues for Reggie. He misses the "security" he had in the penitentiary, and the familiarity with people, places, and routines. In the pen he has managed to get around quite well despite his illiteracy. Here he can't read what's posted on the bulletin board.*
>
> *Field notes*

. . .

This afternoon is a Values, Attitudes and Beliefs session. The topic for today is images of women, and much of the discussion focuses on the way women and young girls are sexualized in society. Several men talk about a TV program they recently saw about the lengths to which parents go in sexualizing their children by having them wear sexy clothing and entering them in beauty contests. There are even websites where people send clothes to these parents, who then have their children model them on camera, they shockingly note. Several men express outrage at this kind of behavior, saying something is wrong with society for promoting this. One of the nurse therapists suggests that these materials are "turn-ons for pedophiles." With this comment I make a mental note that none of the men who so far have spoken on this issue have been convicted of crimes against children. Ian adds that it is "wrong for society to do this" and that "we" must guard the safety of children at all times. He looks directly at Oren, one of those in the circle who, we have learned, is serving time for a sexual assault on a child. Moral boundaries are being established, and those who have offended against children are on the wrong side even in a community of sexual offenders.

The discussion continues with respect to historical and cross-cultural issues of sexuality. Franklin says that all societies have a notion of beauty, adding that this goes back to the Egyptians. Mark adds that society in effect constructs what constitutes a positive look or appearance and that it is not simply free will on the part of women who dress in a certain way. They want to look good, and what this means is determined by their society, even if they do not know it, he explains. But several men disagree with him, arguing that people can dress any way they want. But *how* a woman dresses, Leon clarifies, does *not* indicate sexual availability. One of the nurses nods approvingly. Leon smiles to himself.

"But there is still a double standard," continues Leon, shifting directions. He is frustrated that what constitutes sexual assault or harassment varies depending on whether you are a man or a woman, he explains. "A slap on the butt" of a woman can be conceived of as assault, but this is not likely to be the case if it happens to a man, he argues. Mark jumps in here. "This is what happened to me!" he declares, elaborating that he "touched" a woman on the leg, and now is in jail. Ian picks up on the theme. Two women standing by the water cooler making a comment about a passing man's butt would not solicit a charge, he argues, but if it was two men it would. Much of the discussion is heated, as the men grapple with what they see as the unfairness of this situation. One of the nurses replies that that is just how it is, that there is nothing one can do about it. Society views the issue differently depending on if it's a man or a woman, she clarifies. It can be confusing and ambiguous, but they have to just "suck it up" and work to understand this fact. She chides them for their reaction, saying that they are trying too hard to argue about inconsistencies and not seeing the bigger issues.

CHAPTER 5

"It's *Your* Life Story"

"It's your life story," the therapist tells Sam during his Autobiography. "Try to do it in a neat, chronological way."

Readers will recall this passage from Sam's Auto that opened chapter 1 of this book. Narrative, we know, is never "neat" or neatly chronological unless it has been well planned in advance and, in effect, scripted (Rubin 1995; Ochs and Capps 1996). Sam is being set up here. What he thinks he is about to deliver to the group is *not* what the group, and especially his therapists, are looking for. Sam is thinking narratively, but he is about to be judged paradigmatically.

Most anthropological and psychological analyses of narrative assume an inherent voluntariness to the process, that people readily employ narrative to communicate themselves to the world (e.g., J. Bruner 1986). What they say, and how they say it, is shaped in part by a willingness, if not a desire—and perhaps a compulsion (Lee 2005)—to offer up their stories to others. A fundamental idea behind the appeal of narrative is that the narrator has something to say, something to communicate about himself of which he hopes to convince an audience, be it one or many listeners. This "something" extends beyond a recounting of the facts of events, which exist as little more than the shell over which the real story is constructed (J. Bruner 1990; Good 1994; Mattingly 1994, 1998a). Narrative is not about fact, it is about experience and its meaning. But not all experiences and associated meanings are available for narration. There are some experiences that we choose not to share, that may be too painful for us to recount or that may create problems for ourselves and others. Sam, like most of the sexual offenders in this study, is not particularly interested in telling his life story to the group, and he is fearful of telling the story of his sexual crimes. This is *not* a voluntary narrative; of course, Sam can choose not to cooperate or can even refuse to discuss these crimes at all, but he knows this would lead to his removal from the program, which would in turn negatively affect his chances of parole. As is characteristic of situations of therapeutic intervention, he is required to do it as part of his therapy. If narrative indeed represents "a vital human strategy for sustaining a sense of agency in the face of disempowering circumstances," as Michael Jackson (2002: 15) suggests, what do we make of the therapeutic potential when that very narrative is compelled *because* of "disempowering circumstances," rather than as an act of agency? Can compelled narratives be therapeutic? Perhaps. But as I will show, the inmates typically respond to this form of therapeutic intervention and loss of macro-agency (that is, control over the very issue of rendering the story) with resistance, by seeking to at least control the content that the story contains. Yet here they encounter a new problem: members of the treatment staff already have extensive files on them and their crimes, and any deviation from this official story will be countered.

The way in which narrators generally construct and offer the meaning of their lives through stories constitutes what narrative theorists refer to as "emplotment" (J. Bruner 1990; Garro and Mattingly 2000; Good 1994; Mattingly 1994, 1998a). But emplotment is problematic within the paradigm of forensic CBT. For instance, Marshall, Anderson, and Fernandez (1999: 51), leading scholars on the form of CBT employed in the program in question, suggest that fundamental "cognitive processes allow people to interpret events, their own behaviour, and the behaviour of others in a way that preserves their view of themselves." This idea, of course, is entirely compatible with Goffman's (1969) notion that people normally attempt to manage their "spoiled identities" through presentation of a desirable self; narrative is one means of such presentation. Minimization, justification, and denial, it is argued, represent such "self-serving" cognitive distortions among sexual offenders (Marshall, Anderson, and Fernandez 1999: 51). While this form of identity management is taboo in forensic treatment and will be challenged, from a narrative perspective these "cognitive distortions" look rather like the process of emplotment at work, and therein lie the seeds for conflict.

Treatment staff impress upon the men that only by being "truthful" can they be helped; indeed, this is written into their treatment contracts. This insistence alone forces a focus on objective, verifiable "facts." Yet the issue of the truthfulness of narrative is a complex matter. While David Rubin (1995: 2) argues that the characteristics of autobiographical memory include the "*belief* that the remembered episode is a veridical record of the original event" (emphasis added), I am not convinced that narrators are unaware of invented details in their stories. Rubin and others (e.g., Mattingly 1998a; Presser 2004), argue that memories are constructed through mechanisms such as narrative in response to the very specific context in which the memory is being recalled and related. One does not so much "have" a story, as Presser (2004: 82) explains, as construct a story to fit the context in which it is being told. I would suggest that narrative renderings are always targeted; *certain* stories will be told in *certain* ways for *certain* people, and this would include *certain* fabrications to enhance the impact. Compounding the problem for the presenters is that narrative is, characteristically, sloppy. It is often constructed on the fly and can be inconsistent, contradictory, and incoherent, usually without any dramatic consequence. And since narratives are different from arguments, notes Jerome Bruner (1986, 1991), rather than trying to convince of the truth they seek to convince of their "lifelikeness," establishing verisimilitude.

For inmates, the context in which narrative is generated—in this case prison, with its complex moral codes—ensures that truth remains a flexible, shifting concept that adheres to no fixed, allegedly objective rendering of events that really occurred. To protect themselves, inmates characteristically attempt to persuade others of the details of their lives, their "truth," by employing selective biographical facts and strategic omissions, in combination with verisimilitude, confabulation, and even outright lies, all the while hoping to convince others of the veracity of their accounts. Distortion, embellishment, and invention—the stuff of narrative imagination—commonly appear to characterize each initial and subsequent rendering of the Autobiography and its core elements.

A further complication for the inmates is created by the sheer intersubjectivity of narrative. The reaction of the audience to the story being conveyed exists as an important check on the meaning the story has for the narrator or the message the narrator wishes to convey; in other words, the narrator's account is affected by the listeners' reaction (Kerby 1991; Wikan 2000), and audience members may resist elements of the story being related through a variety of means, such as "minimal feedback, ridicule, denial, and counterversion" (Ochs and Capps 1996: 36). Hence the audience has considerable influence in shaping, affirming/disallowing, and even altering the narrative, both in form and in content, as it unfolds. Further, narrative renderings in human communication are rarely seamless—they are not typically soliloquies—insofar as they invite response, and therefore audience interruptions in the telling of a story are common (Linde 1999). In this sense the performance of the Autobiographical narrative clearly involves a process of negotiating events (or "facts") and meaning acceptable to both the audience and the narrator, a tall order and one that does not necessarily result in balance or detente. On the unit, the audience (therapists and other inmates) are required to be active in the narrative performance; indeed, the inmates are evaluated on the quality of their participation, rendering them in effect not simply interlocutors but coauthors as well as adversaries. Merely listening is not enough. So it is not simply the presenter's story that is delivered, but a story that is often created through a group process in which all have a vested interest.

> *"Even if, you know, I will never get past what she said that I did—and I didn't do it—even if I never get past that, but I get to the point where I hurt her and it wasn't even sexual, you know what I mean? I know that I got charged with sexual assault but there is nothing sexual. She called me a name and she started screaming and I grabbed her I think by the hair, threw her in the car. She got out the other door and I just about killed her right there. There was nothing sexual. But, you can't tell these guys that because then they will automatically tell you, "You are in denial." I hired a hooker to give me a blow job. I mean, she was giving me a bloody blow job! So at what point do you sexually assault?"*
>
> *Interview with Leon*

"BEING NAKED IN THE CENTER OF THE ROOM"

As noted previously, the treatment program for each inmate cohort is constructed around a series of narrative events—the Autobiography, the Crime Cycle, and the Relapse Prevention Plan—wherein individual inmates relate some aspect of their life, including prospective narratives examining how the future might unfold. The core narrative around which treatment is built is the "Autobiography"; all other aspects of treatment seem to be linked to the expression of this narrative, as it represents the initial baseline of personal information to be made known to the other offenders. But here the form of CBT enacted in the program does not envision "life story" in an unrestricted manner, nor does it envision "narrative" in the literary sense; the term *narrative* does not appear in the program at all, and in no way could this be considered a form of narrative therapy (cf. White and Epston 1990). "Autobiography" on the unit is not "narrative," as we shall see; rather, it is imagined as a form of disclosure, a fact that confuses and often escapes most inmates. But even though this "disclosure" is typically embedded within an Autobiographical narrative, the issue of concern to the audience—positioned as the judges and even experts—is not the story value of the narrative or its meaning for the narrator. What they are concerned with is the accuracy of the details that make up the story (their compatibility with the official judicial record) and the interpretations of the details offered (their compatibility with the treatment paradigm). This form of narrative confession is somewhat unique in that the details to be confessed are already known to many of those who will hear the confession: the treatment staff members, who have previously combed through the inmate's records.[1] As a result, the incongruity between Autobiography and disclosure becomes a source of much conflict between the inmate narrator and his audience of peers and staff members when he is told to present "his life story."

Disclosure is not unique to this program, of course; it is a common element in forensic and other forms of psychotherapeutic treatment that provide various avenues for therapeutic intervention. According to Rose (1990: 240), "In compelling, persuading and inciting subjects to disclose themselves, finer and more intimate regions of personal and interpersonal life come under surveillance and are opened up for expert judgment and normative evaluation, for classification and correction." A moral dimension is also at work here, as disclosure speaks to "different ways in which humans have been urged and incited to become ethical beings, beings who define and regulate themselves according to a moral code, establish precepts for conducting and judging their lives, and reject or accept certain moral goals for themselves" (241). The initial Autobiography, then, speaks to the inmate's willingness to disclose accurate details of his life—the institutional "truth"—which in itself is seen as a test of his willingness to engage ethically with the treatment program. Indeed, the willingness to disclose the "truth" becomes itself a measure of moral habilitation for the inmates. As well, embedded within the rendered narrative are what can be seen as other "tests" of his morality: for instance, how he explains the circumstances of his life and especially his crimes and whether he employs cognitive distortions in any manner to evade responsibility—that is, "the precepts for conducting and judging" his life. In practice, the Autos appear to focus more on getting the "facts" correct than on the meaning—moral or otherwise—of the events recounted, leaving the latter for other stages in the program. But a factual and moral baseline is nonetheless established, one that is shared with all present and then employed interactively, becoming "fixed" over the next seven or so months as the inmate is guided toward gaining increased "self-control" (237), the "systematic management of one's natural and social environment" that conforms to dominant moral codes and ethical behaviors.

As suggested earlier, the Auto is a particularly stressful event, for many men are reluctant to discuss their crimes and have been conditioned by life in the penitentiary to keep these details secret. As the Autos are generally done relatively early in the life of a new cohort, the formation of the therapeutic moral community is at a nascent stage. The issue of trust, then, looms large despite the program rhetoric and the terms of the contract. "Scary," is how Ralph describes doing his Auto, "not knowing who to trust." "It was difficult," adds Stan, "because you don't know who to trust in jail. When I came here I was very suspicious of everybody." And, perhaps reflecting the fears of many, Eddie explains of his cohort, "I'm not trusting them all. I know for a fact that a couple of guys are going to go back [to the penitentiary] and will talk. One guy for sure. He's going to be blabbing every little thing I done, what my charges are."

Further, the fundamental principles of CBT suggest that at the outset the inmates will most likely lie or deliberately omit relevant details and will otherwise demonstrate the cognitive distortions of minimization, justification, and denial as they seek to present themselves in a positive light while evading the core details of their crimes. But the fact that the therapists have access to comprehensive file information on each inmate confounds their attempts to avoid responsibility for their actions by omitting details. When cognitive distortions become evident, including deviations from the official facts of the crimes, therapists and other inmates challenge the narrator to reconsider. As part of the therapeutic community concept, the other inmates are expected to participate actively in this process by monitoring the disclosure of the details and offering their own interpretations of the experiences being narrated, including the subjective meaning of those experiences as expressed by the teller. Sometimes the challenge is direct (as in "That's bullshit," a characteristic response of other inmates), sometimes indirect (audible sighs; body language), and sometimes more congenial (as in "Do you

really think a person wants to be treated that way?," offered by a therapist). Sometimes the reaction comes from another inmate in the form of
a supportive or contradictory personal narrative of an allegedly similar
experience. In such cases, inmates in the audience seek to attach their
story onto that of the individual who is narrating in an effort to be seen
by the therapists as engaged therapeutic partners. Such attempts may
be rebuffed by an assertive narrator, who seeks to remain in control,
or they may be accepted and welcomed by a passive narrator, who is
happy to be out of the spotlight, even if only briefly.

The reactions of the audience can signal approval or disapproval of the
content, resulting in shifts in direction and/or backtracking to previous
elements of the narrative to allow for the clarification of details or presentation of an alternative interpretation. Both the content and the meaning
of the narrative, then, become an intersubjective space for negotiation,
and this negotiation has the potential to change the shape of the narrative midstream or at its next expression in another phase of the treatment
program. A man's story can be seen to shift continuously throughout
treatment; indeed, it *should* change if the inmate is engaging therapeutically toward a more coherent, therapeutically sound understanding of
his life. This is not always the case, however, and narratives sometimes
change haphazardly as the inmate tries to find that safe narrative space
that will ensure less conflict in group sessions or a positive evaluation;
these individuals will accept just about any addition offered. The Autobiographical narratives are therefore not allowed to be freewheeling and
unconstrained; they are not "natural" in the Brunerian sense. Rather, they
are structured and constrained by program content and requirements, as
well as the dynamic process through which they are rendered.

On the "Guide to Writing Your Autobiography "instruction sheet
provided to inmates, they are told the following:

> [The Autobiography] allows you to reflect on your past, the interaction
> between you and your environment which worked together to get you where
> you are today. Developing an understanding of this interaction is important
> in treatment as it allows you to focus on the things you need to change,
> both about yourself, your environment and the interaction of the two. . . .
> Other group participants will be more prepared to provide constructive
> feedback to you on your crime cycle and relapse prevention plan if they
> know your history.

From the start, there is considerable potential for confusion among the
inmates as to the task at hand. While their information sheet refers to this
exercise as an "Autobiography," it also states that "the *Autobiography*

also helps you organize your thoughts in preparation for your presentation of your history in *disclosure* group" (emphasis added). The confusion between Autobiography and disclosure is compounded when they are then told, "The following sets of questions are designed to help *you* write *your* Autobiography. It covers the major areas *we* need to know. You may feel that, for you, there are other questions that need to be answered or other areas that need to be covered. Please include them if you feel that it is important to you. The format you use is up to you *and your primary [nurse]*" (emphasis added). The instructions, then, fairly explicitly suggest that what the inmate feels to be relevant about his life is secondary to the concerns of the treatment team. This is further borne out by the fifty-six questions (plus subquestions) that are provided around which to frame the Autobiography, to be organized by the following categories: "Current Status," "Family Life," "School and Friends," "Sexual Development," "Employment History," "Substance Abuse," "Previous Treatment," "Behavioural/Emotional Problems," and "Criminal Patterns." A few examples of these questions are:

- How would you describe your home life?
- Would you describe your parents/caregivers as supportive or unsupportive of you?
- Did you get into a lot of trouble as you were growing up? If so, what kind?
- What was school like? What grade did you complete? Why did you stop going to school? Did you get into trouble with teachers or peers?
- When did you become sexually active? (i.e., perform sex acts with another person). Describe your feelings.
- Describe your sexually offending behaviour (when did it start, how long has it gone on).

The fact that the Autobiographical categories with the most questions are "Sexual Development" and "Criminal Patterns" suggests that this is to be no ordinary autobiography, in which the narrator exhibits considerable agency and control to present his life as he see fit; rather, this is a very directed story that is to be told, one that must meet certain standards to be acceptable. Failure to do so leads to conflict during rendering as well as a negative evaluation on the exercise, and cumulative negative evaluations can lead to expulsion from the program.

The inmate's primary nurse will often work with the inmate in advance of his presentation to the group, as part of his individual therapy. Many men suggest that this input is essential to getting it "right." Several drafts may be produced before the primary nurse feels the Auto is ready for presentation. It is expected that men will ultimately write up their Autobiographies again after presentation, reflecting further insights gained and clarifications requested that emerge from the presentation, and will then submit this to their primary nurses, where it becomes yet another document in their official correctional story. All but the first inmate to present has the advantage of learning the process, and as the Autos unfold over time a collective understanding of what is expected emerges. Occasionally, however, an inmate arrives on the unit and is quickly required to do his Auto in order to catch up with the group. This is typically done to ensure a kind of equal footing, that everyone has been provided with the relevant details of the lives and crimes of their peers. In the several cases where this happened that I witnessed, the inmate floundered terribly, telling a life story in which his criminality played a small, not central, role, and was required to repeat it.

CURTIS'S AUTO

Curtis grabs my arm one day after a group session. "Got a sec?" he asks. "Sure." He turns and walks back to his house. I follow, stopping just outside the door. Peering in, I can see him rummaging through some papers. "Could you check this over?" he asks, handing me several sheets of handwriting. I glance down. It is a draft in the true sense of the word, with scribbling, passages scratched out, arrows going this way and that. "What is it?" I ask. "My Auto," he replies. "Oh, geez, I don't think I can help you with that. You should take it to your primary." "I will," he explains, "but I want to get it right first." I am not sure what Curtis is hoping to get from me, frankly. But I turn toward the day room and, clutching the paper, retreat to a couch. Curtis follows me, sits next and watches me carefully while I try to decipher the combination of poor English and poor legibility. "So?" "Well," I reply, "it sounds okay to me." But anticipating how it will be received, I add, "I think you have to get it more organized, though. It's kind of hard to follow." "Okay," he says, staring down at it. "Could you type it for me?" "No, I can't do that," I explain. "Not allowed." He accepts my answer and turns back to his house.

Over the next few weeks I frequently see Curtis at a unit computer, slowly typing with one finger while gazing across an increasingly larger pile of notes. Not all the inmates take their Autos this seriously. Some come with only a few scratch notes, others talk entirely from the top of their heads (rarely a good thing, as they are often heavily criticized for being shallow and disorganized). But Curtis, like many, is obsessed with the process, the need to get it "right." Surprisingly, then, his Auto is a disaster when he presents it to the group.

It is 8:20 a.m. A brilliant sunshine illuminates the inner courtyard, something the inmates will not appreciate for a while yet; their first exercise period of the day is not until later. No natural light finds its way into the day room where Curtis's Auto is about to commence, a fact that is compounded by the drabness of the inmates' institutional dress. The chairs and couches have been moved to form a horseshoe. It is not a tight formation by any means, with perhaps thirty or more feet from one side to the other. The staff never directs this aspect of the program; it is up to the inmates to arrange the room the way they see fit. I remain surprised that their arrangement, day in and day out, replicates the coldness of the broader prison environment. There is nothing intimate about to happen here.[2]

The session—like all sessions first thing in the morning—opens with "check-in," during which inmates are in turn given the opportunity to tell the group how they are feeling and what might be on their minds. Check-in has nothing to do with the Auto we will hear, and men often use it to complain about the behavior of others or about various perceived injustices they are experiencing with the correctional system. Today, most employ fairly rote expressions: "Doing good," "Ready to get to work," "Looking forward to hearing Curtis," and so on. Curtis sits quietly. "Ready to roll," he says on his turn.

Let me first characterize the overall tone of the session. Curtis is very soft-spoken and often hesitant to speak in groups. He likes to "fly under the radar," according to one of his peers, which generally is considered a negative by both staff and inmates alike. Typically he mimics others during check-in and feedback. He speaks haltingly, appearing to lack confidence. He searches faces as he speaks, seemingly looking for positive affirmation. His narrative is open, in the sense that he freely allows others to help him construct it. Today he has several handwritten pieces of paper in his hands. I deduce that his efforts at typing did not go well, and I feel a little guilty even though correctional rules state clearly that I must not do favors for the inmates. "I don't like talking about the past," he says at the start. He remains seated, looking down at the floor. I notice one staff member look over at another as he speaks. "Cognitive distortion" right out of the gate, I assume they must be thinking. Prepare for minimization and denial.

Curtis begins by discussing his early life growing up on a First Nations reserve. His description, on one hand, is of a fairly uneventful childhood, although he does allude to the tensions and interpersonal conflicts of a small, isolated Aboriginal community. Every now and then throughout the narrative he comes back to this point as a means of explanation. He describes how he wanted to get out and left at around age fifteen or so.

Overall, he tells us very little about his younger years. Curtis does say that when he was younger he had lots of money. He then describes doing lots of breaking and entering. A nurse expresses her confusion over this, saying authoritatively that people commit breaking and entering to get food or things they can exchange for cash because they have no money. Curtis replies with passive responses; there was no good reason for doing them other than that his group of friends was doing them. He also describes a breaking and entering of a police station when he was young. There are guffaws of disbelief among the men, at the audacity of doing this. Why? What were you looking for? Curtis responds that he was just going along with some others, implying that he was not active in the offense. He says nothing was stolen, but some files were burned. Recalling that he came from a small, northern community, I guess to myself that the "police station" in question was in fact a small outpost that was not regularly staffed; in a subsequent discussion Curtis confirms this with me.[3] But at this point I cannot help but think how, from the perspective of the other inmates, the apparent sheer stupidity of this crime will affect his Auto.

Curtis is only a few minutes into his Auto, and he has been interrupted several times with questions. Generally, when the primary nurse works with an inmate to prepare for the Auto they consider the issue of format: Does the inmate want to take questions as he goes, or does he prefer to have all questions wait until he is finished? I assume Curtis chose the former, and as the Auto continues to unfold it becomes apparent that the narrative will be a product of construction by the group, not an individual.

Curtis tries to move quickly into a description of his crimes. "Hold on," interjects his primary nurse. Curtis is then questioned about his first sexual experience. "Oh," he responds nervously. He looks down at the floor. He describes being twelve and being initiated into sex by a nineteen-year-old woman. She showed him how to do sexual things for her, he explains quietly. An inmate asks when he started getting interested in women. He replies, at around eleven.

When did you start masturbating? Curtis looks mortified. "I don't know!" he says emphatically, his voice jumping out of this throat. Then, realizing his outburst, he looks over to his primary nurse. "Sorry." "Just move on," she directs.

A common theme that starts to emerge in the narrative is extensive alcohol and drug use. Curtis has many drunken driving and drug possession charges, he admits. He is glad he never hurt anyone driving drunk. Franklin does mental calculations on the number of charges that Curtis is noting and challenges Curtis that there are many discrepancies. There is considerable discussion, and it takes some time for the group to determine that some charges were dropped and were not convictions. Dealing with this incongruity takes several minutes, and, while the two psychiatric nurses in attendance seem exasperated by this, they allow the discussion.

Curtis now starts to detail his first sexual offense, which was against his wife. "She charged me," he explains. This creates a stir among the men. "How can that happen?" one asks out loud. "It's no different," explains a nurse. "Even with your wife, you have to get consent." Several men ask for the details, to which Curtis responds by talking about the court case, how he was charged and pleaded guilty, and his sentence. He implies that he was innocent but that since he just wanted to get it over with he pled guilty. He does not immediately describe the incident per se, however. Men pick up on this and continue to press for the details. "Did you touch her breast?" asks one. "Did you rip her clothes?" asks another. "No," says Curtis, to both questions. "She just charged me," he explains, a perplexed look on his face. Franklin has a look of incredulousness on *his* face. He says he got one year for touching, so how come Curtis got only ninety days? Something is missing in his story, he suggests. Curtis insists he did nothing more and has left nothing out. "Did you hit her?" asks another inmate. No. He admits that she hit him a lot, though. He mentions one incident where she hit him on the back of the head with a crescent wrench and describes how the blood ran down his neck. At this moment, John jumps in. "I can corroborate that," he declares, "he has told me that before." This is an interesting rescue, in a way, because up to this point there was emerging in the group a sense that Curtis was not being forthcoming, perhaps even lying.

So the men switch tactics here. They want still more details. What was she like? Was she mad at you? Was she getting even? "That's what I told the court," responds Curtis. "Were you a batterer?" asks a nurse. There must have been abuse that his wife was paying him back for, she suggests. Curtis is starting to come undone now. "No," he responds, shaking his head. "I never hit her." He then describes an incident on the reserve when an Elder picked him up in his car. Curtis was drunk, and the Elder chastised him for drinking and neglecting his marriage. "I see you drinking. Trouble in your marriage," the Elder told him. The Elder then proceeded to advise that women were dangerous and he should be careful around them. "They will do bad things to you," Curtis relates. This strikes me as being a form of minimizing, and I wonder if anyone will respond. No one does. Staff members, none of whom are Aboriginal, seem very wary of wading into matters apparently involving Aboriginal culture, and the fact that an Elder was involved here may temper criticism.

The men are having trouble with Curtis's apparent proclamation of innocence. They continue to press for details throughout the remainder of the session. In response to a question, Curtis notes that he continues to talk to this woman and maintains a good relationship with her. Two weeks ago on the phone she told him that she hoped that the sexual offense charge hadn't affected his current sentence. The men guffaw—of course it did! "So why do you still talk to her?" The men are incredulous again. "I don't like to think of the past," says Curtis, repeating what he told us at the outset. He adds: "I have two wonderful children with her." A few heads nod understandingly. Break time.

The men jump up, most dashing to their houses, the only place inside where they are allowed to smoke.[4] Curtis sits motionless for a moment, looking at the floor, then slowly gets up and shuffles over to his house. He remerges just as the session starts up again. He has spent almost ninety minutes so far in the "hot seat."[5]

Curtis opens the second half of the session by discussing his second and third sexual offenses. They all seem to involve women he knows and was having relationships with. Yet Curtis has trouble remembering why he did things and what specifically was going on in his life at the time of the offenses. Men offer ideas, and Curtis happily concurs with their suggestions for what he was thinking or feeling. "You must have been angry at her," offers Andrew at one point. "Yes," agrees Curtis, nodding.

The second offense involved a woman who was sleeping on the floor of a house he was visiting. Curtis explains that he was drunk and "blacked out," meaning that he could not remember what he did. He was charged, whereupon he pled not guilty. He is sketchy on the details of the assault.

The third offense involved a woman with whom he was having a relationship. He was staying at a boardinghouse, and she came back there one night after drinking. He explains that he was also carrying on a relationship with a former partner. When the first woman arrived, he indicated that he wanted to have sex, but she refused. So he decided to go back to the bar where he had been drinking earlier with the other woman. On his way out of the boardinghouse, he told a man he encountered that he could "have" the woman in his room. Apparently the man went in and had sex with her. The inmates are perplexed by this. If Curtis didn't assault her, why was he charged? Was the other man not charged? Aspects of the story are puzzling. Many men shake their heads in disbelief. This makes no sense. And Curtis's style of narrating, offering fragments here and there without connection, is frustrating everyone. The disbelief increases when Curtis explains that he stayed with this woman for several more days during which they had consensual sex and that it was two years later when he was charged. There were no reports of physical abuse, Curtis insists, although he adds that he had been "a little rough" during the consensual sex and had inserted his hand into her vagina at one point, which hurt her.

His language when describing the offenses is tentative, with extensive use of conditional phrasing such as "maybe" and "I guess," suggesting that he has problems with recall. Overall, Curtis fails to disclose many details of these offenses. And several times he says that he has accepted responsibility for what he has done. Several men are confused by this, since he seems to be saying that he has not really done anything wrong. One inmate bluntly rejects Curtis's assertions that the women have done a disservice to him by falsely charging him. "You are 100 percent responsible for your behavior," says the inmate.

Throughout the Auto Curtis's primary nurse is quite persistent in interjecting motives and beliefs in Curtis's narrative. Several times he contextualizes a question by saying that Curtis was living the "high life," partying, or doing bad things, as if this were fact and necessary background for the events that followed. Each time Curtis hesitates, unsure if he wants to agree. The first time, Curtis clearly does not agree with this, saying, "Ahhhh . . ." while he mulls it over, shaking his head as if he is about to say "No." At other times he is a little more ready to agree, looking around at the others as if to seek affirmation that agreeing with the staff's interpretation of his life is the correct thing to do.

Curtis's Auto, like all of them, ends with the story of his sexual assaults. Therapeutically speaking, it seems that nothing that happens from that point forward is relevant to the task at hand, sexual offender rehabilitation. Curtis sits back, looking a little rattled and a little exhausted. But the session is not over. It is time for feedback.

Going around the circle to each man in turn, several men say Curtis has done a good job. This seems rather gratuitous to me, especially since some of these commentators gave him such a difficult time during his presentation. Leon, on the other hand, complains that Curtis's Auto was not at all helpful to the others and suggests that Curtis should have to do his over again just as he did. Leon laughs at his own suggestion. Curtis laughs nervously with him and smiles. No one picks up on this suggestion, however. Oren comments that he too is still confused about Curtis's story. Several others express disbelief that Curtis would receive a five-year sentence given what he disclosed, suggesting that there is something to his story that he is not telling. David attempts a rescue, interjecting that this is Curtis's story and that he has a right to tell it the way he wants.

Curtis needs to determine his "triggers," says Tom. Tom, a tall Caucasian in his early fifties, is frequently heavily medicated, although today he seems relatively lucid. He is doing a sentence for non-sex-related offenses but has a past record of sexual assaults that render him an "untreated" sexual offender. He freely offers his interpretations to Curtis. It is likely that Curtis's triggers are to be found in his childhood experiences, Tom offers. Curtis looks puzzled. Another man, a few moments later, agrees that triggers must be found, adding that for Curtis these appear to be alcohol and drugs. Wilson, an Aboriginal man in his early fifties serving a sentence for sexual assault on a teenage girl, is quite defensive of Curtis. He interprets the vagueness of Curtis's account of the third offense as due to his having been charged two years after the fact.

Curtis is also commended for making a "good first start." One man notes that this is Curtis's first treatment program experience. He will get better as time goes on, he encourages. Another man employs a staircase analogy: "You can't just climb from the bottom to the top. You have to take it one step at a time." I am surprised, again, that those who seemed upset at the lack of details in the Auto are also fairly forgiving, excusing that very lack of details by asserting Curtis's inexperience with treatment. But the painful look on his face suggests Curtis does not feel relieved at all.

One man complains that the constant questioning of Curtis during the Auto was disrespectful. Curtis's primary nurse responds that they always ask the presenter if they want questions during the Auto or after. Curtis said he wanted the questions during the Auto, and therefore they respected his wish. "It was confusing," replies the questioner, not accepting the explanation. Indeed, there has been no continuity to Curtis's story from my own perspective, no flow.

Feedback by the treatment staff, always last, is brief and focuses on Curtis's continued pleas of innocence as evidence that he continues to adopt the position of victim. He should just focus on himself and what he has to do here, he is told, and let go of ideas that he is innocent or that others may be to blame for his problems.

During the feedback Curtis remains quiet, as required. His job is to listen only and to weigh carefully what he hears. He may think of it as his life story, but he does not get the last word; his primary nurse does. As the nurse announces that the session is now over, Curtis darts from his chair and into his house, showing more energy in a few seconds than he has displayed all morning.

In retrospect, Curtis's narrative was constantly disrupted by attention to the specific facts. Small vignettes of his life story were bracketed by questions and answers about details. Curtis seemed to respond to these questions as a means of determining what he thought he should say, perhaps in terms of what he thought the audience wanted to hear. Despite appearing to have been prepared over several weeks, his Auto was fractured and unfocused. This is in contrast to the next Auto, by Franklin, whose narrative is both paradigmatically and chronologically detailed and progresses smoothly, saying what he wants to say, without interruption. Whereas Curtis's Auto is passively iterative and very much the product of group construction, Franklin's appears intentional, rehearsed, the act of a professional, as if following a well-known script.

I am sitting in the lounge with several men when a news item comes on the TV that the police have caught the individual believed responsible for the sexual assault and murder of a young girl. This case has been in the news quite a bit lately, and has been followed carefully by many of the inmates. They have referred to the case as a means to explain their apprehension over how and why things are being "tightened" for sexual offenders, especially in the community context, as a result of public anger.

*Their reaction to the arrest is telling. While they seem to express outrage
at the nature of the crime, they are also concerned that the police have
the "right" man, and they discuss the implications that a false accusation
would have for his life.*

Field notes

FRANKLIN'S AUTO

As I noted in chapter 4, Franklin is a very large man of mixed
Caucasian-Aboriginal ancestry. It is obvious that he once presented
quite a formidable physique; much of the muscle tone is still evident,
though now covered with a layer of middle-age fat. Past his midthirties
now, he has a personality every bit as large as his frame. Over the several
weeks he has been on the unit he has been a very vocal participant
in the groups as well as in the day room during off hours. He comes
across as intelligent and articulate and as someone who, in the sarcastic
assessment of another inmate, "knows it all." My first impression upon
meeting him was that he had researched forensic treatment far beyond
what he would be exposed to in the various prison treatment programs
he had taken prior to coming to the unit. He will not have the "deer-in-
the-headlights" look that Curtis had. But his assertiveness borders on
aggressiveness and is most unwelcome to many of the other men, who
see him as too authoritative, too quick to judge. And there have been
several altercations since he had arrived, with Franklin being accused
of "soldiering," or marshalling allies to promote his influence on the
unit. The bottom line, it seems, is that Franklin is a polarizing influence.
Just before the session begins, as I am retrieving my security device in
the Bubble, a nurse tells me that she is anticipating some trouble with
the men in this session. There could be payback brewing.

At check-in, Franklin says one word, "Confident." When the session
starts, his primary nurse explains that he has requested that there be no
questions until he has finished. Franklin adds that he has a long story
to tell with lots of details. He then looks over at me and, in reference
to an interview we undertook a few days earlier, asks, "How long did
we go? Two and half or three hours?" It is clear to all that he does
not want to be interrupted. In contrast to Curtis, he seems to me to be
employing a strategy to maintain control of the narrative.

Let me first characterize Franklin's session. He is very direct throughout, very articulate, and looks at faces around the room as he speaks,
exuding confidence; given his history, this could well be a means of

intimidation. Only a few men return the gaze, and most stare down at their feet or the floor. He provides great detail, including names and very specific dates; so detailed is his presentation that there is no way I can recall these specific points later when I write up my notes. He floods the room with details. His presentation is more or less chronological as well, but every now and then he falls back and starts a new story and brings it forward as a means of explaining something.

Franklin opens by describing his life in a small northern town. There was no running water or electricity for many people, he explains, and he used an outhouse. It was a very poor place. He recalls having lots of fun as a child. But there was also a great deal of drinking and open sexual activity in the community, and all the men seemed to have extra-marital sex. "I thought this was normal," he says. He describes a little of his parents' background, but although he is part Aboriginal he does not mention this.

Franklin bought his first car at the age of sixteen. It was a Mustang. The norm in his town was for "older" guys to chase "younger" girls, he explains, adding that a car was necessary to "get girls." By "older guys" he means those in their late teens or early twenties, and the girls in their early teens, he clarifies. This is an interesting admission, as Franklin has been openly and intensely critical of pedophiles. His suggestion—that being sexually attracted to early teen girls is acceptable—is not challenged.

Franklin then tells the story of when he was young and listening to his uncle "have sex with" his sister. "Rape," he clarifies. He describes hearing her protests and the slapping of bodies together. As he does so, he continues to scan the semicircle for reactions. There are none that I notice. Most men are still not looking at him. It was hard for him to hear these sounds, he continues, and as he was just a kid he was confused by it. At eleven he was sexually assaulted by this same uncle, who came into his room one night and performed oral sex on him and rubbed his body up against him. Then he carried him upstairs, but Franklin ran back down to his room. The next day, his uncle called down, "Franklin, are you all right," which he thought was an admission by his uncle that he knew what he had done was wrong.

His Auto now shifts gears. "Okay," he says, "let's get to it." A few men look up. Franklin describes his first offense as involving the insertion of his finger in a women's vagina while he was holding her down. This was a woman that he knew and had sex with in the past, he explains, but on this occasion she had rebuffed him. She contacted police, and the result was a one-year sentence, his first jail time. No one in prison knew why he was in, and he worked hard to keep this a secret. He admits to having several prior charges of assault and mischief, and he used these as his cover. Only later in the Autobiography does he elaborate on his long history of assaults.

In the second offense, he assaulted the sister of his partner, with whom he had been having an affair. He explains that he went over to her house to see her and describes her house in some detail. He walked in and went downstairs, where he found her in bed. He describes her bedroom for us in great detail. He explains that he sat on her bed. Then, he says, he "blacked out" from alcohol consumption and does not remember what happened next. Heads snap up around the room. I am already thinking about the incongruity at work here, the very detailed description of the inconsequential and complete amnesia on the crime. I assume this has provoked a reaction in the others as well. Had questions been allowed, he would surely have paid a price for this. But he is allowed to continue, noting that he was eventually charged with sexual assault. He suggests that this may not have actually happened, emphasizing again that he has no recollection. He adds that the woman had made false allegations of sexual assault in the past. Again I wonder what others are thinking. Curtis had been heavily criticized for suggesting that he was innocent.

By this point in the story, we are well past an hour, and Franklin is beginning to look at the clock with some frequency, perhaps anticipating the break. But he does not look at all fatigued despite the monologue. He continues.

Franklin's second sexual assault charge was similar in many ways to the first. It involved an assault on an acquaintance with whom he had a sexual relationship in the past but who in this instance had rebuffed his advances. Like the first one, the story is very detailed up until the commission of the crime. He again tells us that because he was heavily intoxicated he "blacked out" and so does not remember the details, other than what he heard in his court case. His story now shifts to some legal issues and how he was "outed" as someone standing trial on a sexual assault charge. He had told his employer he was taking a week of vacation to explain his absence while going to court. During the trial he would go by work at the end of each day and tell his co-workers what a good time he was having on holidays. But when the truth became known through the newspapers his boss told him that he had to be fired. Franklin was very angry and resentful about this. He was convicted of the offense and sent back to prison.

When he was released from prison on this conviction he found a new job. But one day he was visited by police who thought he might be a suspect in a series of rapes. "That's not my m.o.," he told them, "I don't grab people from bushes." Being questioned by police created some problems, though, as his employer demanded to know why they would ask him in the first place.

"Break time," his primary nurse announces. It has been over ninety minutes, and this is the first voice other than Franklin's that has been heard. Franklin gets up and rambles casually over to his house for a smoke. Several men look at each other and shake their heads. But there is no commentary.

After break, he continues his story. He focuses now on his third and most recent offense. He describes getting very drunk one night while his live-in girlfriend was out. He was angry that she was not at home, he explains, "where she belonged." When she did come home around three in the morning, they argued. "I beat her good," he says, matter-of-factly. When she went to bed, he followed. He blacked out and so does not remember beating or raping her. But when the police showed the photos of her injuries, he was shocked, he tells us. His demeanor seems to shift at this point as he talks about the photos, and he grows contrite. In a hushed tone he describes how badly beaten she looked, and enumerates some of her injuries. His voice, previously strong and confident, cracks a little as he admits, "I'm so much bigger than her." He does not deny that he committed the offense but seems to emphasize the physical aspects of the assault without overtly admitting that it was a sexual assault.

Franklin's Auto now shifts somewhat to a new direction, a more self-reflective analysis of his past. He tells us that he has always had a problem with blackouts. This happened the first time he ever drank and has happened frequently since. He drinks so much he cannot remember what he has done. He explains that part of his problems also related to the stress of debts he was accumulating. As he now sits in prison, he is upset because he is broke and has many debts at various businesses, and even lots of parking tickets. "I'm disillusioned" right now, he says, because he once had so much and now has nothing. He never thought he would come back to prison after the second charge, and now here he is. He says he never wants to come back again.

He has taken dozens of programs in prison, he informs us, and he names them. After his second conviction, by his own admission he acted as a model prisoner, chairing committees and taking programs. But within a few weeks of his parole on the second sentence he was charged with fighting another inmate. He admits that he was doing his laundry after the curfew in the minimum-security unit, against the rules. The other inmate was angry because of this and, according to Franklin, came at him with a knife. So he defended himself. When Franklin went to his parole hearing he was denied within minutes and was returned to the penitentiary, only this time at a higher security level. But with the third conviction, he says, he became "bitter." "I vowed I wouldn't take shit from anyone," he explains. There is steel in his eyes as he looks around the room. "I fought a lot." I have a strong sense that this is not just a reflection on his past but also a warning to those in the room.

Now it is time for feedback. Not surprisingly, no one seems anxious to speak up. Franklin's Auto has been somewhat intimidating, peppered with references to his bulk, his toughness, his willingness to fight, his "take no shit" attitude. The first inmate to speak states the obvious, perhaps a safe thing to do. "I think you have a problem with alcohol." "Tell me something I don't know," retorts Franklin sharply. The next speaker, John, says that after listening to Franklin, he now realizes that alcohol addiction is just as bad as drugs. He adds that he also realizes how many of the men have done these things because of their upbringing. He refers to his own experiences and notes some similarities with Franklin in terms of his relationships with his uncle. He learned both positive and negative things from his uncle, John explains. John is not saying anything *about* Franklin and his Auto; instead, he too is taking a safe route, and by attaching his own narrative to Franklin's he is communicating insight to the treatment staff present.

Several men note that Franklin has given a thorough Auto, with lots of details. A few say nothing at all in feedback. One man tells Franklin that his story is troubling. Franklin has good trade skills, he affirms, and Franklin should seek work in a place where he will not be tempted into trouble, like an oil rig. Only Wilson deems to say anything therapeutically insightful about Franklin. "You're giving yourself permission" to do things by saying that "everyone did it" in your community and your family. Franklin responds sharply, saying that no one in the room could have any idea what it was like for him growing up. "I have a right to be angry!" he shouts, slapping his palm down on the arm of his chair. There are no more comments from the inmates after this outburst. In closing the session, his primary nurse says little as well but comments that in the end it is still the individual who chooses to behave in a certain way. "No one makes you angry," she says. "You make yourself angry."

Later on that day I ask Franklin what he thought of the session. He is disappointed that no one asked him any real questions and that no one challenged him. "But isn't that a good thing?" I ask. "I'm here to learn, man," he replies. "Get better."

In retrospect, it is hard to reconcile this desire to be questioned with the way the Auto was presented. While there certainly were avenues of entry for the audience members, I am surprised that no one seemed to really tackle him with respect to what appeared to be minimizing or denial. A significant portion of his narrative is taken up with his legal woes, and suggestions that he had blacked out and did not remember, and possibly did not even do it. He is treated very differently than Curtis. While this can be partly explained by process—that he is allowed to narrate without interruption—I also think there are many other intersubjective factors at work. Whereas Curtis presents as vulnerable and confused and the others seize on that, Franklin presents as the complete opposite, and the others approach him warily.

Overwhelming the room with details is, perhaps, strategic. He presents himself as very arrogant and conceited, a man who was once fit and strong and had lots of sex. During the session at several points he even informs us what his weight was at any given moment in his life or how big he was. He notes that he was an excellent tradesman and often made high wages. He even describes in great detail the kinds of material goods he has purchased, including the brand names of his washer and dryer and his car and the name of the fancy subdivision he lived in. Add to this that he carries to the unit a reputation for being a tough guy willing to fight, and he clearly sends out "stay away" signals. The men pick up on this.

Various factors, then, seem to explain the differing ways in which inmates approach the offering of their narratives and how audience members respond. It is not necessarily and always an attack on the narrator. The narrator's personality, the manner in which he prepares and addresses the requirements of the Autobiography, implicit and explicit threats made to others, the overall mood of the group that day (including therapists), and previous experiences with the narrator in other groups and outside the sessions all come into play. Some men simply present as more vulnerable, and they often suffer because of it. Others, like Franklin, seem to relish the possibility of confrontation in the group.

Despite his assertion that he is here to "get better," Franklin continues to be a disruptive influence on the unit, threatening others and challenging key antagonists to fight. As a result, he is discharged back to the penitentiary before he can complete the program. He is removed with such haste that I am not able to undertake an exit interview, although I am able to meet with him briefly in another unit in the institution where he is temporarily housed, awaiting the arrival of the bus. He considers his expulsion a "frame job," arguing that others lied to staff about threats and fights and concocted stories about being afraid of him, saying they felt they could not actively participate in the program as long as he was present. Franklin vows to never take treatment again. "My last shot," he confirms.

> *"I would tell him you'd better think twice," David says, in response to my question about what he would tell another inmate considering the program. "I'm being honest with you. If you're willing to pay the price, if you're willing to go through a lot of pain and suffering, if you're willing to go through a lot of challenges and mental abuse and humiliation and you're willing to do all these things, to learn what you can to become a better person, then go. But I will not lie to them. Hardest thing I've ever done. In all honesty, I'm glad I came now. But if I had known in advance exactly what this was like, I don't know if I'd have come. I don't think I could have come."*
>
> Interview with David

STEVEN'S AUTO

Steven is a late twenties Caucasian, thin with stringy, long fair hair. While there is nothing intimidating about his appearance, Steven has a substantial record of violence. My observations of him on the unit so far suggest that he is very sarcastic and quick to take offense. He participates actively in the groups and is often one of the more vocal critics of others' presentations. He has brought along a written version of his Auto, and after check-in he starts to read from it. But, as his session unfolds so many questions interrupt him that he frequently grows frustrated, waving his papers in the air and retorting angrily, "I'm going to get to that!"

Steven opens by explaining that he had a "fairly good" family life. But after a few perfunctory details he changes direction significantly and launches into a discussion of his sexual development. This is a required element of the Auto, as we have seen, though some men seem to get away with saying very little. For the most part, the men do not want to talk much about their sexual development. Steven, however, seems considerably less reluctant.

He was sexually molested as a thirteen-year-old, he relates. He had a part-time job, and his boss fondled him and made him watch while his boss masturbated. Then, when he was a teenager, he went to a party, became drunk, and passed out, only to awake, as he says, "when a gay guy was giving me head." Then, inexplicably to Steven, who adamantly denied the accusation, this man phoned his parents and told them Steven was gay. This prompted Steven to threaten the man, and he tells us pointedly that had he encountered him he would have killed him. He then discusses in some detail his masturbation history. As he does, several men in the group have to stifle their smirks and seem either entertained or embarrassed by Steven's details. Steven scowls in return.

He then begins to describe the history of his adult relationships, which is complex, to say the least. One staff member interjects partway through, opening a debate about time lines and chronology similar to what Curtis experienced in his Auto. She is confused, she says. Steven has described the pattern of relationships he says he had over a period of time. But she has "done some math" and "it doesn't add up." "You couldn't have fit that number of relationships lasting that amount of time into this time period," she critiques. Steven responds defensively. "I'm not lying!" he states emphatically, but follows up by adding that it is hard to get all the details straight. At this point I am wondering about the relevance of this line of questioning, since it seems to me to be rather peripheral. But as the Auto continues to unfold it becomes clear that the issue of truthfulness will be a central theme.

After the break, Steven opens with a recounting of his offenses, and as he does the audience becomes considerably more active. Steven is forced away from his script as he fields question after question, almost all hostile and challenging.

He begins by discussing a crime unrelated to his current incarceration but one that seems telling about some of the broader issues he faces. He describes an earlier weapons charge in which he took a shotgun to high school and threatened a teacher. "What?" Leon blurts out, clearly startled by this admission. "Shhhh!" admonishes Steven's primary nurse, shutting Leon down. Steven then launches into a description of a sexual offense against a five-year-old girl. He had been babysitting the child for a friend, a woman who had gone off drinking for some twenty-four hours. But Steven was also drinking, and at some point he started to fondle the girl while she was sleeping. When he mentions nothing more about this offense, he is taken to task, and more details are demanded. The young girl was "passed out," says Steven in response. Shock waves ripple through the room. Several men challenge him on this. "You said before she was sleeping," challenges one inmate. He replies, "Yeah. Sleeping. Passed out." A nurse interjects that there is a huge difference between the two. "Do you mean you gave alcohol to a child?" asks another inmate in a very indignant manner. "No way," replies Steven, in an equally indignant manner, as if to take on the challenge head to head. The pecking order is being played out; while sexually assaulting a child is a lowly crime, plying one with alcohol first is likely even lower.

Steven picks up his paper and signals he wants to move on. But Ian, a Caucasian in his late thirties with a record of violent behavior, does not let him. He challenges Steven that this story makes no sense. "I'm a parent," says Ian. "A parent would never leave a child with someone who was drinking! No fucking way!" This part of Steven's story was shocking and frankly not believable, judges Ian. Steven tries to defend himself, but Ian is now so flustered that there is nothing more Steven can say other than declare, "She did."

When the room quiets, Steven's primary nurse speaks up. Referring to the police reports and previous admissions by Steven found in his files, she relays that he admitted to oral sex with the girl. You didn't say anything about that, she continues. He denies this vehemently, saying that he never said back then that there was oral sex. "There was none!" he protests. The nurse holds up a part of his files, raises her eyebrows, but says nothing. Steven remains quiet, his eyes darting back and forth from her face to the files in her hands. Both psychiatric nurses in attendance look appalled at this apparent denial, and both start writing in their notebooks as his primary nurse declares that "this part of the story is now over. Go on." Steven does so obediently.

Steven then describes two charges, related to the use of violence in committing sexual assaults on "hookers," for which he is serving his current sentence. It is here that things start to really heat up. "When did you first start thinking about sexually assaulting hookers?" one inmate asks. Steven replies that he didn't really think about it before it happened. It just happened. One day he came across a "hooker" and they went down an alley, although he had no money to pay her. So he put a knife to her throat and forced her to have sex. He relates this to us dispassionately, as if his actions were quite easy to understand. "You planned these attacks, right?" the nurse continues. Steven shakes his head vigorously from side to side. "No way!" Then his primary nurse follows up. "How long have you been angry at women?" she asks. Steven, losing his temper at this line of questioning, says that he has never said he was angry at women. "I am *not* angry with women," he affirms emphatically. The nurse stares blankly at him for a second, then puts her head down and again writes something in her notebook. "I'm a protector of women," he protests as she writes. His girlfriend was once assaulted at work, he continues by way of explanation, with the result that Steven began to keep an eye on her. But this attempt to extricate himself fails terribly, as several other men interpret his actions as controlling behavior, followed by his nurse, who suggests that this was not about protection at all. Steven looks disheartened.

Mark and Steven then engage in a debate over these crimes, during which Mark repeatedly refers to them as "rapes," which clearly makes Steven uncomfortable, then angry. Mark is a disruptive force on the unit, barely tolerated by the other inmates, who freely refer to him as a "psychopath." His record of violence, both in the community and in prison, speaks to the kind of life he has lived. His current sentence is for a sexual assault of a woman at a party. When Steven continues to use expressions like "I committed a sexual offense" or "I had sex with . . . ," a nurse jumps in, supporting Mark's contention that Steven is minimizing by not referring to them as "rapes." Steven responds glibly, "Sex, rape, same thing." The room erupts with condemnation! His primary nurse, looking shocked, emphatically admonishes Steven that "they most certainly are *not* the same thing," adding that Steven "has some obvious work to do."

During feedback, the general theme of the comments and questions is that Steven is not being upfront and truthful. There are too many inconsistencies in his story. He is denying or minimizing, several men suggest, and he shows little insight into his behavior. When asked by one inmate why he is in the program, Steven replies, "To learn why I do these things." The therapists thought this feedback was excellent overall, I suspect because it was very compatible with the CBT paradigm. While somewhat harsh (and harsher than many I witnessed), the feedback still ends on a positive note, with several men commenting that Steven has done his best, that he should be here for himself, and that he needs to work with his primary nurse much more. Ian even apologizes for his profanity-laced outburst.

As the session ends and the group breaks up, Steven can still be heard protesting that he wasn't being evasive and that he really couldn't remember all of the details. It seems to me that his Auto is not all that different from some others I have observed in terms of the details offered. In this instance, however, his primary nurse was really focused on the facts, and kept going over them trying to count up and order events. This was disruptive to the flow of the Auto, and the inmates in particular seem to view confused narratives as evidence of cognitive distortions, especially since they lack access to the correctional files, unlike the staff. The nurses, on the other hand, despite their own frequent complaints regarding confused narratives, do not use narrative flow as a key criterion by which they judge the adequacy of these narratives. For them, disclosure of key facts that are compatible with the official record seems to draw much of their attention.

. . .

"[My primary nurse] couldn't really shape my Autobiography because my Autobiography is pretty much *my* story being told, and she doesn't know my story," an inmate tells me one day. "But with the reports that she has on me in my file and . . . the charges that I've had, all my past charges, all that's on record. So she can go into that and have a rough idea. But I still have to add the pieces." In sexual offender treatment, however, the narrator's attempts at emplotment—the "pieces" to be added, as this inmate suggests—provide the site for considerable debate, and justification of any kind represents a taboo rhetorical strand.

Disemplotment, whereby the meaning of the life story and its associated facts or events is dismantled, begins with the Autobiography. This goes beyond the simple "reframing" of a patient's story, a strategy used in cognitive psychology in which "new narrative accounts of self and others that can sustain more successful social behaviors" are engendered (Kirmayer 2000: 154). What is at stake here for the inmate is his ability to control his life story, and having to fit one's story into the parameters provided by the fifty-six questions represents a significant discursive trimming of narrative agency. Getting it "right"—both factually and morally—adds a further problematic dimension, since these narratives are not just consumed by an audience but challenged and judged. Eventually, to be successful, some offenders such as Curtis give up on emplotment and "surrender" to the audience of staff and inmates (cf. Frank 1995), providing their life story in a format that may or may not have therapeutic meaning to them but has significant meaning to members of the audience. Others, such as Franklin, appear to make an effort to deliver what they think—or have learned—is required, what the audience wants to hear, and to do so in a manner that allows them to maintain a significant degree of control in the narration. And there are those, like Steven, who scrap, argue, and fight their way through the Auto, refusing to give in yet failing to respond in a manner that would reduce criticism. It is a learning process, and those inmates, like Franklin, who have more insight and perhaps experience in treatment than others seem better able to render a story compatible with CBT.

"Success" in the overall treatment program, then, is based on an evaluation of the extent to which reemplotment has occurred in a manner prescribed by the program. Another way of looking at it is that "success" speaks to the extent to which the Autobiographical narrative comes to reflect both the factual details of the life lived, as previously authorized by the judicial system, and the moral and ethical principles taught in the program, which are themselves derived from the broader treatment theory. Yet the Autobiographical process is not repeated as such unless the inmate does so poorly he is required to do it over. Instead, the program moves forward to parse the inmate's life and focus especially on the crimes themselves and the criminogenic factors believed to be associated with them. He never gets to tell his story again, never gets to show off his therapeutic progress as he rethinks his life, and hence this initial Autobiographical offering takes on enhanced significance.[6] The stakes are high indeed.

The Autos of Curtis, Franklin, and Steven represent three different types of experiences, but they do demonstrate agreement on one key point. From the perspective of forensic treatment, the "Autobiography" is not meant to be a narrative, despite how the inmates interpret it; it is a disclosure, a form of confession, and the point of the disclosure is to admit guilt to the crimes by accepting the "facts" without qualification. Our idea of narrative structure is subverted: instead of the facts providing the structure over which meaning is laid, here we see that subjective meaning as it is typically rendered becomes the stuff that clouds the facts, gets in their way, makes them "distorted." This lends itself to an overarching concern with the truthfulness of the details recounted. In the hands of the inmates, and sometimes even the treatment staff, this often seems to result in a microscopic examination of the minutiae, a search for consistency and inconsistency in the details. While compatibility with the official record is important, so too is compatibility with what might be called the "plausible record," the understanding of sexual offenses and CBT more generally that is developing among the inmates and that they employ like a grading template in judging the quality of the Auto they are hearing. Verisimilitude at this time is more important to the other inmates precisely because they, unlike the staff members, lack the factual details.

For the inmates, the Autos, because they are the first presentations, establish the factual baseline against which a narrator's subsequent performances will be judged. By the time they move into the second major component of their treatment programs, the production of Crime Cycles, the paradigmatic emphasis on falsification can be seen to dominate in the reactions of the inmates to their peers. But though inmates, under the watchful and hopefully approving eye of the staff, increasingly invoke a more positivist framework to critique each other's Crime Cycles and then Relapse Prevention Plans, with a greater focus on "historical truth," in their own presentations in these two components they continue to fall back on the narrative mode, hence providing the fodder for each other's critique.

"How to Say 'Fuck Off' Politely"

"Anger Management" and "Assertiveness," common components of many kinds of psychotherapeutic modalities, including those with prison inmates generally, are two psychoeducational groups that typically follow "Cognitive Skills" and "Values, Attitudes, and Beliefs." In Anger Management, the inmates are taught "what anger is, when it becomes a problem, and the importance of managing anger effectively," using a variety of cognitive and behavioral strategies (Treatment Manual, 35). Assertiveness is seen as a component of anger management, although it is handled in a separate module. Lessons on impulse control are also included. Linkages to the Cognitive Skills and the Values, Attitudes, and Beliefs modules are made clear: the inmates are told that "our actions [are based on] self-talk, [which is based on] our core beliefs" (Patient Manual).

Instruction in this module includes the "Five Factors That Tell Us We Have a Problem with Anger: 1) when it is too frequent; 2) when anger lasts too long; 3) when it leads to aggression; 4) when anger is too intense; 5) when anger disturbs your work or relationships" (Patient Manual). To make this lesson more concrete, each inmate is directed to complete his "Anger Cycle," linking in clockwise circular fashion the following:

- Environment/Event/Trigger ("List all the situations or events that trigger your anger")

- Negative/Distorted Thoughts ("List your negative or distorted thoughts that are associated with the triggers")
- Feelings ("List how you feel about the situation or the thoughts")
- Anger Arousal (Physical Signs) ("What is happening to your body? What are the signs?")
- Defence Mechanisms ("Examine the defence mechanisms we discussed and list the defence mechanisms you have used")
- Behaviours ("What are the behaviours you have carried out—either towards yourself or others?")

The "Five Ways to Deal with Conflict" are also explained, including the "Rules for Fair Fighting."

The anger management module often resonates with the men, who seem readily able to recognize anger issues in themselves and others. They actively engage with the sessions, and therapeutic insight is often gained. "You know," explained Stan during an interview, "I was very, very, very, very surprised to see how many triggers I had out there, some of the warning signs I have. I didn't realize they were, like, an anger problem. I thought anger was like someone gets me mad, that's it, I'm angry. You know? But I didn't realize anger reflected all these other things. They affected all these other things in your life! And then I started to learn." Then, demonstrating the possible impact of the program so far, Stan provided an insightful assessment. "I realized things about myself through some of my thinking errors I have, like from Cog Strategies, I started to realize my attitudes and what type of thinking always got me in trouble. I was very, very surprised when that happened."

Assertiveness training seems more difficult for the inmates because it involves strategies of interaction and not just cognitive skills. In assertiveness training, the inmates learn "appropriate communication skills, including active listening, giving and receiving feedback" (Treatment Manual, 36), or, as the inmate quoted at the beginning of this chapter-ette explained more colloquially, "how to say 'fuck off' politely." This module extends the lessons learned in Anger Management by describing the "differences between passive, assertive and aggressive responses" to situations and providing alternative assertive responses and conflict resolution strategies.

One of the central components of Assertiveness is the importance of using "I" statements to avoid aggressive or passive-aggressive responses. "'I' statements tell a person that you have a concern," the inmates are told in the Patient Manual. "'I' statements tell a person how you feel about a situation." There are three parts to the use of "I" statements. First, "tell the person how you feel (I feel . . .)"; second, "tell the person the situation (When . . .)"; and third, "tell the person why you feel that way (Because . . .)." As an example, consider this "inappropriate" comment: "You are a lazy jerk. Why can't you do something about this mess?" A more "appropriate response," the inmates are instructed, would be "I get very angry when I have to clean up after you because I think we should both do our share."

Part of the problem for the inmates in this and in other aspects of the program is that they often identify contradictory behaviors in relating to the staff members that confound them. David, for instance, explained that "I can give an example of a facilitator in the group who lost her temper with me right in the group." He continues his story. "Started to swear at me. Accused me of being in denial and all kinds of other things. Because I challenged her! I didn't do it in a disrespectful way, but she was behaving in a manner that . . . that was not the way we've been taught in the program how to handle situations. And so I took the program material that I had been taught, when she started behaving like this, and I tried to use that material on her." David's tone turned more reflective:

> That's about the worst thing you can do. The worst thing you can do. They tell you what to do, they tell you how you should look at things, and . . . and how you should react in numerous situations. How you should handle different things, be it thoughts, words, or behaviors. And yet when they act outside those things, and it happens. Not with all of them, it would not be fair to say that, it's not all of them. There's two or three here that do it. And we're in a position where they carry the big stick, and if you question them or you try to use the very things that they've taught you on them, then you're in deep shit! And it's happened to me a couple of times. I thought, okay, this is good! If you really believe in what you're teaching me, then why are you not using it yourself? And yet you expect me to do it? Somehow that doesn't seem right. Do what I say, not what I do?

So while the inmates typically engage to varying degrees with anger management and assertiveness training, and often find that the lessons resonate with their own lives, an important issue that arises is that the skill sets and responses they are taught seem so foreign to their situation as prison inmates. During a teaching session one day, this matter comes up, and quite a debate erupts about how useful the anger lessons are for the men while in prison. There is significant resistance to the lessons, such as the idea that one has "choices" when confronted with situations that provoke anger. "Choice," the reader will recall, is a central element in CBT, the idea that the men have considerable agency and "choose" to commit criminal acts and therefore can "choose" not to as well. Several men stress that the skills and strategies of anger management and assertiveness might work on the street, in "happyland," as the nurse describes it, but do not work in prison. "You have to meet aggression with aggression," states one man, and many agree. "It's dog eat dog in here," he adds. Several men join in. If a friend is being beaten, you have to intercede. Heads nod in agreement. If you are being attacked or pushed around, you have to respond; failure to respond makes you a target. But another inmate disagrees. "I beg to differ," he says, and explains that while he has been in "the system" almost his entire life he has never had a fight. He has good skills at reading people and thus has avoided conflict, he claims. Several men respond that such a position makes him "passive," and they have learned from the program that this is the opposite of anger and also to be avoided. Surely he has been hassled for this stance, it is suggested. He denies it, but the others seem unconvinced.

"If I used my 'I' statements in the pen," Billy explains to me one day, "I'd probably get killed!" This is an interesting dimension of the con code, in which an "I" statement is likely seen as an aggressive act, one that calls for a response. "Oh yeah," agrees Stan during an interview, "I'd get eaten if I tried this assertiveness stuff in prison. It's different there. If you got a beef with someone you gotta confront them, you know? Or else turn your back, and be a victim the whole time you are in." Aggressiveness is a means to survive in prison. "I" statements "are for normal people, like you, Jim!" explains Stan, laughing. Indeed, this is but one example of the incommensurability of many treatment lessons with life on the inside.

> Board game frenzy has taken over the unit. Several men have become intensely involved in a particular military game in which one tries to conquer the world with one's game pieces. Every nonprogram moment, it seems, sees the men rush to the table to resume play. Today during play one inmate accuses another of being too "aggressive" in his efforts to conquer a third man's territory on the board. Program language erupts. "Yeah, I do not like it when you play like that," says the target of the

attack. "It hurts my feelings." "Well," replies his antagonist, equally as calm, "I do not like it when you play like a fucking moron." There is laughter all around.

Field notes

. . .

Today during an assertiveness training session, the treatment staff presented a scenario of a party where one man is talking to another who finds the conversation boring. What goes through the first man's mind as he is being bored, one nurse asks the group? She provides three categories of potential responses for consideration: passive, aggressive and assertive. Possible ideas for each are written on the board as they are offered. For instance, a passive response might be, "This guy is boring but I cannot get away," suggests one inmate. An aggressive response might be to insult him and walk off, another contributes. An inmate suggests as an assertive response simply telling the man that he is boring and that one no longer has an interest in this conversation. Here the nurse notes that while they are being taught to be truthful, this tack could hurt the other man's feelings. So being honest and forthright must be balanced with the need to respect the feelings of others, she explains. The men seem puzzled by this, since it adds a dimension that complicates their understanding of assertiveness. The nuances of the lessons are often lost on them, as they tend to approach mastery of the material in a fairly rote manner.

CHAPTER 6

"Feeding Frenzy"

The cold and spartan atmosphere of the interview rooms on the unit may be intentional: three walls of cinderblock, one of glass. This is an interior room, and the constant hum of the ventilation system is distracting. Even though the rooms are small, the acoustics are terrible. "Do you think that some of these guys can fool the staff?' I ask. David, sensing this problem, leans forward toward my tape recorder. He speaks in hushed tones.

"Oh yeah," he replies, nodding and grinning. "You mean the staff can be tricked, they can be fooled by a bullshitter?" I clarify. "Oh yeah, for sure," he reiterates, but then, pausing as if for effect, adds, "but for only so long." David looks at me and smiles slightly, then continues. "Like, they have contacts beyond belief. I know that. I knew that coming here. A lot of guys don't know that. A lot of guys don't know that I know that, because I have been here before and I know." "What do you mean that they've got 'contacts'?" David shifts in his seat, his eyes now darting back and forth from the glass wall out toward the Bubble, where several occupants are visible. The correctional officer appears to be looking right at us. David proceeds cautiously, quietly. "Well, police reports, for example. The *real* thing." "So, they know about you before you get here?' "Right, exactly," he replies, "reports and everything else." Then, perhaps recreating a scene from earlier in his treatment, his tone changes, and he speaks in the voice of a staff member. "Oh, okay, if he doesn't say anything about this, oh, I wonder why not." Returning to his own voice, he clarifies the consequences. "Then, it is put on you: 'You are this, you are that, you did this, didn't you?' What are you going to say? Well, you can either bullshit them or give them the truth. It is right there in black and white." Tapping the table with his index finger, he adds, "it's on paper, pal."

THE TRUTH, THE WHOLE TRUTH, AND NOTHING BUT THE TRUTH

From the moment he is arrested, the question of "the truth" dominates an offender's life. Every time he is questioned—by police, by courtroom lawyers, by case management workers, by parole boards—the quest for "truth" is central, and what the inmate says becomes part of his official record. This information is collated alongside information acquired from other sources, documents such as police and court records, psychological and psychiatric evaluations, and reports from prison correctional officers, and together it serves to generate the official judicial-correctional profile of the offender. The "facts" of the crime take a central place in the electronic dossier, but a more general profile of the inmate also develops, a profile that weaves all these various sources of information together to form his official "life" story, including his life in the penitentiary. The file follows the inmate around as he moves through the various levels of the justice and correctional systems, with new information added at each step. His file has been read even before he presents himself to the correctional treatment staff members who will now have significant power over his life.

The inmate arrives, therefore, not as a stranger but as someone well known—at least on paper—to security and treatment personnel. Key elements of his "story" have already been told through these official channels. Yet as we saw earlier the first major activity he is required to undertake in treatment is to stand before staff and his peers and tell his story to them. What makes this process especially difficult for the inmate to navigate is that the two target audience categories—the staff and the other inmates—do not *share* the same initial knowledge about him, nor do they assess the validity of his narrative using the same criteria. Compatibility with the official facts and theory of CBT dominates in the assessment of staff members, whereas for the inmates verisimilitude in combination with a nascent and emerging understanding of CBT seems to be invoked. For the most part, what the other inmates know about each other is based on what they have learned during the presentations of the Autobiographies, and as we saw these can often be characterized as the fractured and fragmented products of group construction. The institutional memory about the inmate, then, consists of both written and oral accounts, with the former being more central to the evaluation by staff and the latter more central to evaluation by the other inmates. As the inmate moves forward through his program, the "truth" of his life story becomes more complex as a result, consisting of not only the information in his official records, but now also information added or extracted by his therapists and other inmates during the Auto, information he himself has delivered orally to the group, plus any additional information he may have confided to associates during nonprogram time in the broader therapeutic community context.

In chapter 5 we saw the tension that develops between the inmate's Autobiographical reflections upon a life lived and an imposed script of biographical details and meanings, both of which are mediated through the theoretical lens of CBT. This tension continues as the inmates move into the second major performative aspect of their program, the Crime Cycle, where matters of fact are now more directly joined by matters of cognition and affect. The presenter is still very much in narrative mode during the Crime Cycle phase, reworking reality "in order to make it bearable," as Michael Jackson (2002: 16) might suggest, and this reworking characteristically involves the inclusion of "counterfactual or fictional" facts and episodes, including confabulations. The "facts" presented earlier in an inmate's Auto may seem less remarkable, that is less worthy of remembering, for the inmate than the meanings and interpretations that he wished to communicate to make his story "bearable." Recall may be even more problematic where the "facts" were, in reality, fictions, or where they were interjected by audience members and passively accepted by the narrator. Such "unstable" details, having been employed in a decontextualized manner, often prove resistant to recall later on (Berrios 1998). The audience, in contrast, tend to focus most of their attention on their own notion of what was remarkable about the presenter's story; they concentrate on the "facts," consisting of events, people, time frames, and chronological sequencing, but add a new dimension, compatibility with CBT theory.

It is here that the idea of a falsifiable "truth" and narrative memory begin to clash most clearly. *Memory* in this instance refers not only to the ability of the presenters to recall events and associated affects and cognitions of many years prior but also to their ability to recall what they actually told the group during their Auto, or what was collectively agreed upon as their story was co-constructed. This in turn is compounded by what the group members themselves recall of what was said, since of course this too is subject to the vagaries of listening skills and inclination as well as memory. Together, narrator and audience continue the process of disemplotment and reemplotment, the disconstituting of facts and meaning in preparation for replacement by the official facts and more CBT-compatible meaning.

We can gain insight into this process of memory and narrative by turning to cognitive science, where memory in particular has proven to be a fruitful yet controversial field of study. Some cognitive scientists have employed "fuzzy trace theory" to suggest that, over time, people generally do lose sight of specific details—contained in "verbatim memory"—while retaining the "gist" of the experience (Reyna 2008). Indeed, the neuroscience of this phenomenon suggests that "different brain regions are activated when gist and verbatim representations are encoded and retrieved" (851). Valerie Reyna (2008; see also Brainerd and Reyna 2002), a leading fuzzy trace theorist, compares gist and verbatim representations in intriguing terms for me here. She writes that "a gist representation is vague and qualitative; it captures the bottom-line *meaning* of information, and it is a subjective interpretation of information based on emotion, education, culture, experience, worldview and level of development." In contrast, she explains, "a verbatim representation . . . is precise and quantitative, and it captures the exact *surface form* of information (i.e., it is literal)" (850–85; italics added). Fuzzy trace theory, then, suggests that actual lapses in memory demonstrated by these sexual offenders—as for all of us—are normative, not pathological; as specific details fade over time, their appeal to gist memory, communicated via narrative, seems likewise normative. Further, according to Elizabeth Loftus (1992: 121), "People are particularly prone to having their memories modified when the passage of time allows the original memory to fade." As the inmates become self-conscious about their abilities to accurately recall, their memories become pliable, open to varying degrees of modification, including the insertion of "counterfactual" and "fictional" details by themselves and others. The addition of such "unstable" details further facilitates the imposition of paradigmatic-like standards applied to the issue of the truthfulness, and hence validity, of the narratives rendered.

The "archive" approach to memory, that is, the idea that memory represents storage, an archive of past experiences, is a dominant paradigm in the history of cognitive research. However, the "traditional model of memory as a static and stable place of storage, where past perceptions and experiences are retained and from where they can be retrieved," is in the process of being dismantled, according to Jens Brockmeier (2010: 10). Indeed, fuzzy trace theory supports Brockmeier's assertion insofar as it advocates for the logical and normative erosions of the content of the archive. And research on brain neuroplasticity contradicts the idea of a permanent memory, he notes. Brockmeier, however, is less concerned with this idea of erosion because it still appeals to some extent to the archive model. Of significance to my work here, he suggests that contemporary neuroscience shows how, neurologically, "we cannot separate 'real' acts of remembering from acts of 'imagined' remembering. . . . Even if such acts create fictive or even fantastic scenarios, they still are carried out by 'real' neurophysiological activities" (23). He points specifically to the contentious issue of "false memory" as an example, arguing that "although on a neurobiological basis we may not be able to testify that memories are 'right' or 'wrong' we certainly can prove that they are 'real.' That is, in either case, they come with a solid neuronal correlate" (23). Neurologically speaking, then, "real" and "imagined" elements of memory are indistinguishable. Further, Brockmeier, echoing what many narrative theorists have also argued, suggests that "every act of remembering mingles elements of experience from the past with elements of experience from the present." Again in neurological terms, "All new experiences, that is, new neuronal input, encounter neuronal networks that have already been shaped by previous encounters with the world. This preexisting 'neuronal knowledge' powerfully influences the way new experiences are integrated, shaping the content, texture, and emotional quality of what we 'recall' of the moment" (24). Memory, in other words, is a generative event occurring in the present but shaped by the past, and not an event retrieving a fixed set of details stored somewhere in the brain.

What this research seems to suggest, then, is that when the inmates stand before their therapists and peers and engage in memory events, the recalling of details, cognitions, and emotions pertaining to historical events, they, like the rest of us, are subject to both processes of detail erosion and the vicissitudes of memory construction in the temporal present. What is historically "true" and what is imagined emanate from the same neurological processes and quite possibly blur together in many instances; "It is possible to confuse imagining something with remembering it," notes Wertsch (2011: 25), "and the same neurocircuitry may be involved in both." "Memory mistakes" are problematic for the inmate because the dominant treatment paradigm, and dominant lay models of memory, are both based on the archival model that suggests humans have a capacity to accurately recall details, even though much psychological research suggests otherwise (Wertsch 2011). As Brockmeier (2010: 26) has noted, within Western thought such "memory mistakes" have been viewed as "sins" because of the "belief that one's memory ought to be, and in principle was, able to provide reliably a correct and permanent replica of past experiences." "This morally and religiously charged vision of memory and its 'sins,'" he adds, "seems to linger on even in the thinking of leading contemporary neuroscientists." We might add here that, when such mistakes are seen as the product of a more deliberate effort to obfuscate, as is often the charge when inmates forget or fail to disclose "fully," the sin is doubly damning. And of course sometimes—perhaps quite frequently—the inmates just plain lie, a major moral fault and one that is considered an innate character trait of such criminals.

THE CRIME CYCLE

The Crime Cycle narrative exercise follows after the Autobiography. Having spent considerable time probing aspects of an inmate's broader life and crimes, the Crime Cycle moves to focus attention on the crimes themselves and the proximal factors that, combined, seemed to have contributed to the commission of the sexual offenses. The idea of a "Crime Cycle" is that "seemingly unimportant decisions" can be part of a chain leading to the commission of an offense (Marshall, Anderson, and Fernandez 1999: 129). Recognizing the links in that chain is an important step in avoiding reoffending in the future, and therefore the development of a Crime Cycle is the first step in the development of a Relapse Prevention Plan, which will be the subject of the next chapter.

In the Crime Cycle, offenders are required to dissect their past crimes "in order to define both the characteristic steps in their chain and the high-risk factors or situations to which they are particularly vulnerable" (Marshall, Anderson, and Fernandez 1999: 131). The "offence chain, it should be noted, involves not only the behavioral steps leading to an offence, but also the corresponding thoughts and feelings" (131). This latter requirement adds a whole new, complicating dimension for the inmates. While ability to recall the brute "facts" of their offenses is challenging enough, trying to recall what they were thinking and feeling at the time of the commission of the crime proves daunting, especially given the role of alcohol or drugs in their actions. As Donald Spence (1982b: 49) suggests, "Feelings and attitudes leave few traces." One might question whether they leave any traces at all.

The idea of the Crime Cycle is explained to the inmates in the Treatment Manual handouts as well as by the staff through direct instruction. "Sexual assault is not considered to be an isolated act," states a handout. "It is the end result of a series of events the offender has experienced. The offense cycle can be described as the sequence of thoughts, feelings, events, circumstances, and arousal stimuli that are activated in the offender prior to his committing an offense." The goal is to "identify problem behaviors which contribute to sexual offending." "Behaviors," they are told, "includes actions that are observable," and they are asked to "identify the behaviors that contributed to the events or problem patterns that led to the sexual offence." Examples given include "viewing pornography, getting drunk, hitting a loved one, staying awake all night." "Thoughts" include "words, images and/or perceptions that we say to ourselves, or that pass through our mind." "Our behaviors and feelings influence our thoughts," they are told. They are then instructed: "When developing your Crime Cycle, focus on your perceptions and interpretations of events or problem patterns that contributed to your sexual offending. These thoughts are often identified as Cognitive Distortions." Examples provided are: "She owes me sex; she's asking for it by the way she is dressed; that little girl came on to me." Finally, "feelings" include "any emotions you experienced at the time." "Again," they are directed, "focus on the feelings associated with or preceding problematic behaviors."

To assist them, they are advised to generate a list of categories to help identify what was happening in their lives before the commission of the offenses; they are provided with possible categories ahead of time. Examples include "relationships," "work," and so on. Of particular relevance to my argument here, the inmates are cautioned, "**Remember, ONLY choose categories that are related to your offending behavior. This is not a Life Cycle, it is a Crime Cycle**" (capitalization and bold original).

> Kevin is angry. He had a "hot piss" test, he says, meaning he tested positive for drugs. "Yeah, I smoked one joint in the yard," he admits, "just after arriving" at the institution, about a month ago. He shows me his discharge letter, which also notes that, in addition to the test, he has demonstrated disruptive behavior on the unit, including "soldiering," and that he has refused to explain how his drug use fit into his Crime Cycle.

He wrote an apology and gave it to his primary nurse, and was told that this is not what they meant. He has now written several pages explaining how his actions do indeed fit into his Crime Cycle, but fears he is too late. He has appealed for another chance to complete the program, but he does not hold out much hope. Indeed, he is bussed out the next week.

Field notes

CURTIS'S CRIME CYCLE

Curtis spent more than two weeks on his Crime Cycle, producing three versions. I was not surprised by this admission. After his Auto experience he had seemed to dedicate himself to determining what was expected of him and to delivering it. We met often over the ensuing weeks, informally, while he bounced ideas off me and sought my feedback about his Crime Cycle presentation. Always cautious, I tried to react not as some kind of professional but rather as if I were a member of his group. How might they respond? My assistance had little impact on his insecurity, however. Referring to a written draft of his Crime Cycle, he explains during an interview, "The first one I didn't do right. Talked to my primary nurse, and he said that he didn't want it that way. He wanted a 'big picture.' And I did another one that took me another two or three days. Then I presented that to him, and he turned around and told me that wasn't right either. And he says he wanted a 'big picture.' And the third one I finally hit it right on." Now at the end of his treatment program, Curtis reflects back upon his Crime Cycle experience three months earlier. "I think I did very, very good." Such a positive evaluation does not easily jibe with my notes from the session, however, perhaps a good example of the reconstructive nature of memory.

"It's my birthday," Curtis announces at check-in. He beams, and a few men clap. That is about all the goodwill he gets, it turns out. Curtis's Crime Cycle presentation is actually characterized by extensive debate over the events and meaning of his life. As directed, he opens with a recounting of his sexual crimes, a kind of refresher for the group but also, I note, an opportunity to check this version with the one previously told during his Auto. Curtis explains that there were three offenses: sexual assault against his ex-common-law wife, another against his wife, and between these crimes one against a female friend at a party. "All adults," it is noted by his primary nurse, as he looks around the room at the various faces. Curtis admits that all these offenses involved his drinking.

For purposes of the Crime Cycle exercise, Curtis's early life experiences are of little interest. The crime "cycle," apparently, is so narrowly defined as to force out of the narrative salient life experiences such as foster placements, sexual abuse, and violence. So the first "category" that he employs in his presentation is called "As Good as It Was," the period just prior to his lapse into criminality linked to his current chain of offenses. Most men are encouraged to start with this category, sometimes also referred to as "As Good as it Gets." Curtis begins by listing the things that were positive in his life before his crimes started: job, nice family, friends, "good times." He talks a little about his wife and kids and a time when there was no drinking. His sexual needs were being met, he adds. On the whiteboard is a chronology of this period, which he has written out prior to the session. He directs our attention to it as he traces over a period of several years.

A discussion of the chronology ensues, and a short time later one of the inmates comments that things must have been deteriorating in the year prior to Curtis's first major crime. Another inmate agrees, followed by a third, who jumps up to write it on the board. Curtis sits blankly and gives no indication he is going to intercede. His nurse points at him and says, "You should speak up. It's your Crime Cycle." The nurse seems to be acknowledging that Curtis risks losing control of his narrative and giving Curtis permission to dispute the claim. But Curtis remains silent. The man at the board, interpreting Curtis's silence to be nonagreement, returns to his seat without writing anything down. But the discussion of Curtis's downward spiral continues.

The deterioration in his life began as he started hanging out with his old friends, explains Curtis, drinking and then cheating on his wife. He says that in his small Aboriginal community there were a very large number of boys born in the same year as he was, and they all grew up together. "Best buds," fishing and hunting together, he says, but also breaking into houses and causing other kinds of trouble. His primary nurse motions with his hands, finger pointed, making circles, a gesture we all interpret to mean "move on." As Curtis returns to a discussion of his deterioration, Franklin comments that Curtis must have gotten "bored" during his "As Good as It Was" phase. "Bored with your family life, I bet," he elaborates. Franklin continues by relating his own story about how he would get bored when he was not drinking and how he would drive by bars where he knew his friends were all having a good time. He would wish he could join them. Eventually he gave in, just as

Curtis must have, he surmises. Curtis nods knowingly. "Yeah," Curtis says in agreement. "That's it. I was bored, for sure."

The next issue that arises is where to draw the line between "as good as it was" and the downward slide into crime. Our attention directed back to the board, we explore the chronology again. A nurse notes the pattern that, when things were going well, he was getting what he wanted and so, presumably, was his wife. When things deteriorated, he continued to get the things he wanted, but slowly this began to happen without consent and lawful behavior. Curtis listens but does not respond. The nurse writes all of this on the board. Curtis watches, still silent. What was the "trigger" event, then, Ernest asks? Others nod in agreement with the question. Curtis, generally slow to respond to any question, opens his mouth but is cut off by one of the nurses, who says that there is no "trigger." It's a process of deterioration, the nurse says. It's not like one day Curtis woke up and no longer was content with his life. Curtis stares blankly at the nurse who is offering this interpretation of his life. The nurse nods at Curtis to continue. The tone for the session is already clear.

"Were you having any problems at the time of your first offense?" asks the nurse. "No," says Curtis, and shakes his head. "What? Wait a minute!" Leon is incredulous. In his Auto Curtis had suggested that he was worried about losing his job at the time of the offense, Leon reminds the group. "That must mean you *were* having problems, and you knew it!" Curtis, looking uncomfortable, initially nods in agreement, and Leon jumps up and heads toward the board to write down this fact. But then it seems that what is being said sinks in, and as the discussion starts to move in a new direction, Curtis blurts out, "Did I say that?" Yes, he is first told. "Then I take it back," Curtis says meekly. He clarifies that he was *not* afraid of losing his job, actually. But then another inmate speaks up, admitting that it was *he* who said that Curtis was obviously worried about his job. Then one of the nurses adds that she thinks *she* was the one who said it first. Another inmate agrees. Finally it is resolved by the group that Curtis did not say he was worried about his job, others did. Curtis seems confused but relieved, and I sense that he is now way off track. Betrayed by a whiteboard he inscribed so carefully the night before, he reaches into his jacket and pulls out some papers. His eyes search while we wait. His nurse eyes the clock and calls for break.

After the break, the emphasis is on how Curtis gave himself "permission" to commit offenses. Others relate how they have done this as well. One nurse notes how Curtis was used to having his way and took what he felt he wanted. Curtis nods in agreement. At this point Leon interrupts and begins to relate a story about his life, when he too felt the world owed him everything and he could just take what he wanted. He does not get very far into the story before he is stopped by the nurse, who reminds Leon and the rest of us that we are here to focus on Curtis. But later when Tom does the same thing, he is allowed to ramble on, almost incoherently due to his medication, until he runs out of thoughts. Curtis sits patiently through all of this and does not seem to mind that he is not the center of attention.

As Curtis's presentation ends, I make a mental note about how to characterize it. Raucous. Lots of interruptions. People talking over each other. Debates about Curtis's life that didn't involve Curtis. A confused-looking Curtis, sitting quietly and only once really rising to defend himself against an interpretation of his life with which he disagreed. Slow and not necessarily thoughtful responses to questions, allowing plenty of time for others to offer possible answers. A willingness to let others define and interpret his life.

At feedback, Ian begins by conceding that "some of us think a little slower" than others, and it's hard to think when so many questions are being directed at us. It is clear he is speaking about Curtis and this session. Ian's rescue of sorts continues as he instructs that we should allow the person to answer one question at a time. Treatment staff members nod in agreement, although I note that in this session they are as guilty of the apparent chaos as the inmates, if not more so given that they are in charge. But Ian is not pointing fingers or naming names, and he is quite calm as he says this. Several men note how well Curtis has done. He is commended all around for his hard work. Although Curtis is not supposed to comment during feedback, as the session breaks up and the men start to reorganize the chairs, he credits Franklin for helping him the night before in putting his Crime Cycle on the board. "He went over it with me too," he says. But Franklin is quick to respond that he only added three or four things and that the rest is Curtis's work. Curtis stands, shuffles forward with his papers and pen in hand, and begins to make notes before the board is wiped clean. He will submit what he hopes is his final Crime Cycle to his primary nurse, to be placed in his file.

I return to my research office to make my notes. This is the second time I have seen Curtis in action, and it has become clear that he is very passive and, with only the occasional exception, content to allow others to shape his narrative performances and his written reports. He seems willing to acquiesce to the expertise of the nurses but struggles to understand what is expected of him. During his presentations he frequently glances over at the staff, as if gauging their reaction to what he or another inmate is saying, searching for the "right" answer, the thing to say that will be acceptable. Otherwise, he seems most happy when members of the group are so engaged in debate about him that he is forgotten.

> *"And then when you're giving your Crime Cycle, they bombard you with questions," explains Paul. "It's constant! Continuous, constant questioning. I had an easier job in the courtroom when I was in front of the prosecutor. I'm not exaggerating this! When I was doing my Crime Cycle it reminded me of . . . a feeding frenzy!"*
>
> *Interview with Paul*

TOM'S CRIME CYCLE

This morning Tom is about to present his Crime Cycle. Tom is an active presence in the group sessions but has developed a bit of a reputation for being a "space cadet," in the words of one inmate, often saying things that seem remotely linked to the topic at hand. Tom at times seems to live in his own world. Since he arrived on the unit he has been on and off medication for both anxiety and depression. Some days he simply looks wasted, with glassy eyes and slurred speech. Other days he fires off commentary at rapid pace. He seems to be having a good day today.

As always, the session starts with check-in, mostly platitudinous, with "Feeling good" and "Ready to work" responses dominating. But the formulaic opening is disrupted when Franklin announces, "I'm pissed off." "About what?" asks a nurse. "I'd rather not say," he replies. The fact that Franklin refuses to provide any explanation casts a pall over the group. This is manipulative, and such bold efforts usually engender ill will. After the session I learn that Franklin was involved in an altercation with another inmate, with Franklin allegedly issuing a challenge that his antagonist enter his house and "rock and roll." There will be an investigation, and Franklin knows he is already on thin ice for his aggressive behavior on the unit. As the session unfolds this morning, it becomes apparent that Franklin's check-in was advance warning of his mood and demeanor.

Tom opens his presentation by saying that he is not in the program to get parole "like you guys." David's head snaps up. The goal of parole is the public secret (Taussig 1999) of the unit. Almost everyone is thinking about it, most are there to achieve it, but it is not appropriate to state it as bluntly as Tom suggests, and especially in such an accusatorial way. I sense that Tom, by mentioning it, has broken another one of the moral rules of the group. A couple of men shake their heads side to side, as if disavowing the sentiment and silently saying to the treatment staff, "Not me." "I just signed the papers two weeks ago," Tom continues unabated, declining his right to a parole hearing for another two years. He has been in jail for several decades already, for a homicide unrelated to sexual crimes. He says he has come to the unit for his own "piece of mind" with respect to prior, undisclosed sexual offenses.

Like Curtis before him, Tom has spent some time in advance of the session writing his Crime Cycle on the board. Following the template he has been given, there are four categories: "As Good as It Was," "Thoughts," "Feelings," and "Behaviors."

He opens with "as good as it was" and warns us that he has had many "negative" experiences, such as an alcoholic father and sexual abuse (later we learn that this was probably done by his father, but he is not absolutely certain, as he insists that he has "blackouts" from this period of his life). It is not uncommon for the men to have mostly negative items in this category despite its heading. Those that do mention something positive are often quite vague as they move quickly to talk about transitioning into problematic behaviors. Tom is one of those that does not have much positive to share, and he suggests that he had problematic behaviors even when younger. His "as good as it was" begins at age ten—there is nothing at all before this—and goes until age twenty. Confusingly, his sexual abuse of children also began around age ten, he explains, and continued until his early twenties. From his point of view, there were no "good times" that he can recall, no restore point that would characterize what is meant by "as good as it was."

Tom seems reluctant to disclose anything more than that he offended against children. "This is your Crime Cycle," reminds Wilson. "We can't help you without the details." But Tom admits to having trouble remembering the details of his past, and specifically asks for help from the group in recalling not only the events but also relevant thoughts and feelings. As the Crime Cycle unfolds, Tom proves to be very receptive to integrating ideas from the group, perhaps because he himself has so little to offer.

Following up, Franklin asks Tom about his victims' ages. I note that Franklin has a look of disgust on his face, a look he commonly reserves for child abusers. Franklin has shifted his eyes over to Tom as he raises his question but has not swiveled his head at all, which is slightly forward and tilted to the right as if actually looking away. Tom sits at a forty-five-degree angle to Franklin's left, making this posturing somewhat visibly awkward. Franklin has been scowling since Tom commenced, and he clearly refuses to show him respect by turning to address him directly. Tom returns the disrespect by responding without looking at Franklin, provides the ages of his victims in general terms ("I can't really remember"), and admits that he "groomed" them, mostly by playing with them, "but I didn't offer them treats." He was never violent with them, he only fondled them, he further clarifies. No intercourse either. Franklin rejects this. "All sexual abuse is violence," Franklin declares, adding that this is what they have been taught in the program. Tom is "minimizing," he accuses. Tom's nurse intervenes that this is not what Tom means, that he is talking about physical harm and force. Franklin responds by demanding to know why the same rules don't apply to everyone, why sexual abuse is "violence" for some in the group but not for Tom. "I may as well stay in my room," Franklin declares cynically. The nurses ignore him and continue with Tom.

From this point onward, the men in the room take an active role in the session, peppering Tom with questions and seeking clarifications. Tom does not fare well. Ernest, seeking to make a link between Tom's past crimes and his current status, asks Tom about his sexual fantasies while masturbating. Tom replies that he mostly fantasizes about adult women, and less so children. In response to more questions, he clarifies that he does not fantasize about males and that he never fantasizes about violent or coercive sex. He admits to being bisexual, however, and expresses that he has had much confusion in his life over his sexual identity, a product of childhood experiences, he believes.

When a nurse asks if an emotion he had was "excitement" or "anticipation" with regard to sexual fantasies, he agrees. The nurse, who has been busy redrafting Tom's Crime Cycle on the board, adds this in. But when David then says it makes no sense to say that he does not ever fantasize about sex with men when he admits having a sexual attraction, the nurse announces, "Let's move on," not allowing Tom to respond. Ernest then asks about the age at which Tom started to abuse children. Franklin jumps in and begins to answer, but Ernest interrupts him, pointing at Tom and saying, "Let him answer." "I already told that," replies Tom. "It's when I was fifteen or so." "You said 'ten' before,' corrects Andrew. "Oh, okay. Yeah, ten," agrees Tom. "No, I think it was closer to fifteen," adds his primary nurse, rummaging through parts of Tom's file that have been resting on his lap. Tom nods in agreement. The nurse continues to root around in the papers while asking him about his sexual fantasies involving children, and Tom replies that he will get to that on the next board. But the nurse insists it is relevant now, and Tom agrees and discusses it.

So far in the session Tom has been quite congenial, even with Franklin, appearing to do his best to answer questions while offering very few details, and accepting interpretations offered by others without much resistance. He has not taken the bait that Franklin and a few others have thrown in his direction; he is not going to argue with those who do not like or respect him. As the first half of the session winds down, I also note how Tom seems to insist on telling stories about the thoughts and emotions detailed on his list, unlike many inmates who often just read the lists and count on others to question them for clarification or elaboration. Tom also frequently answers questions with a narrative. When telling such stories, he is again and again interrupted by staff, who do not allow him to develop them or make his point. They seem to be hustling him through the process.

After the break, Tom's demeanor changes in the face of more interruption and criticism. He becomes more argumentative and the audience more frustrated by his inability to give straight, simple, and consistent answers to questions. Men roll their eyes or collapse back in their chairs, sighing loudly in apparent exasperation as Tom launches into yet another story. Several men, and especially Franklin, show obvious impatience and constantly interrupt Tom, insisting that he just answer the question. When one of the nurses defines Tom as a "follower," Tom rejects this vociferously. He admits that he is "easily influenced" by people, that people can get him to do just about anything they want, but he is not a "follower." Several men throw up their hands, as if to suggest that Tom's own words prove the point. The matter of his being a "follower" resurfaces again later when he explains how some of his crimes unfolded, and this time the nurse writes "Follower" on the board, as if it is now confirmed.

Tom admits to being a substantial drug user in his adult years. "Did you sell them?" asks a nurse. Tom does not directly answer the question but instead launches into another story, this time about a friend who would sometimes bring drugs to him. Tom would "skim" some and then sell the rest. The nurse cuts him off at this point and states emphatically, "You were selling," then writes "SELLS DRUGS" in large capitalized letters on the board and forces Tom to move on.

The discussion of his sexuality picks up again as he starts to move into a more concrete presentation of his current, nonsexual offenses. Under both the "Thoughts" and "Feelings" categories on the board are several references to him having great sexual prowess and being a "gigolo." "Women would pick me up," he says matter-of-factly, "often just walking down the street." He implies that they even paid him for sex. This is too much for some of the men, who loudly scoff at the absurdity of this idea. Any woman could get ten guys lined up for sex for free, declares Franklin. One of the nurses frowns but does not challenge Franklin's cognitive distortion. After more challenges, Tom admits that most of the women did not actually pay and that most of his prostitution money came from men. Did *you* pay any of the women? he is asked. No. He then admits to blackmailing some of his male clients, which brings out some more incredulous laughter. Even the staff members are startled by this admission and laugh. Tom explains that he would try to extort money from them if they hid their homosexuality. He carried a gun, he admits, as if this bolsters his claim.

Tom also informs us that, during this period of his life, he was working. In what appears at first to be a minor detail, he provides a description of the hours he worked. But Ian challenges him by saying that he also worked for the same company (though likely a different branch) and that the work hours were different from what Tom suggested, implying that Tom is lying about working there. Tom clarifies that the nature of his job was such that it had to be done at an unusual time. He emphasizes that he is telling the truth.

Tom is then questioned about why he would carry a gun. He says it was for "protection." Franklin is surprised to learn that Tom would put it down the front of his pants. Wouldn't your clients see this? he asks. "Yes," agrees Tom, "I told them I had a gun." There was no attempt to conceal it. Others too seemed surprised that Tom carried a gun. Leon then asks for specific details about where in the city Tom did his "stroll." They briefly discuss particular intersections but are cut off by a staff member, who says the details are not relevant. Leon looks upset at this but stops talking. A few minutes later in Tom's story it becomes clear that Tom was working as a prostitute in a particularly tough part of the city and that most "hookers" in that area carried weapons. "That's what I was getting at!" exclaims Leon, looking vindicated.

Tom's behavior was, apparently, quite normal given his occupation and place of business.

Tom's efforts at extortion ultimately led to the murder of a former male client who would no longer pay him for his silence. Tom used a club he found at the scene. There is some quibbling at this point over the premeditated nature of the killing. Using the club suggests that he was not planning to commit the murder, suggests an inmate. Why not use the gun, asks another? Tom explains that the gun would have been too noisy. Franklin challenges Tom, stating authoritatively that the kind of gun Tom had would not have been that loud. Tom disagrees, and they argue back and forth for a minute or so before Tom's nurse puts an end to this line of discussion. Tom shifts direction, and in response to a question about why kill, and not just intimidate, this client, he explains that he also needed money and took it from the dwelling after the killing. "Wait a minute," interrupts a staff member. "Earlier you said you were doing okay financially. So this doesn't make any sense." There is a strong suggestion that Tom is again not telling the truth, and he seems to be getting exasperated by this. Leon helps out. "Could it have been that at the time you were short money and didn't want to work the street?" he offers. Tom accepts this interpretation readily. "Yeah, exactly."

There is much discussion of Tom's murder charge, an act that Tom says he was talked into committing by his girlfriend. "Denial" accusations rain down. No one can make you commit a crime, he is reminded. Tom now seems to be getting agitated about the constant questioning over the details. These are not relevant to his being on the unit, he argues back. But, for reasons he will not explain, he will not disclose the details of his sexual offenses. His nurse assures him that this information is not needed. Clearly something is going on with Tom that the rest of us are not privy to, since everyone else in the program is forced to disclose the details of their sexual crimes. Several men in the group look perplexed, but no one questions the nurse's decision.

The feedback for Tom is surprisingly quiet. Franklin, again not looking at Tom, simply announces, "I have no idea why you're here." Most others note that Tom is "courageous" for wanting to deal with the issues behind some fairly old offenses. None of us really knows what those crimes were, however.

A key issue in Tom's overall presentation is that it was confusing, and the repeated interruptions, while adding certain particular details, disrupted whatever narrative flow Tom was trying to establish. My recounting of the session here adds considerable organization and smoothness in order to share at least some aspects with the reader. What is clear is that while Tom attempts to use a narrative approach to explain his Crime Cycle, he is repeatedly derailed by a focus on specific details, some of which seem tangential if not irrelevant to his Crime Cycle, along with overt refusal by the treatment staff to allow him to tell stories as a means of explaining himself. In a subsequent interview he explains that he found this frustrating and was not certain he had obtained any positive therapeutic value from the exercise. His willingness to allow others to ultimately dictate key elements of his Crime Cycle parallels that of Curtis described previously.

> *"Like they want me to talk about things that happened twenty years ago. I can't remember what happened yesterday! You know what I mean? I was trying to remember three days ago. I couldn't remember what year I was born. I was trying to remember. Shit! Just like your name, I couldn't remember your name. I can remember [his primary nurse's] name good now. But I don't remember what-do-you-call-his-name very well. The little short one."*
>
> *Interview with Eddie*

EDDIE'S CRIME CYCLE

At check-in today, Leon and Mark sit next to each other, joking around, making it look like they are buddies. This is surprising, since these two alpha males have been knocking heads for weeks, both in the program and outside it. One staff member, returning today from a brief holiday, feigns a double take and remarks laughingly about how much things have changed in a week!

Eddie has elected to remain in his usual seat along the side of the horseshoe, rather than near the whiteboard and in front of everyone as some men do. His primary nurse sits at the front, though, ready to write on the board as Eddie begins. The board is empty.

Eddie opens by quickly reviewing each of his offenses, the age of his victims, and his age at the time. "You know all this from my Auto," he explains. But this is not sufficient, notes his primary nurse, and Eddie is asked to break down the offenses and address each one in terms of the categories "Behaviors," "Thoughts" and "Feelings." There is no mention of the "As Good as It Was" category. Despite an appeal for a chronological rendering, however, Eddie almost immediately starts to jump around in detailing each crime. He admits to being attracted to teenagers and to cheating on his wife. At this point Ian interrupts to suggest that Eddie must have done so because his wife—whom he had married when they were teenagers—was aging and no longer looked like a teenager. Eddie denies this, but his nurse seems intrigued by the idea and writes it on the board.

Eddie has memory problems, he explains to the group, and asks for their help. Indeed, he notes that some of his crimes happened a long time ago and that he himself is an "old man." This ongoing struggle over recall dominates his Crime Cycle session, and the staff and other men spend a great deal of effort trying to pin Eddie down as to the facts. At one point, exasperated, one staff member bluntly asks for a "true" or "false" response to a question, adding that there is to be "no guessing." Eddie, as he has done on many occasions during his Auto and again today, responds that he does not know. His explanation for memory loss, however, moves away from the simple erosions of time to what he no doubt thinks will be a more plausible explanation. "I was drunk at the time," he begins to say in response. The other men partici-pate in this as well. After Eddie describes a phase of his life dominated by drinking and meeting women in bars, one man asks if Eddie was the one "hitting" on the women in the bars or if they were "hitting" on him. He wants a clear answer that, by implication, suggests Eddie was in every instance either the "hitter" or the recipient. Eddie cannot easily answer this question and again notes that he was drunk in the bars when he was doing this. The ambiguity that pervades aspects of his presentation appears to frustrate many. Yet Eddie does not readily come across as evasive; rather he seems genuinely puzzled. He often says "probably" or "I guess" in response to questions, demonstrating a willingness to agree with whatever fact or interpretation is offered. Of course, by claiming that he cannot remember many details he effectively eliminates his ability to argue and in effect opens the door to the others to fill in the blanks of his story.

As Eddie reviews some of his crimes, it becomes evident that he is sexually attracted to teenagers, that he provided some with food and shelter and, in return, was provided with sex. It is suggested that he focused on vulnerable girls for this reason, and one inmate declares that Eddie was their "sugar daddy." While alcohol was involved in his earlier offenses—and he admits to drinking quite a bit—he had quit drinking by the time of his last two assaults. No doubt Eddie feels that this is an important positive point to make, that he can beat his alcohol problem. But to his surprise his primary nurse takes a different tack, pointing out that this makes him "high risk" because at the time he could no longer claim to have impaired judgment. It is suggested that while with his earlier offenses the alcohol had facilitated his actions, over time committing these acts became easier, to the point where the alcohol was no longer needed. Eddie seems a little stunned by this interpretation. "I was just helping these girls," he insists weakly. "I didn't ask for it," he adds, in reference to the sex. "They coulda' stayed for nothin'."

Eddie's use of the term *girls* creates problems. When he subsequently also refers to his many sexual partners over the years as "girls," his primary nurse spins around and writes "GIRLS" on the board, in quotation marks, reminding that Eddie's victims also tended to be quite young. His nurse suggests that Eddie's use of this term seems to provide some insight into his offending behavior. Eddie nods but looks puzzled, and I am not sure he understands what is being suggested. One inmate advises that Eddie should get the phallometric testing, which measures sexual arousal (more on this in the next chapterette). Eddie agrees that it is a good idea and that he plans to do this "to prove I'm okay." But he does try to explain why he is attracted to teenagers. He says it is physical. "They *are* women," he protests. I look around anticipating, but there are few reactions. A couple of men nod understandingly. However, others suggest that teenagers are easier to control and maybe that is why he is attracted to them. He is reminded by Leon that during his Auto he admitted that he liked the "inexperience" of the young girls. In fact, at several points during the description of his crimes Eddie is challenged that what he is saying today is not compatible with what people recall from his Auto.

Although Eddie jumps around quite a bit in explaining his crimes, he saves until the last the one that most troubles him. In an earlier interview with me, he refused even to mention it, telling me he was "not ready" yet. In his Auto two months earlier he likewise refused to discuss the details. Today he reluctantly discloses the nature of the crime, noting that the victim was a young relative. Asked to recall his thoughts and feelings at the time, he says, "I guess I was lonely," adding that the victim "must have" reminded him of his wife, from whom he had recently separated. These suppositions are hardly evidence of affirmative recall, especially for a man who complains at length to have memory problems, and the language he uses clearly speaks to plausibility and possibility, not factual recall. Yet he is not challenged, probably because these thoughts and feelings are compatible with CBT theory. He *is* challenged by several men, such as Floyd, who fail to hide their outrage at the idea of committing a sexual offense against a child. Badgering Eddie to get him to relate the specific details and nature of his relationship with the victim, Floyd, in prison for the sexual assault of an elderly woman, ultimately gives up hoping for an acceptable answer and announces that he simply cannot understand how Eddie could have done something like this. Several other men also seem to have great difficulty with Eddie's assaults against this young girl.

Eddie, passive for the most part even when outright refusing to answer questions, starts to get testy. Mark, returning to the matter of his offense against the relative, offers some unwelcome insight into the nature of this crime. "Your victims seem to be getting younger," he suggests. "Maybe you have a thing for young girls." Eddie, visibly angry, turns to the staff and asks, "What? Is he a psychologist?" His primary nurse replies that, no, Mark is not a psychologist, but that Eddie should listen to what he is saying anyway because he is correct. Mark elects not to continue, however. Eddie, his face red, stares down at his feet and waits silently until his primary nurse encourages him to move on. There will be no rescue this time.

At the end of the session, Eddie concludes by again reminding everyone that he has trouble remembering the details of his crimes because some offenses took place so long ago and that therefore he is offering what he believes he "should have been thinking" because of the circumstances. "I should look in my file," he adds, suggesting that his official records would be of assistance. His primary nurse ignores this suggestion and tells Eddie he should take down the notes from the board, which is now a jumble of text and arrows, to use in writing up his Crime Cycle for submission. "Do the best you can," Eddie is advised. "Don't make up stuff."

During feedback several men complain that Eddie's Crime Cycle was confusing and that he appeared to be minimizing his behavior by always saying he was drunk or couldn't remember. Eddie clearly does not like to hear this but when he tries to respond he is silenced by his primary nurse, who holds up a hand and points to the inmate speaking. Several others simply add that Eddie had done a "good job." "It's hard to remember," says Leon supportively. The last speaker, before Eddie's nurse concludes the session, says simply that Eddie should take from what he has heard whatever works for him and discard the rest.

The issues of memory and recall were a dominant theme in Eddie's Crime Cycle presentation. At one point his primary nurse even told him that they did not expect him to remember exactly, only recall generally what was happening. In other words, there was some accommodation for the importance of gist memory. But this accommodation did not play out consistently during the session. At times there was indeed a great deal of insistence on the details and the recounting of specific memories, and the audience consistently challenged Eddie to relate what he was thinking and feeling at the time of the offenses or just prior. Suggestions that he was lying were frequently hurled his way, and of course it is entirely possible that he was claiming some memory lapses instrumentally to avoid scrutiny and even responsibility. But when Eddie continued to appeal to his memory problem, the inmates and staff members alike sometimes offered what appeared to me to be CBT-compatible plausibilities, almost all of which Eddie was willing to accept, even if lukewarmly.

> At one point as I am sitting in the day room, talk turns to the Jerry Springer and Jenny Jones shows. These shows seem quite popular, and I have seen men watching them frequently. There are often jokes about the shows that link into the treatment program. Yesterday, for instance, while Sam and several others were watching the Jenny Jones show about sexual perversions, another man hollered out jokingly, "Sam, you're cycling!" Today, Stan suggests that they should all watch Jerry Springer and identify the "cognitive distortions," and he chuckles at the idea. Leon responds, "That entire show is a cognitive distortion." Laughter erupts.
>
> Field notes

. . .

Eddie is not alone in struggling with his memory, and as all three case studies in this chapter demonstrate, the Crime Cycles, like the Autobiographies before, emerge as the product of group construction where fact, cognition, affect, and even meaning—or, in a word, experience—are collectively determined and employed to fill alleged holes in recall. Yet the focus on recall of details is somewhat problematic in that it suggests that "normal," "moral" people would be capable of recalling similar details of experiences even many years removed from the event and that therefore the apparent inability to recall represents by definition either a cognitive distortion or a disinclination to be truthful. Cognitive research on memory demonstrates the fallacy of such logic. When the forgetful inmate visibly struggles to avoid appearing evasive, he tends, ironically, to appear just that, as his honest efforts at recall blur with his efforts to invent plausible details or lie outright.

To be successful in the program, then, the inmate must engage in a process of negotiation over the set of details that are to be considered therapeutically meaningful and that should remain consistent throughout their treatment programs. But forgetfulness and "memory mistakes," whether genuine or not, creates a fertile void for new details and memories, including "misinformation" and fabulation, to rush in. Confabulation logically follows. The overriding concern with accurate recall of details, thoughts, and emotions, and with the truthfulness of such recollections, then, is actually somewhat of an artificial distraction in that these "truths" are hardly stable through time and are amended constantly as new elements of truth are added into life narratives throughout the various stages of treatment. This instability simply fuels more challenges. But the preoccupation with details also exists as a vehicle for the imposition of the CBT theoretical paradigm, since holes in memory provide a space for the introduction of institutionally and theoretically validated details and interpretations and mean fewer points of contestation between the inmate and staff. This preoccupation also provides an avenue for the inmates as a whole to demonstrate learned mastery of the theoretical paradigm by accurately recalling the details, often introduced into their narratives by others, whether or not they believe them to be true. The issues of "truth" and recall that become more pronounced in the Crime Cycle process, in comparison to the Auto, continue to dominate the final, major performative stage of treatment, the Relapse Prevention Plan.

"Peter Meter"

"Downright pornography," as Oren describes it. "But if that's what staff's idea is of going through the mud, right, to get what you need and to better yourself, then okay, fine and dandy. Take me to the 'peter meter.'"

According to information provided to the inmates, "evidence of deviant sexual arousal" leads to an offer to complete a phallometric assessment (Treatment Manual, 39). Such evidence may consist of either self-report or, more likely, offense history. This assessment, they are told, is "voluntary," and if they refuse "it is simply noted that they did not volunteer for the assessment"; they are not removed from the program for refusing to volunteer. However, the reports of the phallometric test, one way or another, go into the inmate's record and will be of interest to psychologists, psychiatrists, and parole boards who will be called upon to judge the extent of rehabilitation of the inmate and, especially, their risk to reoffend. And several inmates in my study reported being directed to do the test by their primary nurses. If the inmate does undertake the test and "deviant sexual arousal" is noted, then a variety of approaches are taken to treat this problem, including "orgasmic reconditioning, covert sensitization, thought stopping and other sexual arousal control techniques" (Treatment Manual, 39). Changing masturbatory fantasies to involve only appropriate partners and contexts is one of these techniques, and existing fantasies are often the subject of much interrogation—and snickering—during group therapy sessions.

Inmates who agree to be tested are taken off the unit to a small room equipped with a reclining chair and audiovisual equipment. The room is also equipped with a penile plethysmograph, or "peter meter," as the inmates call it, which is a device designed to measure blood flow to and the circumference of the penis. It looks very much like a rubber band but contains mercury, which measures the changes in the penis's girth as the inmate is shown a variety of images and video. Testing is typically often done over several days; the first two days involve an assessment of arousal patterns, and on the third day the inmates are requested to try to control their arousal, typically to images that elicited arousal earlier if these are considered "deviant." It is recognized by experts that some inmates can manipulate their response to the images by, ironically, employing "cognitive strategies aimed at distorting actual interests" (Marshall, Anderson, and Fernandez 1999: 112).

I have never seen the images used and have never asked to see them, but the descriptions provided by the inmates suggest that they can be very graphic. They show both adults and children of both sexes in various stages of undress and sexual activity, including scenes involving the use of force, such as rape. Novices to the test are often rattled by the images that they are shown, sometimes unfamiliar images that may challenge their moral sensibilities. "It was degrading," explains Perry. "They start out with naked women and then they go down to children, and then they go back to women, and then they go down to children again." "It was the images that bugged me the most," adds Clifford. "Seeing the children in certain stages of undress, you know, or in certain positions, and having to look at them. A lot of times trying to look away, not wanting that in my head. I found it degrading . . . traumatizing." Ryan agrees. "Some of the pictures are very disgusting. How could they show something like that? It's humiliating." The impact of the test may linger as well. "It is very emotional when you come back to the unit," explains Ryan further. "You don't really want to talk to anybody. You just want to be left alone, and just go into your house. The pictures were in my head. I asked my primary [nurse], 'Does it go away?' And she says, 'Yeah, it will go away.'"

Some inmates report that they fear the results of the test, as they may be unaware of how they will react to "deviant" images of sexuality, especially if they have never seen these before. This seems to be particularly the case with respect to images of children. Other inmates, however, approach the test with a sense of confidence and bravado, as if it is a challenge of sorts through which they can show the treatment team that even though they have committed sexual crimes they are, in effect, "normal" deviants with socially appropriate sexual arousal patterns and not "deviant" deviants. Still others simply do not know if they have deviant sexual tendencies and are genuinely interested in finding out. David, who had offended against both adult women and teenagers, was interested in the test precisely to determine if the younger victims represented a particular problem for him. "And when my testing was done," he explains, "[the technician] says, 'Well, you're still more attracted to adult females. You're not attracted to young females or adolescent females.' To me, that's a relief," David concludes. "That's the main reason why I went through testing, to make sure that I don't have a serious problem." Keeping an eye on an ultimate goal, such as parole or even family visitation with one's children, helps inmates navigate through the process and assess the risks that doing or not doing the test entails.

The phallometric test certainly allows the inmate to learn something about himself that may have hitherto been unknown, such as that he is sexually aroused by images of children or sexual violence. While empathy per se is not a part of the testing and follow-up (more on empathy later), empathy lessons often emerge as the inmate is afforded an opportunity to watch as other individuals are victimized. "Watching the video, especially the audio," says Christopher, "it is very loud, very intense. Very at the strain of what the victim goes through. I was thinking back of what I put my victims through. I could put myself on those tapes and probably make one," he added.

Douglas is worried about his peter meter test. "That staff member who runs the test is hot," he explains matter-of-factly. "What if I get a bone just walking down there?"

Field notes

CHAPTER 7

"My Rules for Staying Out of Jail"

Tom's primary nurse begins to push him about his Relapse Prevention Plan, employing repeated "What will you do if . . ." questions. "If you are out and feel the urge to have sex with kids, what will you do?" Tom looks perplexed, and responds, "I don't know. I'm not sure." "See a psychologist?" offers a fellow inmate. "Yeah," agrees Tom. But what if you can't get in? "Social services," Tom says, offering what he assumes is the next logical recourse. What if they can't help? Tom is blank.

The two nurses in the room shift direction and now take turns with question after question about how Tom will satisfy his sexual needs until he finally declares that, if all else fails, he will masturbate. "To what?" asks an inmate, in reference to fantasies. "Men?" the inmate inquires. "Kids," admits Tom. Uproar ensues. Several inmates start talking, almost yelling, all at once. Nothing has changed, the men insist. You have not changed! Tom needs to use "appropriate" fantasies, they chasten. "Okay," agrees Tom simply. He will masturbate to fantasies of adult men and women. Acceptable, nods his nurse.

The Relapse Prevention Plan is the third and final dominant performative component of the treatment program. Built upon a platform constructed initially in the Autobiography, and then the Crime Cycle—in conjunction with the psychoeducational groups I discuss throughout this book—the Relapse Prevention Plan initially appears to be the least conducive to a narrative rendering. Indeed, it is here that all that the inmates have learned is expected to come together as they grapple with hypothetical challenges to their pathological tendencies. But dogged "What will you do if . . ." questions lead many men to continue to struggle for control over what are, in effect, prospective narrative episodes, while others seem finally to have resigned themselves to the loss of narrative agency and allow the group to actively contribute to the building of their future plan more or less unfettered.

THE RELAPSE PREVENTION PLAN

Relapse prevention models joined with CBT in the treatment of sexual offenders in the mid-1980s. CBT's "emphasis on the role of cognitive distortions and decision-making processes," along with its approach to "social learning," seemed compatible with the idea of relapse prevention training (Marshall, Anderson, and Fernandez 1999: 128; Mann 2004). The idea of relapse prevention was borrowed from addictions treatment, where it was noted that while individuals often demonstrate positive change during treatment, once the program ends, challenges often lead to a relapse. Relapse prevention planning is designed to identify potentially problematic behavior and situations and provide measured responses to alter the course.

The idea of a relapse plan in this treatment program begins initially with the notion of an "offense process," often also referred to as a "cycle" or "chain." It is here that information gleaned initially from the Autobiography—providing relevant background factors—and then reworked in the Crime Cycle—a detailed breakdown of the offenses—becomes particularly relevant. The Crime Cycle is conceptualized as consisting of "seemingly unimportant decisions," each one actually a link in the chain that can lead to offending behavior (Marshall, Anderson, and Fernandez 1999: 129). This chain consists of not only behavioral steps but also the corresponding thoughts and feelings. The Relapse Prevention Plan model emphasizes that each link represents an important moment where the cycle can be broken. The goal, then, is to help the offender recognize when he is in his "cycle" so that he can call upon a limited repertoire of strategies to break the chain and avoid reoffending. Framed differently, Relapse Prevention speaks to the processes of "self-control" and "self-inspection," as Rose (1990: 237) defines them, which include "systematic self-monitoring and record keeping, showing the occasions on which desired and undesired behaviour occur, and the construction of a detailed plan programme for transforming conduct, not through airy and overambitious hopes, but through little steps, with achievable goals." This is not so much a matter of will power, according to Rose, "but of the systematic management of one's natural and social environment ('stimulus situations') in order to transform the likelihood of pleasurable concomitants of particular types of conduct." In this case, the success of relapse prevention—its "pleasurable concomitants"—is found in the issue of recidivism.

The Relapse Prevention Plan model typically includes three components. First, the offense chain is determined. Second, a plan is developed to deal with future scenarios that the offense chain indicates may be problematic; the plan includes specific strategies to be employed. And third, warning signs that the offender is slipping back into problematic behaviors and ways of thinking are enumerated. Each step in the chain is identified and dissected, and the relationships among behaviors, thoughts, and feelings are examined. These "risk factors" also include interpersonal and situational contexts that can be problematic, such as continuing a relationship with criminal friends, passing by schoolyards, or going into bars. This is best done by reviewing specific past offenses, on the assumption that the essential elements of the Crime Cycle are not specific to any particular crimes but rather underscore a more problematic cognitive outlook and associated behaviors that are, in themselves, the issue. This, in turn, leads to a plan to assist the offender in recognizing these problematic situations and calling upon his repertoire of strategies and alternative actions to avoid offending. Significant others in the offender's life, such as family, friends, employers, and parole officers, are expected to share in the plan and to utilize a set of observational criteria or "warning signs" that indicate possible slippage to challenge the offender. So relapse prevention often requires that the inmates disclose the nature of their sexual crimes to others, that is, noninmates in the world outside prison; that they have been required to do so in such minute details while on the unit is an obvious stepping-stone in helping them become more comfortable with this.

"The goal of Relapse Prevention is self-management of problematic behavior," the inmates are told in the Patient Manual. And then the warning: "It is important to remember that Relapse Prevention is **NOT** a cure" (emphasis original). Indeed, awareness of "your potential to reoffend" is essential, they are told. "Relapse prevention will only work if you take an active role in managing your problem behaviors." The linkage between the Crime Cycle and the Relapse Prevention Plan is emphasized. "A simple way to think of the Crime Cycle is the 'building blocks' for your Relapse Prevention Plan. When building Relapse

Prevention Plans, you need all the pieces in order to complete the job. . . . If you leave out important information about your cycle, you will be missing important pieces of the puzzle." Much of this "important information," as we have seen, is found in the offender's extensive correctional files. But it also consists of information provided orally during the Autobiography and Crime Cycle presentations, plus other comments offered by the inmate during and outside treatment sessions.

The production of the Relapse Prevention Plan typically comes some six to seven months into the program, by which point there is a great deal of shared information available to the group. The presentation of these plans follows the same format as the Autobiographies and Crime Cycles. The narrative element is somewhat different, however. These performances not only call forth retrospective narrative, as was the case in the presentations of the Autobiographies and the Crime Cycles, but also include prospective narrative, as the inmates relate plausible future events or narrative episodes and their own likely or hoped-for corresponding behaviors and reactions. In effect, the inmates must deduce and relate a proper response to a plausible yet hypothetical problematic future event or sequence of events that is compatible with both previously related personal information and the relevant elements of CBT and Relapse Prevention theory. As David suggests in the title of this chapter, the inmate must demonstrate that he knows how to stay out of trouble upon release from prison.

> "After the one group I had a guy come up to me, you know, 'What the fuck are you doing,' you know? 'You don't have to ask that stuff.' He was lying about [his crime]. The guy had assaulted an eleven-year-old girl and was trying to say that she was a prostitute, and not taking responsibility for [it]. It's a child! It's not a prostitute! It's a child! You are a child offender, you know? And he didn't like that being put on him in group and he got very upset with me. Too bad. That's what you are."
>
> Interview with Ernest

SAM'S RELAPSE PREVENTION PLAN

The session this morning does not start smoothly. There is considerable confusion over what the session is about and when it will start. The program schedule posted on the bulletin board suggests that Sam's Relapse Prevention Plan has been switched at the last minute, from the morning to the afternoon, when psychoeducational groups are usually held. The men assemble at 8:30, as required, not certain what they will be doing. But nothing happens. About twenty minutes later a staff member emerges from the Bubble and announces that they will be starting at nine with Sam after all. Sam jumps up and hurries over to his house, returning a few seconds later with his papers. There is much grumbling about this. The inmates never lose an opportunity to complain about any disorganization or late start to a session, as they are heavily criticized when they themselves are disorganized or late. Several men suggest that they should start without the staff, and two declare that I should lead the group. I decline, of course.

The whiteboard is empty, perhaps because Sam did not expect to make his presentation this morning. As he begins, he walks over to it and picks up a marker. He seems calm and ready to document his plan on the board. Given Sam's previous presentations and the conflict they engendered, I am a little surprised that he seems so relaxed. He will not make it all the way through the next two hours like this.

As Sam starts to talk, he sits back down. Another inmate volunteers to work the board, and Sam agrees. The first half of the session focuses on Sam's short- and long-term goals. Under "short-term" he discusses his continued prison experience, noting that he anticipates relocation to a minimum-security farm after completion of his treatment program, in advance of release into the community. His "long-term" goals assume he is on the street and involve the basic things that all inmates discuss in their plans: the need to find a job and a place to live. He also declares that he will attend Aboriginal sweat lodge ceremonies in the community. Sam, as I noted earlier, has a very loose affinity with his Aboriginal community. His plan to attend "sweats" is surprising because he has rarely even acknowledged his Aboriginality in his earlier presentations and has expressed to me a lack of interest in pursuing these Aboriginal activities, which have become elemental to much forensic programming for Aboriginal people (Waldram 1997). I wonder what he is up to here. Treatment staff sometimes encourage Aboriginal men to meet with the Elders that work in the prisons and to pursue sweats and other "traditional" spiritual or treatment approaches as an adjunct to their program on the unit. Sam's resistance to this advice has been noted before. Perhaps he is now delivering to the staff what he assumes they would like to hear. His primary nurse seems pleased by this part of his plan but asks Sam for specific details as to how he will actually make this happen on the street. Sam replies that in the city where he lived before incarceration there are several sweats that happen and these are open to anyone. This answer seems satisfactory.

Sam's long-term goals also include staying away from alcohol and drugs, again a rather rote offering that all the inmates include in their plans. "How?" he is asked. Sam seems unprepared for this rather obvious question. "I won't buy any," he replies, shrugging his shoulders at what I am certain to him seems like a logical answer. "Well, what if you are at a party and there is alcohol?" "I won't drink any." "But what if your friends insist?" "I'll say 'no.'" It goes back and forth like this for a minute, with each response by Sam seeming more and more implausible to the group. "Why not avoid parties altogether?" he is asked. "Oh." Sam pauses. "Yeah," he agrees. "That is something to work on in your plan," concludes his primary nurse, pointing at the papers in Sam's hands.

Sam continues, moving into the area of relationships. When asked how he will expand his social contacts on the street, he says he doesn't know. "You *should* know," critiques his primary nurse. Other inmates try to help out. "How about the library? Or the grocery store?" Sam chuckles noticeably. I assume that both Sam and the others are thinking primarily in terms of meeting women, and Sam does not come across as a library or grocery store kind of guy. When he is then asked about his desire to establish a romantic relationship, he states bluntly that he is not interested in having one when he is released. Instead, he would like to have sex with as many women as possible. Alarm bells go off around the day room. A different nurse, recalling Sam's Crime Cycle, explains that promiscuity is clearly a problem behavior for Sam. So his goal of having multiple sex partners represents a risk behavior. But he does not want a relationship, he reiterates, just sex. Sam's primary nurse then points out that in his other presentations, especially his Auto, Sam suggested that he believed he was evaluated as a man in terms of his sexual prowess and how frequently he had sex. This, the nurse suggests, is a cognitive distortion, and therefore his continued interest in promiscuity is clearly a risk behavior. An inmate also suggests that Sam is probably concerned about his sexual prowess. Sam is reminded by Leon that he told them before how he had sex with a woman who had passed out at a party. Leon wonders what kind of "sexual hero," which Sam seems to be suggesting he is, would have to resort to sex with an unconscious woman. When asked specifically by Alfred what his thoughts were about having sex under these circumstances, Sam hesitates to respond. Alfred jumps into the silence and suggests that perhaps Sam figured it was okay because she wouldn't know. Sam responds, "Yeah, probably." "Was that a thinking error?" asks his primary nurse. "Yeah," Sam replies weakly.

It is concluded by the group that Sam faces a dilemma in his Relapse Prevention Plan. How will he obtain sexual gratification if he does not have a relationship and must not engage in promiscuous behavior? One inmate offers the suggestion that masturbation is the logical thing to do. Sam smirks. His macho demeanor is clearly at odds with the idea of masturbation or, perhaps more accurately, talking about masturbation. The inmate continues, asking Sam's primary nurse if going to a "hooker" would be "high risk." "Yes," she responds emphatically, because the woman would be just servicing his sexual needs. "What's wrong with that," the nurse is asked, "if it's consensual?" "It's always wrong when a prostitute is involved," she responds tersely, without additional explanation. Referring back to Sam's Auto, she reminds us that he has a problem with treating women as sex objects and that acknowledgment of this should appear in his Relapse Prevention Plan. Sam nods in agreement.

Despite Sam's obvious discomfort with the topic, the issue of masturbation will not yet go away. "How often did he say he masturbated?" asks one inmate to the group as a whole, not even looking at Sam. His primary nurse jumps in and asks Sam point blank: "How often did you masturbate?" Sam mumbles that it must have been only occasionally. It is then suggested by one inmate that masturbating too frequently upon release would be a warning sign, as would having sexual fantasies about women. Another inmate challenges this, saying that sexual fantasies themselves shouldn't be seen as a warning sign; rather, the frequency with which he has these fantasies is the issue. A general discussion ensues among the inmates and staff—but not including Sam—about whether the issue is frequency of fantasizing or the content of the fantasies. His nurse responds that the content is more problematic of the two. Sam is then asked if his fantasies involve consensual sex. "Yes," he replies, the first thing he has said for several minutes. Have you ever fantasized about raping someone, an inmate asks? "No." Sam shakes his head as emphasis. Have you ever masturbated in unusual places, like in public or in washrooms? "No!" again, more emphatically. And nothing more. Break time.

During the break, Sam disappears into his house without saying a word to anyone. But he is one of the first to return to his seat. The break lasts longer than usual, about twenty minutes, and there is some grumbling about this. Several men complain that breaks are supposed to be only fifteen minutes long. They are all sitting impatiently, including a very fidgety Sam, when the two nurses emerge from the Bubble to continue the session. Nothing is said on either side about the delay. Sessions start when the nurses say.

Sam now launches into a more detailed description of his offenses. He explains that one of them involved a woman he met at a dance, in which he became sexually aroused while slow dancing with her. An inmate offers that perhaps dancing is a risk behavior for Sam, but others balk at this. Dancing is innocent, even healthy, says another. But when dancing is combined with other things, such as alcohol consumption, as in Sam's case, then it can be a problem, adds a nurse. Several inmates agree among themselves that for Sam this is a risky combination.

Time is running down, but Sam's plan, now detailed somewhat haphazardly on the board, is not finished. Despite his protests, Sam's nurse directs that it is time for the discussion. When the topic of risky thoughts and behaviors is mentioned, several items emerge that are not detailed on the board. The assumption, it seems, based on the reaction of others, is that Sam has missed key elements in his plan. But Sam is quick to defend himself, jumping in and declaring that these things are on his paper, which he has had a firm grip on throughout; he points to it for emphasis. His nurse nods in agreement.

During feedback, several men comment that they had to help Sam out quite a bit with his plan. One says that, at the risk of being blunt, Sam would not have gotten through the presentation without the help of others. Rather than arguing, Sam thanks the group for their help. As the session breaks up, Sam scoots over to his primary nurse, papers in hand, and points, presumably to those areas that he was unable to cover in the session.

During his Relapse Prevention Plan presentation, there were several instances in which members of the audience referred back to Sam's · Autobiography and Crime Cycle sessions as a source of information with which to compare the Relapse Prevention Plan. Items from earlier sessions that were omitted by Sam were added in by the group where they were seen as integral to the exercise. Overall, Sam seemed accommodating, accepting these bits of assistance. His plan, though shallow in the details, seemed very "by the book" insofar as he followed carefully the required categories as laid out in the Patient Manual. Later in discussion he explained to me that he had also learned a great deal about how to do it from watching others. But he was befuddled by one thing: it seemed that when he was most honest, such as when he said that he did not yet want to settle down, but rather preferred to continue having many sexual partners, he was challenged most intently. In Sam's mind, it seemed, brute honesty—telling the "truth"—should be a shield, and clearly it was not. Perhaps it was safer to hedge a little more than he did, he wondered, an issue with which Alfred too would need to come to grips. The "truth" does not always set you free.

> *At check-in today, one inmate presents a story rather than simply saying how he feels. He says that yesterday at canteen he wanted to buy his usual two packages of cigarette papers. The clerk gave him four and the receipt. He walked away, and a short time later looked at the paper and saw that he had been charged for only two. He went back, and put the paper in front of the clerk. "How many did you charge me for?" he asked. The clerk looked at the paper. "Two" the clerk responded. "Well you gave me four," the inmate replied, and he put two down on the counter and walked away. "I felt good about that," he tells the group, smiling. His primary nurse smiles back.*
>
> *Field notes*

ALFRED'S RELAPSE PREVENTION PLAN

There is a lot of sickness on the unit today. In such a closed environment, with no fresh air and very tight quarters, this is not really a surprise. Viruses often rampage through and seem to take forever to subside. There was a lineup at the meds window when I arrived this morning, something I have never noticed before. Most were getting pain relievers and other cold and flu medicines. As we get ready for check-in, several men are missing. They are given considerable latitude to declare sick days and absent themselves from the group sessions.

Alfred has already written his Relapse Prevention Plan on the board. It appears neat, well organized, and color coded by category. It seems to follow quite faithfully the template that the inmates are given and to cover the main points that are likely to arise. Very comprehensive, I think to myself. Indeed, the whiteboard is full, as if to discourage any audience-generated additions. Nevertheless, at the outset Alfred is sending signals that he will be cooperative and compliant.

Alfred begins by saying that he will start where everyone else seems to start, at short-term and long-term goals. Again, they are rather rote: get parole, find a job and a place to live, maybe a relationship. Nothing surprising here, and no controversies arise. As he moves into a discussion of his "high-risk thoughts," one inmate suggests that he add to his list "sarcasm." Alfred is famously sarcastic in group, and I am not sure if this inmate is trying to be helpful or funny, or is taking a swipe at Alfred. Alfred ponders this for a moment, issues a sly smile, but refuses to take the bait. He says he will write this down on the board—he does—but adds that "I'll put a question mark beside it," which he does as well. Later, after break but before we start up again, Alfred asks the inmate who suggested this if he meant sarcasm toward Alfred or Alfred's sarcasm toward others. "Toward others," the inmate clarifies. Alfred smiles again but says nothing.

His discussion of relationships comes next, and he explains how he believes that in the past everyone who loved him had left him. Therefore, in his relationships he tends to be the first to leave, before they do it to him. His secondary nurse notes that, while the latter sentiment is on the board, Alfred has not included the former as a high-risk thought. Alfred squeezes "People leave me" into the appropriate column. His primary nurse then asks if learning to trust should also be on the board. Alfred responds that he obviously trusts now, as demonstrated by his comfort at presenting in front of the group. When he first arrived at the unit he would not have been able to do this so openly. He did not like to talk much at the start, he admits, to which others nod in concurrence. His sullenness and occasionally flippant behavior were somewhat of a distraction to the other men when he first arrived, several have told me. Alfred was not likable, and despite his efforts today I get the sense that this is unlikely to change.

Next, Alfred moves into a discussion of his "high-risk behaviors." Drinking is a problem, he notes. He proposes as a strategy that he consume only nonalcoholic beer but then adds insightfully that he may just be fooling himself in thinking that the taste of beer, and not the alcohol, will be sufficient. Others agree that this is a problematic idea. Still another high-risk behavior is his use of "porn," he admits. He informs us that he likes to buy lots of magazines and masturbate frequently to them. In his plan, he states clearly that he will not buy porn anymore. But he will continue to masturbate. Some men feel that perhaps he engages in excessive masturbation and that this is a risk factor. He admits that his masturbating has sometimes been at the expense of sex with his girlfriend, and one inmate notes that this is problematic. But Alfred clarifies that his masturbation is not excessive and that he does not accept that masturbating generally is a problem. Unlike Sam, Alfred seems quite comfortable with this topic. His primary nurse adds that it could be a problem in certain circumstances, such as when it affects a relationship.

Relationships are indeed a problem, it becomes apparent. Several of Alfred's high-risk thoughts and behaviors include his controlling attitude toward women, how he needs to know where his girlfriend is at all times, and how he easily becomes jealous if she talks to other men. He says that he will try not to be like this in the future and will attempt to recognize that she can have "her own life."

Alfred also tells us that another high-risk behavior is walking around at night, looking for women who will be sex partners. He adds that this was "sort of" what happened in his offense. His primary nurse interrupts to clarify that this is "exactly" what happened, in that he attacked a complete stranger passing by, and that Alfred needs to consider alternative ways to meet women. "Night time is for sleeping," Alfred responds affirmatively but with a tinge of sarcasm, "not going out."

For the most part, things are going well for Alfred. Having interviewed him several times, and talked with him at length informally, I cannot help but think that he is demonstrating considerable restraint, putting on a performance for our benefit. During an interview following his Relapse Prevention Plan session he admits that he learned what was expected. "I had had the opportunity to sit through a few of them before mine actually got presented, so I had a better idea of the areas I had to go into and what I had to identify," he explains, "the things I had to do to prevent them from happening again." Despite this planning, however, Alfred does crack and opens up a significant controversy for himself.

"Okay, I expect to get jumped on for this," he tells the group. We are still discussing his high-risk behaviors. He will continue to play cards, he declares. He is good at it, has been doing it for years, and loves it. It's "like a job" because he frequently wins money. But he admits that because of his unruly, drunken behavior he has been banned from many high-stakes games in his hometown. So his only option now is to play in other places, such as casino bars, that hold major games. He will take a "trusted friend" to ensure he stays away from alcohol and trouble. At this point one inmate interjects that expecting someone else to take care of him is unfair, and wrong too. Alfred shrugs off this criticism. His nurse then points out that his criminal record shows he has serious trouble with alcohol and that this represents a pattern in his lengthy criminal record. Alfred acknowledges this problem as long-standing. He will not drink in the bars, he continues to insist, but admits that he might go into bars sometimes to "test" himself. Several men scoff at this, and some laugh out loud at such a preposterous idea. His plan represents a huge risk to reoffend, they argue. What if he loses, they challenge? He can't win all the time. How will he handle losing? Will he end up drinking? One inmate reminds Alfred that, the previous week during his own Relapse Prevention Plan session, Alfred was very critical of that inmate's alcohol use. Returning the favor, he accuses Alfred of being a hypocrite. And if card playing is his "job," why not just get a real job where there is less risk, asks another? Alfred replies in turn that in one evening of card playing he can make as much as minimum-wage earners do in two weeks. "Rationalizing," one inmate responds, more diagnostically than accusingly. "You're rationalizing." "You're just justifying your behavior," adds another.

There is much discussion of this issue among the group. After listening for several minutes, Alfred retreats somewhat, saying that "maybe" he should continue to think about the issues of cards and bars and discuss it further with his primary nurse. His nurse nods in agreement. But he is not backing down completely, he adds, and concludes that he still believes that this is a viable option for making a living.

Alfred's final category is "positive thoughts" about himself, an opportunity for some self-affirmation. He notes that he is not at fault for what happened to him as a child, the abuse he suffered. "I am special," it says on the board, "because God don't make no junk." "Are you a Christian?" one man asks. "Not really." A thoughtful pause. "Sort of." Another pause. "I believe in God," Alfred explains further. So maybe you need to consider going to church, suggests the inmate. Alfred is noncommittal. Another inmate attempts to help him out by stressing that there is a good Aboriginal program in Alfred's hometown that includes Elders and sweats and that they could really help him when he is released. "I'm not really into my Native heritage," Alfred responds dryly, almost dismissively. You should still give it a try, encourages his nurse. Alfred agrees to at least think about this. An inmate points out that it is time for "walk." The nurses agree and the group breaks.

When we reconvene, feedback commences. Not surprisingly, Alfred's plans to play cards and avoid alcohol figure centrally. Several men again note that Alfred needs to think more about his postrelease plan. There is widespread skepticism among the men and the nurses. Alfred is not being realistic, they say. He will not be able to play cards where there is alcohol without running the risk of relapsing. Card playing for big money is rife with the criminal element, he is reminded, so there will be lots of negative enticements. While some comment that he has done an excellent job in laying out his plan, many continue to take him to task on the matter. Not permitted to respond, Alfred simply smiles that smile of his and absorbs the barrage.

Alfred's intransigence is interesting because he clearly knew at the outset that he would be challenged and admitted as much. It would have been easier if he had just given in and presented the therapists and other inmates with details that were compatible with the narrative schema of treatment. This was his third presentation to the group, and after almost eight months in the program, he had an acute sense of what would be acceptable and what would not. By his own admission he had seen other Relapse Prevention Plans. He seemed so well organized that he probably could have gotten through relatively unscathed. So why not keep this plan to himself? Why throw out this clearly inflammatory idea? Afterward, when I ask him about this, he explains that it was important to him that he show the others that he could go into bars and not drink and that he could play cards without getting into trouble. When I push him, and note that he could easily have avoided a negative reaction if he had just left this out, he responds simply, "I just like to hit things head-on." I think he was trying to maintain some control over the relapse plan narrative, digging in his heels on a matter of some personal significance despite understanding that he would receive a poor evaluation as a result. In the eyes of the therapists, Alfred's interpretation of his card-playing, alcohol-drinking life probably represented a cognitive distortion. Yet to Alfred, his interpretation was not negative at all: it provided meaning to a life in which, despite other setbacks, he was an accomplished individual.

A few weeks later, only days before the conclusion of the program, Alfred was caught gambling on the unit and was discharged back to the penitentiary. He had successfully completed all of his programs, yet this infraction meant he was now an official treatment failure.

> There was an incident this past weekend when Ned was cleaning the fish tank on the unit. One of the fish died during the process. When Mark walks into the lounge this morning before group starts he is very agitated, paces back and forth, and mutters that Ned is an "animal abuser" by killing the fish with too much chlorine. Ned's response, muttered to me but in a way that Mark can surely hear, is that "not only am I a diddler," in reference to his convictions for sexually assaulting a young girl, "now I am also a killer." He chuckles as he says this and shakes his head in mock disbelief.
>
> Field notes

STEVEN'S RELAPSE PREVENTION PLAN

Steven is chatting away loudly as the group assembles, calling across the room to other inmates. The typically wide gulf across the span of the horseshoe created by the lounge chairs seems even wider today. Perhaps this is because Steven's cohort has been whittled down to only seven men. The setup of the room has never been raised as an issue in any of the group sessions I attended. The men seem quite comfortable not being huddled together.

Steven moves quickly through the discussion of his short- and long-term goals. One of his short-term goals includes going back to church. There is some snickering in the room, possibly a reaction to the stereotype that all inmates "find God." Perhaps this offering is too obviously pandering to the treatment staff, I wonder. Even one of the nurses appears to quietly chuckle; they are not naive. Under questioning, Steven's bluff is called; he admits that he has not yet started going to church and fails to offer any explanation for this. There are regular services in the institution, he is reminded. He also says that he plans to go to Aboriginal sweats on the outside and points out that this *is* something he has been doing in prison. Steven is not Aboriginal, however, and although non-Aboriginal men can indeed attend these ceremonies it is highly unusual. There are no more questions about this.

The presentation then moves to "high-risk thoughts." Steven reminds us that he offended against a sex worker and a young girl. With the "hooker," he explains, it was because he wanted sex but had no money. He had a girlfriend at the time but would use "hookers" when she was away. Discussion ensues, and the men conclude that Steven seems willing to take what he wants without considering the consequences and that it was easier for him to force sex upon a "hooker" than it was to work for the money to pay her. Sam, who is in charge of the board while Steven remains in his seat, turns and writes, "Take what I want." Steven continues by admitting that another high-risk thought is that he sees women as sex objects. Not having money and carrying a knife are problems as well. The issue of the knife seems to pique the interest of many. Asked why he carries one, he repeatedly offers no answer other than variations on it being "a habit," or "for no particular reason." Several men argue that there has to be a reason, but Steven refuses to back down. We are still early in the session, and Steven's temper, noted in earlier sessions (as well as in his file, I subsequently learn), is starting to become a problem. His pale complexion is now red, and he is wrapping his knuckles on the arms of his chair. His primary nurse persists, noting that Steven used a knife in his offense against the "hooker," and suggests that he carried it as a means of intimidating so as to get his way. Steven has trouble with this. No one seems to accept his explanation as to why he carries the knife, a nonexplanation really. The issue is no longer relevant anyway, he continues, almost pleadingly, as he is prohibited by law from carrying a weapon. But this seems to miss the point that he is willing to go to certain lengths to get what he wants, the law notwithstanding, his nurse comments.

Next Steven opens the discussion of his sexual assault on the child. What were his thoughts? "Revenge," he says unabashedly. He had babysat for the girl's mother on several occasions, he explains, and although he got lots of free alcohol he was not receiving the expected cash payment. So he wanted revenge against the girl's mother, who he notes seemed to find the money to go out with her boyfriend. Steven's primary nurse comments that this was not really revenge, because Steven admitted in his Auto that the girl was asleep and that he anticipated that she would never know what had happened, or that if she did she would not tell. These were his "thoughts" at the time, Steven clarifies. "That's what I was thinking. I'm not saying it was right." Steven is challenged by an inmate that there must be something else to this matter. Under further questioning, he finally admits that the girl was "good looking" and that she often walked around the house somewhat undressed. His primary nurse picks up this line of inquiry and iteratively coaxes Steven into admitting that the girl was "sexually arousing," despite actually behaving like a normal child. Then, having done so, the nurse scribbles something on the stack of papers on his lap. "That's a cognitive distortion, right?" asks an inmate. "Oh, yeah," agrees the nurse, nodding his head.

So babysitting is a high-risk behavior, concludes one inmate. "It should be up there," he continues, pointing at the board. Steven waves his papers in response. "I haven't gotten to it yet!" I am sitting next to Steven, and he turns to me and points at the relevant text. He indeed has "babysitting" written down, and I nod to the group in confirmation. The board by now is busy anyway, covered in blue ink—to identify items Steven has offered—and red ink—to identify items added in by the group. The balance is starting to look even. Steven has not actively resisted the addition of new items up to this point, often consenting to have something added "if you want" without strongly agreeing to it. This explains the many new items and the cluttered board.

Several men call for a break, perhaps sensing that Steven is getting heated. The nurses agree, and during the break both nurses sit with Steven as the others leave the lounge. Steven is looking flustered; toward the end of the first half of the session he had grown increasingly angry at the inquisition. I suspect the nurses are trying to calm him down. But when the session resumes Steven still looks tense.

One issue that emerges immediately is his attraction to female children. Steven admits that he didn't know he had this until the phallometric testing here at the institution showed it. He seems to feel that he is able to control these urges, that it is not a problem. He is asked why his plan does not include staying away from children. He agrees that he will add that in. Discussion then centers on a comment he made about cutting through schoolyards. He says that he will continue to do this to save time and that there is no problem from his point of view. Several men challenge him on this. One asks, Why not leave five minutes earlier and go around? Steven replies that where he lives cutting through one particular schoolyard saves him half to a full hour. "That's a pretty big schoolyard," comments one inmate in a disbelieving tone. Another man asks what he would do if a well-developed schoolgirl asked him for help. He says he would brush her off and keep walking. The belligerent tone in Steven's voice is palpable.

As the discussion of Steven's high-risk thoughts and behaviors continues, Leon repeatedly raises the idea that a high-risk thought would be wanting to have a drink and that this is not on the list. Steven, getting frustrated with this pestering, jumps out of his seat, stomps up to the board, and circles the word *alcohol* that is already there, under the label "High-Risk Thoughts." He slams the marker down on the ledge of the board. As Steven returns to his seat, another inmate interjects that we have just witnessed an example of the belligerent attitude that Steven has shown throughout. Steven silently scowls. But the issue of alcohol will not easily go away.

Both Steven's sexual offenses were committed while he had been drinking, it is noted by his nurse. At several points he is asked to recall his thoughts and feelings at the time of these incidents. Steven is mostly vague in response, suggesting that he can't really remember. He does indicate that he no longer has a desire to drink. Others point out that since he committed his offenses while drunk, it must still be an issue. The desire just doesn't simply go away. Steven is combative on this point. He repeats firmly that, while he occasionally thinks about drugs, he does not think about alcohol. So alcohol is not in his relapse plan in any meaningful way. "If you don't think about it, why put it there," he is asked by an inmate, pointing at the board. Steven is cornered by the inconsistency between what he is now saying about alcohol use and what he has previously written on the board. He is not going to get away with this, of course. More discussion ensues, and eventually his primary nurse instructs Sam to write "alcohol," this time under the category of "High-Risk Behaviors." But Steven himself will not let go and tersely states, "Fine," but adds that his long-term plan does not include Alcoholics Anonymous, though it does include Narcotics Anonymous. He would rather use drugs, and thinks about them more, than alcohol, which he continues to insist he never thinks about. Alfred reminds him that he has been living in a "controlled environment" (i.e., prison) for some time and that his access to alcohol has been necessarily curtailed. Steven denies that prison restrictions have been a factor in his lack of interest in alcohol. What would you do on the street, where there are bars, and the stresses of work and daily life? "I don't drink anymore!" he replies angrily, almost shouting now.

Alfred is the first to respond during feedback and opens by saying that he will begin with "something negative." "I can see your relapse," he declares. He then goes on to explain that Steven has produced little in the way of a meaningful plan and that the biggest hole is his refusal to deal with the alcohol issue. Alfred does not accept that Steven will simply be able to say "no" to alcohol, or that it will simply not be a problem. Job and personal stress will put him at risk. Steven interrupts, proclaiming loudly, "I'll challenge you on that later." It is unclear what he means by this, but as he is not supposed to say anything during feedback, I assume he means outside group.

Many men note that Steven was too defensive in his presentation and that he has a lot of work to do on his plan. Some say that this defensiveness is frustrating. It is recalled that Steven walked out of his own Crime Cycle presentation because of his defensiveness, speaking to the issue of a pattern in his behavior. Steven doesn't listen, they agree. Leon echoes Alfred's observation that Steven has not developed a very good plan. Steven looks very angry at this repeated assessment, and he and Leon clash. Indeed on several occasions during the morning the two have been at odds, and feelings are running high. Another man intercedes and reminds Steven that this is *his* release plan and that the others are just trying to help him. Steven, accepting the conciliatory tone, agrees by pointing out that they have in fact been helpful by teasing out his feelings toward the young girl. Another inmate, perhaps reacting to the tension, speaks about how they are all there for the same goal, to help each other and themselves. They are not there to cause trouble for each other. Steven's primary nurse agrees with many of the comments offered by the men. Steven has made some progress, he notes, but adds that he has also received some good insight from the men.

Steven is tense and combative throughout his session, often refusing to accept others ideas or else accepting them in a backhanded way that suggests that he does not really agree with them. Many ideas on the board at the end are put there at the direction of the staff, or else are allowed to be written down by a very reluctant Steven. He struggles throughout to maintain control of his Relapse Prevention Plan, and his recalcitrance is noteworthy to both the other inmates and the treatment staff in attendance.

· · ·

The Relapse Prevention Plan as a form of prospective narrative requires the inmates to call upon past experiences as the building blocks for strategies to deal with plausible, though hypothetical, future experiences. All that the inmates have disclosed and otherwise spoken about in earlier sessions sets the evaluation criteria for these plans. They must be consistent with past details but also theoretically insightful. It is here that the impact of the treatment program must be most clearly demonstrated. They must be able not only to identify their own cognitive distortions but to employ their newly acquired cognitive skills and understanding of relationships, assertiveness, anger management, and so on as they narrate acceptable strategies for avoiding trouble. Some clearly struggle with the hypothetical basis of the exercise, and many respond in such apparently disingenuous ways that it is hard to see much evidence of sincere "buy in." The question of their sincerity is even more dramatically raised as they move into the final, most emotionally disturbing aspect of their program, empathy training.

"The Most Emotionally Draining Thing I Have Ever Done in My Life"

Inmates in the treatment program are required to undergo empathy training as one of their final treatment modules, and in many ways this is where all the moral lessons of the program come home to roost. The experience for them is both emotionally rewarding and challenging. It is in the Empathy module that the "victim" of their crime finally comes to play a central role, after some seven months of treatment. But this "victim" emerges in a disembodied, ephemeral way as a vehicle for empathy training, for of course he or she is not present and does not engage with the inmate in any way. The "victims" are likely unaware that they are so centrally, if amorphically, involved as part of their perpetrator's treatment program.

Can empathy be learned? Empathy, as I understand it, speaks to an intersubjective moral capability, but is such capability inherent to the individual, or can those who appear to lack empathy by some standard be trained to embrace it? As we have seen so far, much of the treatment program is aimed at moral habilitation, and it can be argued that the rules of fair play in interpersonal relationships, for instance, are indeed learnable. But empathy is different, however, as it typically speaks, in part, to the ability of one individual to in some way understand the experience of another (Stueber 2006). Further, I argue that empathy involves both understanding *and* being understood; that is, true empathy is defined by a relationship in which both parties obtain some kind of psychological or emotional benefit. So if "empathy is an ongoing, dialogical, intersubjective accomplishment that depends very much on what others are willing or able to let us understand about them," as Hollan and Throop (2008: 394) suggest, can it even exist in such a nonintersubjective context as this, where "ongoing interaction" between inmate empathizer and victim empathizee is not possible and the confirmation or disconfirmation of the other's "emotional states and perspectives" (Hollan 2008: 476) is theoretical, derived entirely from a therapeutic paradigm?

An underlying assumption of the Empathy module is that the inmates lack a sense of empathy, which allowed them or "gave them permission" to commit their crimes without concern for the suffering and distress of their victims (Marshall, Anderson, and Fernandez 1999).[1] It is further suggested that such offenders have difficulty recognizing certain basic emotions in others, such as surprise, fear, disgust, and anger, and that since these are emotions linked to experiences of the victims, the offenders are correspondingly unable to feel empathy, unable to understand what their victims experienced. Empathy training, then, is important as a key to preventing sexual recidivism; it is assumed that the offender who can read the emotional state of the victim, and who can feel his or her pain, will not knowingly want to inflict this pain and suffering. So the inmates are told quite clearly that empathy is not innate and therefore immune to modification, that it is in fact itself an "emotion" that can be learned. Not all inmates in my research accept this assertion. Admittedly, I am not convinced either, and I think their experience of the Empathy module suggests that, at least within a carceral context, I may be correct. Justin expresses his own doubts. "You try to treat it as serious as possible, but that doesn't mean that's the way the victim actually feels, because it is hypothetical, you know? It's just a big theory. You know, you don't really, really, truly know exactly how that victim really feels. It's all a guessing game."

The treatment staff, of course, appear not to endorse such a perspective, especially that last part, since they go to great lengths to instruct the inmates about cognitive and emotional responses to the trauma of sexual assault, a necessary part of sexual offender treatment. I do not think Justin is off track, however, considering Clifford Geertz's (1976/1984) observation that what anthropologists frequently label "empathy" is essentially just the projection of one's thoughts and feelings onto another. But what is the basis for such a projection? It is partly an intellectual exercise, for sure. This kind of empathetic projection, however, is best invoked when the experiences of others trigger emotional memories in us; it is not so much that we feel *their* pain, it is that we are reminded by their experiences of *our* pain. Two processes seem to occur in the Empathy module, then. First, the inmates learn what thoughts and feelings are *likely* or *plausible* given the nature of their crimes, which allows them to intellectually project to some extent onto their victims without the need for allegedly similar experiences. Second, for some inmates, Empathy invokes their own painful past experiences, which they emotionally utilize in their efforts to understand the pain that they have caused while, in many cases, simultaneously seeking resolution of their own distress. However, recourse to one's own, allegedly similar experiences, which seems normative in empathy, creates problems for the inmates, as I shall show below.

A variety of different topics are covered in the Empathy unit, such as definitions of empathy, shame, guilt, and forgiveness, and inmates explore in considerable detail the immediate, short-term, and long-term consequences of sexual crimes on victims. They also learn about emotions, what they are and how to both express them and read them in others. As in all aspects of the treatment program, emphasis is on "the connection between thoughts, feelings and behavior." There is considerable role playing in this module. During one session in which Floyd was asked to role-play "anger," he was so convincing that an alarmed corrections officer and another nurse ran out of the Bubble to investigate. Inmates also "examine their own blocks to empathy and how these blocks have influenced their behavior" (Treatment Manual, 37). This includes an exploration of "the harmful effects of physical, emotional and sexual abuse," a topic that opens the door somewhat for self-reflection, since many of the men have themselves been victims of sexual crimes and other forms of abuse. However, this apparent appeal to personal experience as a means through which to comprehend and develop empathy is highly circumscribed and creates in the men much confusion over the role their own experiences are to play in successfully completing the Empathy module.

> "This guy had his house searched yesterday and today. That's harassment, man. I almost put in a grievance for that guy, you know? Me, my house, two days ago, a dog came into my house and sniffed my house, to see if I had been touching dope or something like that. Stupid! And, it was

during group, Jim, during group! Right in the middle of Empathy! A guy is crying and guards walk right into the room to go and search his house. How's that?"

Interview with John

WRITING EMPATHY

The Empathy module "is often very difficult for the offender," the inmates are warned. The main reason is that the most central component of the module, and the one that creates the greatest stress for the inmates, is the composition of two specific letters. These letters are generally composed toward the end of the module, after the instructional sessions. The first letter is written from the inmate to the victim, taking full responsibility for his actions, and thus represents a theme that is reinforced from the beginning of the treatment program. These letters often provide very detailed descriptions of the assaults and empathetic speculation about the consequences for the victim, but they must not contain references to the offenders' own experiences of abuse that could be seen to justify their subsequent criminal actions. The letters are confessional in tone, and although not actually sent to the victim they are shared with the group. Inmates stress over leaving out details of their crimes for fear they will be accused of minimization or denial. By the time they offer these letters, of course, they have gone through the Autobiography, the Crime Cycle, and the Relapse Prevention Plan modules, and the members of their cohort are well versed in the details of their crimes and poised to jump at the first indication of an alteration or omission from previous renderings. The second letter, also shared, is even more challenging in that the inmate is required to view the crime through the eyes of the victim and, imaginatively assuming his or her voice, to send a letter to the inmate explaining the consequences of the crime.

The letters have "criteria" that must be met if they are to be judged acceptable by the treatment team, and a template of sorts is provided to the inmates in handouts. I will explore in greater detail here the letters written from the "victims" to the inmate, as these are the most analytically insightful and the ones most dreaded by the inmate. The criteria for these letters include the following:

a. Will usually express anger. May say that the offender
   i. deserves to be raped or beaten
   ii. is sick or abnormal

  iii. deserves to remain in jail for longer
  iv. deserves other punishment
 b. Will usually take a contemptuous and disgusted tone
 c. Will usually describe life before assault
 d. Will usually describe feelings during assault
 e. Will usually describe impact of his assault
  i. short-term
  ii. long-term
 f. Will usually contain the most damaging details
 g. May mention treatment to prevent other victims
 h. Will not usually express concern for the offender

The last item in the list again references the fact that the inmate is not the focus of the letter-writing exercise; his life and his experiences are not relevant and would be seen only to detract from the attention to be paid to the victim.

  The inmates are given the opportunity to read an actual letter by a victim of sexual assault that was published in a newspaper, and it in conjunction with the template seems to create a model for empathetic expression that is somewhat rote and emulative. The letters tend to be similar, as a result, except of course with respect to specific details. The delivery of the letters in the group, in contrast, evokes a variety of emotional responses among reader and audience, from unemotive and deadpan to highly animated and emotional. I observed numerous sessions where these letters were read to the group, and several inmates offered me copies of their letters. Here I juxtapose an actual letter with the experience of its reading as I observed.[2]

  Paul remains seated as he unfolds his paper. The room is quiet, more so than for any other type of group. The air seems thick with apprehension, anticipating the possibility of strong emotions, emotions not normally witnessed among inmates. Before Paul even opens his mouth, I sense the discomfort among all. More so than with any other part of the program, I feel like an intruder today, about to bear witness to a moment that characteristically would not be shared with mere acquaintances. Given the nature of this exercise, I always make it a point to seek explicit permission from the presenter to attend even though the group as a whole has already granted me carte blanche. Paul thought it was crucial to my work that I do so.

  "I am writing this letter to you to tell you how I feel about the shit you put me through and how it fucked up my family and my life," Paul

begins. It is his voice, but also a sanctioned, indeed mandated, appropria-
tion of his victim's "voice." "Before you came into my family I was caring
and trusting. I thought the world was not such a bad place to be. You
destroyed all of that for me and stole it all away. You are the sick . . ." Paul
hesitates for a second, swallows hard, then continues. "You are the sick
son of a bitch that abused others and went to jail and came back to abuse
more people and then included me in your sickness and destruction."

Paul's voice quivers. His tone is hushed, serious. "You sucked me in
by buying all kinds of gifts and I was fooled into thinking you cared,
and you abused me. You put your dirty hands into my pants and on
my body, taking what was not yours to take."

I look around the room. Most men have their heads down, staring at
the floor. The two nurses are not looking at Paul either; they are looking
off in separate directions to some distant place. Paul, it seems, is being
provided the maximum amount of privacy possible in a group of twelve.

"The guilt and shame you have put me through became my reality
and still is today. Then when I turned fifteen years old you fucked me,
your own stepdaughter. How could you do such a sick, cruel, fucked-
up thing?" There is glassiness to Paul's eyes now as they moisten. "I
am still so very angry I could cut the hate with a knife. I think I will
always feel this way. I even felt somehow responsible for your sick
behavior. I was powerless and could not tell my mother because she
had betrayed me by allowing you into my life. I still feel pissed off and
angry at my mother and my relationship with her still suffers today
and I find it hard to even trust her opinions and judgment. You even
fucked that up for me."

Paul stops, reaches for water, and drinks slowly. He clears his throat,
and continues, pushing through to the end, his voice a little firmer.

"Even sex with my boyfriend now has been affected because we see
you there. You have screwed up my ability to have a relationship with
others because I don't know who I can trust. There are also certain
ways I don't like to be touched because of you, you bastard. There is
an emptiness inside of me that hurts and I do not know how to fill it.
People like you should have to feel the pain and hurt and confusion
and frustration I feel. I wish you could stay in jail forever, then you
might know how our prison feels like. You would get a taste of how it
feels to lose the things you value, to have them taken away from you
forever. How could anyone be so fucking evil? I will always feel this
way. Will the pain and suffering ever go away? Will I ever be able to
have a normal life in any way? Will I ever be able to be at peace with

myself? Will I always and forever be different? Will I ever trust again? I hope you feel real shitty, you should. I did not deserve to have you fuck my life up this way. What did I ever do to you?"

Paul puts his letter down. There is some shifting in chairs. Few look up. The uncomfortable silence is broken by his primary nurse. "Good," she says simply, quietly. "Comments?" She looks around the room. Nothing at first. "Did you have any blocks when you were writing the letter?" she asks. Paul replies that there were several, especially because of the close relationship to his victim, and that he still has trouble understanding how he could have violated her trust. The nurse nods approvingly. In Empathy, unlike all the other group sessions, the men are loath to comment in any way about the content of these letters. Most of the feedback for Paul is quietly supportive. "Good job."

Paul's letter follows the template fairly closely and is typical of the kinds of letters I read and heard during the research. In contrast to the letters *to* the victim, these letters "from" the victim are characteristically devoid of specific details of the crimes, focusing instead on the emotional, psychological, and physical suffering of the victim. While so much of the treatment program up to this moment has focused on disclosure of these details in combination with processes of verification (against both existing written records and the oral record), it is considered "revictimization" if the inmate puts expressed details in this letter. The key issue, they are told, is to focus on the thoughts and feelings their victim may have had and may still have, and not recount the crimes in detail. Oren, for instance, takes about forty minutes to read his letter, and is instructed to cut back on the details dramatically. How much detail is needed? The inmates struggle with this. When Tom starts his letter with a vague, "To Whom it May Concern," he is soundly criticized by the group, one of the few Empathy presentations I attended in which both criticism and defensiveness were expressed. Douglas also struggles with this when he presents his letter to the group, describing his crime with the words, "and then you did what you did to me." "Is that acceptable?" he asks. "No," replies his primary nurse, "you have to give *some* details." "Use 'sexually assaulted me,'" she suggests, or better, "You raped me." Douglas accepts these suggestions, adding that he did not want to appear to be in denial. "You cannot have empathy and be in denial or minimizing," clarifies his nurse. "That would be contradictory."

It is a quiet morning on the unit. No program sessions are running this morning—Empathy was canceled—but the men are not allowed to sleep

*in. They must be up "working" no matter. Most are in their houses and,
I can see as I pass by, some are indeed sleeping. A few come and go, to
the kitchen or the Bubble. A couple of men are playing on the computers.
One inmate is watching TV, the volume almost inaudible as if he does not
want to disturb these moments of quietude.*

Field notes

UNREQUITED EMPATHY

"Marked" empathy, it is suggested (Hollan and Throop 2008: 394), is a form that emerges "at just those times and places in the social fabric where more direct, explicit forms of understanding are limited by politics, anxiety, fear, or ignorance." Is this the form of empathy necessarily invoked in the treatment program, given the physical and communicative segregation of inmate empathizer and victim empathizee, and the fact that the appeal to one's own experiences is necessarily covert? Is truly grasping an empathetic understanding of the experiences and feelings of victims, then, even possible in such circumstances?

Only an imagined intersubjectivity is possible here, I suggest, and therefore only an imagined, unrequited empathy, and this is not true empathy in my book. But this does not mean the exercise is not potentially beneficial for the inmates. As Hollan and Throop (2008: 394–95) suggest, empathetic encounters "sometimes allow people to know and understand things about themselves that they would not know or understand alone." Perhaps such is also the case of unrequited empathetic encounters. In some respects this may be a more enduring product of the Empathy module, but one that is fraught with complications for the inmates.

Ralph, for instance, began the process of empathy training by crafting a victim impact statement to understand his own victimization as a child. "It helped me open up how they would have felt," he explains. "Once I opened up for myself it gave me a way of seeing them." Tellingly, however, he did not inform the treatment staff that he had done this. To an outsider, calling upon one's own experiences would seem to make sense in striving for empathy, as opposed to sympathy. But as we have seen so far, in the overall treatment program the inmates are actually discouraged from utilizing their own experiences to understand those of their victims, as this may lead to a focus on themselves and thus subvert the basic tenet of the treatment paradigm, that the inmates accept without qualifications responsibility for their crimes. So, while many like Ralph find the appeal to their own experiences unavoidable, especially during Empathy, they must be careful that these experiences do not obviously intrude into the imaginative letter-writing exercise. Paul's letter above avoided all mention of his own abuse as a child, a good example of how this plays out.[3]

The cathartic element to the empathy exercise is another possible benefit, but again something that is not easily brought into the public aspects of the Empathy sessions. Jerry, for instance, explains that Empathy was particularly tough "because of all the stuff that I was repressing all these years. I was holding it all inside. With 'Empathy,' I couldn't run anywhere so I had to deal with it head on. I was just emotionally worn down. And then I cried and cried for three hours [in my house]. All that ugly stuff that happened to me." Jerry's voice sinks as he continues in a hushed tone. "Incest in my family." Few know of this aspect of his childhood, he explains, and he has not informed the treatment staff. He pauses, and looks away before he continues. "So I was scared [to do the letters], really emotional. It was anger coming out, So that helped me put myself into the shoes of my victim."

Leon also recognizes the importance of distressing experiences in grasping empathy. "What Empathy does," Leon tells me, "is teach you to isolate those feelings of anger and to express them and to recognize them in another person. And then in order to show empathy for somebody, you have to mirror their feelings. It's a good thing. I hate taking it because then you have to feel all these emotions and deal with stuff that I've never dealt with in twenty years."

So while Empathy emerges as one program where, albeit vicariously, their own experiences come to be meaningful as they attempt to understand those of the individuals they in turn victimized, they must appeal to these experiences somewhat furtively. These allegedly similar experiences are conceptualized as "blocks" to empathy to be surmounted as opposed to psychological and emotional issues to be managed therapeutically; this leaves open the possibility that any issues that may arise from this largely unavoidable self-reflection are not resolved, especially in the little time left in the program before the men return to their parent institutions. There is no doubt that the treatment staff are aware that many inmates appeal to their past experiences of abuse during this and other phases of their program, as the men are constantly reminded not to do this. And while some issues may be dealt with during private counseling sessions, most inmates I interviewed expressed dissatisfaction with the limited amount of such counseling available to them. The modus operandi of the treatment program is group, not individually, focused. Any public display of program engagement in groups must adhere to the strict regulations against appealing to minimization, justification, or denial. For inmates, theirs is an empathy that must not be too obviously linked to allegedly similar personal experiences. One wonders, again, Is this really "empathy"?

Empathy is a core psychological (that is, cognitive and emotional) construct of humanness and speaks to our inherent morality and sociality. People have a need to be understood (cf. Hollan 2008), especially in moral terms. They do not just want others to listen to stories of their experiences; they want others to *get* them, to feel as much as possible what it was like for them to have that experience. People want others to appreciate the meaning of their life on an emotional level, not just a cognitive one. This requires the establishment of some kind of empathetic relationship, and it is just such a relationship that is impossible to convene given the carceral context of the treatment program.

We have no way of knowing how the victims would feel about the manner in which they are represented, or how their victim status is employed in the treatment of their victimizer. I would think some would find the Empathy training, and especially the letters, rather creepy and possibly offensive, which perhaps explains in part why the letters are never actually sent. Empathetic understanding, for the victim, is probably derived from other resources: family, friends, social services agencies, and especially victim support groups. After being sexually assaulted, and then undergoing the often emotionally disturbing experiences of a trial, that a victim would not want to ever again see or think about the offender makes perfect sense.

We might ask, though, What is to be gained for the inmate empathizer by engaging in this exercise? I return to the suggestion that in any empathetic relationship the empathizer also seeks to be understood and, more importantly, seeks personal insight, meaning, and understanding through engagement with the empathizee. The empathizer seeks to define his experiences as similar and then attach them to the empathizee's narrative in a kind of "me too" moment; indeed, we see this process at work constantly throughout all the group sessions as audience members seek to interject their experiences into the narrative event of the inmate on the "hot seat." It is then largely up to the empathizee to determine the legitimacy of the analogy and accept or reject it. Of course, we do not have an empathetic relationship to manage in the Empathy module, so the question is more complex. The victim and the inmate are not positioned to negotiate a shared narrative. Yet

I do think there is a potential benefit to the inmate to be found in the process of imaginative empathy despite its unrequited nature insofar as it often encourages a focused reconsideration of one's past experiences and their meaning in contemporary context, even if these must be largely kept private. There are risks to this too, of course, as I have noted above, particularly in that the nature of the exercise inhibits opportunities to seek resolution of personal issues that are called up during the imaginative empathy process.

These contradictions in the Empathy program create an enduring dilemma for the inmates. Within both science and popular culture, emotions have often been conceptualized in contradictory ways. They have tended to be considered as irrational and dangerous, leading to erroneous judgments and uncontrollable actions. Yet emotions are also seen as potentially controllable, that they can be "reasoned away" (Lutz 1986: 293). This, of course, is precisely what CBT attempts to do. The treatment program first seeks to teach the men how to think rationally by identifying erroneous thoughts and cognitive distortions. The Empathy module, near the end of their programs, then explores the meaning of emotions and their role in the inmates' lives, perhaps encouraging more of an intellectual than personal approach to the topic. The letters, however, represent a highly emotionally charged exercise, and their reading generates strong feelings in all present, but most certainly within the inmate reading the letter. And recall of their negative experiences invariably is emotionally evocative despite its covert nature. The module does create a space for emotionality, then, but it is highly circumscribed and regulated, sometimes entirely performative (as in the role playing), and it often discounts the personal experiences of the inmate empathizer. Indeed, at least among the men I interviewed, expression of appropriate emotionality during the Empathy sessions is seen as an essential ingredient to a "successful," that is, therapeutically validated, program experience. Inmates who fail to show an emotional response during letter reading are thought to be therapeutically unengaged.

In effect, the treatment program emphasizes a kind of rational, cognitively controllable and prosocial emotionality, and in the Empathy module, as in many other aspects of the program, it is left up to the men to comprehend the nuances that such emotionality entails. It remains unclear how such rationally conceived cognitive processes and emotionality are to be balanced. This is a complex and perhaps impossible task, beyond the reach of most inmates (and, I would think, most of us too). Empathy, as taught, seems too "hypothetical," to use Justin's words, too theoretical, as Jodi Halpern (2001) might suggest, generating at most a degree of "detached concern," perhaps better thought of as a combination of sympathy and remorse for past actions that may not transfer to future situations. As in other elements of the program, the inmates seek not this theoretical understanding but rather a pragmatic, context-based knowledge that they can apply. Appealing to their own experiences seems like a logical means to do this, yet this is discouraged. The ambiguities inherent in any discussion of "appropriate" emotionality confound them; they are taught to recognize emotions in others as legitimate but not to act on their own emotionality without thinking first if their response is appropriate. This complexity suggests the possibility that inmates are inclined, if not inadvertently directed, to engage with Empathy, and the overall treatment program, more strategically and instrumentally than therapeutically.

One might suggest that the Empathy module, approached cynically, involves a punitive element insofar as it typically invokes strong and troubling emotions and memories in the inmate. Many feel pain, both emotionally and physiologically, regardless of whether they themselves have had similarly abusive experiences. The conjuring up of this pain may be seen as a clear marker of the success of the Empathy module. However, I suggest that the existence of psychological and emotional distress expressed by many inmates during the letter sessions, which may or may not be genuine, is insufficient for the creation of empathy precisely because the inmate's own issues are not dealt with. In the absence of some therapeutic closure the inmate is often left seeking some kind of resolution to the psychological problems caused by these sessions. For empathy to be truly created, *all* parties must receive understanding, all must receive tangible psychological benefits. The victim clearly does not in this context, as his or her voice is appropriated, unknowingly, by the perpetrator of his or her suffering. I would also suggest that there are great risks that the inmate will not benefit either. For inmates, empathy is unrequited: they can neither form an empathetic relationship with their victim (or any victim, for that matter) and negotiate a shared narrative leading to closure or reconciliation, nor easily call upon and therapeutically resolve their own experiences of victimization.

Further, it seems that many of the lessons of Empathy, like other aspects of the program, are not suitable for life in the penitentiary. "Empathy is the last part of the program," notes Rick. "You're right at the end of the program, and then next thing you know you're finished the program and you're out the door. You don't get a chance to, you know, really settle down. But some of the guys actually are hurting by the time they're finished Empathy. And then they're walking out with no support, going back to their old attitudes. Because when you leave here," Rick clarifies, waving his finger around the interview room, "if you go back to your mother institution, a lot of them are rough joints and you got to go back to putting the walls up in certain areas to protect yourself. Because you can't walk around there like you can here, because guys would knife you."

. . .

Empathy training for sexual offenders is an excellent example of habilitation. The goal is to safeguard the public by teaching the inmate to feel the pain of past and possibly future victims, rather than to engage therapeutically with the inmate's distress that may stem from his own victimization or may arise through his efforts to appreciate the pain he has caused others, even when this distress emerges as a product of the Empathy exercise. Moral habilitation, moreover, is clearly linked to the community beyond the walls, and there is no place, it seems, for community notions of morality in the penitentiary, perhaps the greatest paradox of prison treatment. We care mostly about how inmates behave when they are released into our world, it seems, and less about how they behave while in their own.

CHAPTER 8

"A Pretty Shitty Place Out There"

Mark starts to chuckle at my question. "The way the public's going off right now?" he laughs. "I'll be hounded. I'll have these, uh, vigilante groups. I'll have media following me. I'll have police harassment. In between all of that I'll be having to try to adjust to the changes that . . . you know, the world has come to since I came in, right?" Mark and I are sitting in an interview room, talking about his future. He will leave the institution in a few days, going back to his home penitentiary to wait further judicial processing.

I have asked all my participants the same question at both the beginning and the end of their programs, "How do you see your life unfolding from this day forward?" As in my research overall, I have not asked them to specifically address their crimes, and hence these prospective narratives take on a very different appearance than the Relapse Prevention Plan narratives, which, as we have seen, must address directly the individual's life as a criminal. This invitation to offer a prospective narrative seems to have sparked in Mark a significant degree of apprehension. He has been in prison for several years, and much has changed in the world since. "You know," he continues, "9/11 has happened since I came in. Big changes with that, all kinds of security, lots of police upgrades so there's a bigger police presence everywhere. More restrictions. The DNA thing has come in now so you have no privacy . . . Once you're convicted of a sex offense they can pull your DNA from you any time there's an offense now. They're trying to establish this national sex offender registry, so they're going to be adding all that kind of stress.[1] Any time any kind of sex offense happens, what do you think's going to happen now if that goes up? They're going to come to your work, they're going to come to your home, they're going to arrest you and take you down for questioning. Uh huh! To tell you the honest to God's honest truth, it's . . . looking like a pretty shitty place out there now."

That prison might provide a degree of comfort and security will perplex many readers, but it makes perfect sense to inmates like Mark. "I've learned how to survive in here," he explains. "I've got my own little world. I have my, you know, eight-foot-by-eight-foot cell with my TV and my stereo system. And I get my three meals a day. And that's almost looking better than all the stress and harassment I'm going to have to go through out there now." Then, contrasting the panoptic nature of the prison with the synoptics of life in the community, Mark surprisingly concludes, "You know, I've got more privacy in here now, with the guard coming around every half hour or every hour, and staring in a window and looking at me, than I will when I get out."

Linda Garro (1994: 776) reminds us that autobiographical narratives are "best understood as reconstructions rather than reproductions of past events." "The present," she elaborates, "is explained with reference to the reconstructed past; and both are used to generate expectations about the future." This chapter is about the future, for, as Garro and many other narrative theorists suggest (e.g., Ricoeur 1980), the future is envisioned in a manner that links it narratively to past and present. This "chronological dimension" (Ricoeur 1988) to narrative temporality is foundational, yet medical and psychological anthropologists have not paid as much attention to prospective narrative as they have to retrospective or autobiographical narrative. In this linking of past and present with future—its "unity," to use Ricoeur's expression (1980: 171)—significant purchase can be gained on the meaning that the first two—past and present—have for the individual. Ricoeur (1988) referred to this as "phenomenological time," time experienced in terms of past, present, and future together, in contrast to "chronological time," the linear progression of time and events that so befuddles the inmates when sharing their Autobiographies. Sense of self is exposed in this process—"narrative and self are inseparable," write Ochs and Capps (1996: 20)—and as Landau, Greenberg, and Solomon (2008: 94) note, "Individuals sustain prospective continuity by perceiving the present self as meaningfully leading up to or setting the stage for significant future outcomes, and extending the self from the limits of a finite existence to something enduring." Since prospective narratives concern hypothetical events not yet experienced, of course they are inherently different in character from retrospective narratives, where the narrator is able to reflect on his past within the context of the present. In this research, where inmates were asked to imagine the future, past and present remained as forceful reminders of the conditions under which the future was likely to be lived. While everyone has a "past," not everyone's past is likely to result in the kinds of state and public scrutiny that accompany a convicted sexual offender's release from prison.

As I have shown so far in this book, much of the treatment program involves a critical engagement with the past, the assumption being that what is learned about the inmate's past provides the key to identifying dysfunctional modes of thinking and behaving as well as lessons for the future on what to avoid. I have also shown how, for the inmates, the present encompasses the somewhat conflictual roles of "inmate" and "patient" within the context of often competing regulatory regimes of penitentiary, hospital, and con code. The immediate present, of course, is dominated by the treatment program. The future has a more circumscribed place in the program and daily lives of the inmates and is engaged most obviously in the Relapse Prevention Plan process. The prospective narratives that I solicited, then, can be characterized by the extent to which they focus on the future, as opposed to the past and present. Some narratives concentrate on the near future, the completion of the treatment program or the overall prison sentence, while others look beyond prison to life on the outside. There are differing degrees of pragmatism versus romanticism evident, as well as differing engagement with ideas of relationships and family. Matters of agency are also raised, as some men express a complete lack of control over their future, in contrast to others with varying degrees of assertiveness in directing the next phase of their lives. Let me explore some of these issues as we listen to the words of several of the men that we have already met in this ethnography.

"SKELETONS IN MY CLOSET"

First off, some men seem unable, or unwilling, to engage with the idea of a future. These individuals are pessimistic or, at most, cautiously optimistic about the future, with the result that their narratives are primarily present oriented. The best articulation of this can be found in the pronouncements of those men who are haunted by their past, declare that they live their lives "one day at a time," and present few if any ideas for the future.

Tom, doing a life sentence, demonstrates this "one day at a time" philosophy in fatalistic terms during his initial interview with me:

> From right now into the future? You know, that's . . . that's . . . that's a big subject all over. You hear that all over these days. What is the future going to hold for me? Well, you know, I could be like a millionaire one day, and like . . . on Skid Row an hour later. Right? I mean, sure I can plan, and have hope, right? But . . . is it going to come true? I don't know. I . . . I may be stepping off the curb and the bus flattens me. I'm dead. Right? So . . . all I can do is, like I say, plan and hope [that] things will go better for me in the future, right?

In his exit interview Tom is less fatalistic but still devoid of any real plans. The influence of the program is evident as he appeals to truth discourse as a kind of sanctuary to make things better:

> Well, you know, from what I am getting and for what I am feeling, and I am doing the program, and I am working the program, I will get there. You bet I will get there as long as I am sincere in doing it. I am not hiding anything. I am sincere in what I am doing. Last time I was out there, yeah, I screwed up, yes, I did this and I did that, yeah.

Alvin, also doing an indeterminate sentence, similarly expresses a lack of hope for a future. Given that it remains unclear when he may be released, this is not all that surprising. "I'm in limbo," he explains. "I can do nothing until, you know . . . I feel nothing . . . I won't allow myself to hope. I won't allow myself to despair. It has been a long road to get here and I am just taking it one hour at a time doing what I have got to do to survive."

Yet even those doing defined, shorter sentences sometimes fail to express much future orientation in their prospective narratives. Alfred, doing considerably less time than Tom and Alvin, is as fatalistic about the future as they are. In his intake interview he explains:

> From this point forward, I see it as, well, I'm a person who doesn't really believe in looking too far ahead. I like to take things day by day. Like, 'cause I could say, "Well, I'm gonna live a great life, when I get out. I'm gonna live a perfect life. I'm gonna treat my children great, you know, I'm gonna love my family, love my relatives, you know, look after them all, teach them great and wonderful things," you know. I could say all that. And yet tomorrow

I could die. And then what do those words mean? Right? So, what I like to say is, I like to say, "Today, I'm gonna to try to get through today to make it to tomorrow. If I can make it through tomorrow, I'll try to go for the next day and the next day." I mean, sure, I have my wants and likes for what I think my future should be like. I'd like to live alcohol-free, drug-free, abuse-free. To have the type of life where people look at me and say, "Hey, there's someone who's doing something with his life. There's a successful person." You know, I don't feel that I'm ever gonna be able to do that unless I deal with all the skeletons that are in my closet. Once I can put all those skeletons to rest, then I can start to look towards the future. I have to deal with the here and now before I can deal with the future. And dealing with the here and now is gonna get me to the future. So when you ask me what do I think of my, what do I expect of myself from here? In the future? All I can really say to you, is I just expect myself to live day by day. Try to make it one hour to the next.

Alfred's views have not changed significantly at the end of the program either:

Not going to look that far ahead. I don't know what's going to happen tomorrow. I don't know what's going to happen next week. I sure as hell don't know what's going to happen in the future. So . . . what happens, happens, I guess. I guess I just got to live for today. Treat each day like it's my last, I guess. Don't worry about tomorrow, what tomorrow's problems bring. Worry about today and what today's problems are.

Sam, also doing a relatively short sentence, similarly relates his aversion to planning for the future at the intake interview:

I don't look at that [the future] right now, I don't . . . I don't want to look at . . . build myself up and then not . . . do what I say I'm going to do. So I'll just look at my life as it is, as the days come, like one day at a time type of thing. I don't want to . . . say something and then not do it. Because things change over time. So I just take it one day at a time, pretty much, right now.

At the exit interview, after some eight months of treatment, his view of the future also remained unchanged:

It's like they say in Alcoholics Anonymous, "One day at a time." So I've just got to take it one day at a time. And then when the day is through, just sit back in the evening and just think about the day, like look at the day, how your day went. So, that's about the only good thing you can do if you want to look ahead of yourself, is just go through the one day and then at night, just look back at the day.

In a sense, individuals like Tom, Alfred, and Sam fail to provide much of a prospective narrative at all. The chronological dimension, as Ricoeur (1988) might define it, is largely absent. There is little plot, and there are few if any details. The future seems to hold no appeal, and we can surmise that their "one day at a time" philosophy is a direct reflection of a difficult past and present, including prison time, when such a present-only approach was and remains thoroughly pragmatic. While their future projections seem to be devoid of the stuff of narrative, meaning, in contrast, is striking; these are individuals in a liminal stage, to adapt Victor Turner's (1967) use of this concept—"in limbo" in Alvin's terms. Therapeutically speaking, they should be in transition from a "sick self" to an "imagined future healthy self" (Lester 2007: 370), but, unlike those undergoing Turner's notion of rites of passage, these individuals articulate few prospects of a transition through time to a new stage of life. Having been removed from society through abjection, the product of criminal convictions of a particularly heinous type, they are apprehensive that they will be allowed to rejoin as new moral habilitates. The sheer passivity and fatalism, with little evidence of a sense of agency, are also striking: the future, to be experienced one day at a time, will just happen.

This kind of narrative depression is less salient for others, especially over the length of the treatment program. Justin, also doing an indeterminate sentence, perhaps logically finds planning for the future somewhat irrelevant to his current situation, since he has no idea when he might be released from prison. When asked during his intake interview how his life might unfold, he replies, "Oh, that's a difficult one, 'cause I only go day by day now. I try to use basically hobbies or waiting for programs to do. I don't sit there and try to think too much about the future, you know. 'Cause I'm not really in any rush to basically, uh, make any quick decisions." But unlike Sam, Justin, by the time he was close to finishing the program, was much more concrete, with a more clearly defined chronology. He explains:

> I think a lot of it's going to be good. Like I got a lot to look forward to. I'll be in [name of prison] around the Mental Health Unit for only six months to see how I manage my meds for six months, and if it goes really good for six months I go to [name of another prison]. Then from there I just stay there and apply for my visiting for my girlfriend, or fiancée, to visit me there. Then I got to write a lot of support letters for parole, like John Howard Society, Lifer's Group. And there's a sex offender program there, I can take three or four times, so, you know, just to basically prove that I like to learn about my own behavior that I did in the past.

But even here we see that Justin's prospective narrative, while suggestive of a plan, does not extend beyond his prison sentence. His life, as he sees it unfolding, involves a series of prisons, brief visits with a loved one, and more treatment programs.

Of those individuals who are more willing or able to project into the future, the temporal horizon often stretches just barely to include completion of their treatment programs. This is especially apparent in the intake interviews. A fairly daunting task lies before them when they arrive on the unit, and of course this will preoccupy the minds of many. Some men, therefore, have a short temporal horizon and difficulty simply looking beyond the program; others, like Justin, look not much further than the completion of their prison sentences. Stan is one such individual, commenting during his intake interview:

> Well . . . now from today, you know, continue to doing the program here, you know, and completing it in the eight months' time. So I hope I do get a . . . I feel I will get a successful completion, whatever my security rating will become. Hopefully it'll . . . it'll go down to minimum. I'm confident enough I will complete this course. Like, I'm not going to quit or drop out or anything like that, you know. I'm very confident I will complete this course. It's almost a given. And I hopefully . . . I see myself getting down to a secure rating of "minimum." And maybe while I'm here hopefully apply for parole as well too, to get out maybe before my "stat" [i.e., statutory] release. And get home to my family, because that's what I'm . . . I'm really longing for. That's two things I got right now that are motivating me, are completing this program, you know, and getting help for myself basically, is one; and the other one is getting home to my family.

As his program comes to a close, and a successful evaluation is assured, Stan is able to be more concrete about his future. His sense of agency is "hopeful":

> Hopefully [my life will unfold] really well. I got me and my wife. Hopefully I'll get my school lined up before I get out. Want to get that career going, that I've always wanted. Maybe have another child. Own my own house and my truck or whatever. And I'll be able to go hunting when I can, fishing when I can, and stuff like that. And I will just enjoy life, really, you know. Just don't stress out and you know, just enjoy it with my family and whatever, and friends.

Stan's hopes are pragmatic and entirely plausible and probably are not unlike those of nonoffenders. The temporal horizon on the exit interview is much longer than on intake, as he now envisions an expansion to his family.

Still, the lack of temporal diversity in the narratives above is noteworthy. Certainly the intensiveness of the treatment program encourages men to immerse themselves in the daily routine of group and individual therapy, punctuated by occasional periods of respite to engage in recreational activities. The con code, still very much a part of their lives even in treatment, necessarily focuses some attention on the exigencies of daily living, to make it through each day safely. "Doing my own time" and "living one day at a time" are two sides of the same existential coin for these inmates. Thinking about the program is what they are encouraged to do, not only in therapy sessions but also after hours, when they are expected to be completing homework assignments.

Contemplating a future outside prison, however, is programmatically shaped, in part, by the development and implementation of strategies to avoid reoffending. Their focus is as much on recognizing cognitive distortions and correcting them, and implementing strategies to extricate themselves from problematic situations that their Crime Cycles suggest may lead to criminality, as it is on those aspects of living relevant to nonoffenders: food, shelter, employment, and companionship, for instance. Further, when these issues of basic living are brought up in group, very often it is in the context of their being implicated as risk factors to reoffend, relational and situational contexts that are seen as problematic rather than supportive. Even their lessons in moral habitation have a certain ethereal quality to them as the men are taught how they *should* behave in future, hypothetical social contexts. Simply put, for some men their foreseeable futures involve treatment, treatment, and more treatment, followed by more prison time, and possibly followed by an ongoing struggle to avoid reoffending in the community.

As narrative theory would suggest, some inmates call more directly upon their past as they seek to respond to my question. Unlike those above, whose sense of self is clearly anchored in a fragile and present-limited temporality, others seem almost handcuffed by their past, so much so that thinking concretely about the future involves directly addressing, even rectifying, the past rather than escaping it. The treatment program certainly does not allow them to escape their past, and so the preoccupation with the past that many men exhibit is not surprising. But the past is clearly a liability for some, in that they are so consumed with anger toward a justice system that they believe has unfairly treated them that they are unable to articulate a more positive view of the future and often have difficulty settling into the program as well. Despite their treatment contracts, and ongoing admissions to the effect that they are fully responsible for their actions—both required in the program—a few men still argue their innocence, and many men who accept their guilt nonetheless have serious concerns about certain details of their convictions that they feel reflect badly on them, and they often struggle to keep these thoughts private. For a few, lawsuits and revenge color their view of the future. Ned, despite ostensibly discussing his future, focuses almost entirely on the past when he relates his views of the system that put him behind bars:

> When I committed this offense I was already on an eighteen-month proba-
> tion, okay, for exposing myself to an eight-year-old child, okay, and inviting
> her to touch me, which didn't happen. But thanks to our open-minded justice
> system, children don't lie. They, they have this, this, this, uh, blanket, this
> covering belief, okay, that children do not lie when it comes to sex. They
> could lie about everything else, but when it comes to sex, and somebody
> harming them in a sexual way, in any way, okay. It could even be as much
> as touching their arm, okay, if they didn't want it to happen, they said, "no,"
> or they just have to go to whoever, the powers that be, okay, and say, uh,
> "He touched me in a . . . I felt uncomfortable way, I was scared," you know,
> that was a sexual assault. You know, you can be charged the whole nine
> yards. And it's downright scary. I was freaked when I had to be faced with
> that. Our overall justice system as to "You're innocent until proven guilty,"
> okay, it's not there. I found that out the hard way.

While Ned cannot let go of this element of his past, Leon, in contrast, appeals to past injustices as he shapes his future. He is conflicted about revenge, a struggle that dominates his prospective narrative during his intake interview:

> Well, I can probably see fighting with the cops for a bit, you know. When
> I get out of here I might go fight with them, I might go destroy them. In
> the sense of in court. See, I got the goods to . . . to take them down, you
> know? [Here he relates specific details of his case, which he believes shows
> problematic behavior by investigators.] So how many other cases haven't
> they screwed up? How many murder trials and stuff like that? Haven't
> they been deceived, and deceiving these juries and these judges? I come in
> there and I can use their own words against them. It'll maybe cost me a
> little shame and a little humiliation, on the grounds that I got to come out
> there and say, "Hey listen, I'm a sex offender, yeah, yeah." But you know
> what? I've got more going for me than they have got going for themselves
> . . . And if I can turn around and show their transcripts with their own
> words, you can use them against them, flip them over in court. Destroy
> 'em. No more credibility with them. So I might charge them, might go
> after their careers. Ah, that's what I might do, you know. I don't want
> to be the type of person that wants to go out hunting for revenge, but

I don't think that they should be allowed to do stuff like that. There's a problem. You've got conspiracy within the police department, to hide and manipulate evidence.

Despite having a legal right to do so, those men who continue to fight their cases from the inside are seen by other inmates and the treatment staff as too distracted to commit fully to the program. Generally, the program tends to temper men's attitudes toward the past as well as the justice system. Thoughts like those expressed by Ned and Leon do not get an unchallenged hearing because of the cognitive distortions assumed to be embedded there and the conflict between their views of the crimes and the official record. Both the other men and the staff will usually criticize an individual who says he is innocent or was framed, or who prattles on about lawsuits, and there is no patience for such attitudes when expressed in the group setting.

Leon's exit interview demonstrates how his view of the justice system, and his victim, has become less strident after seven months in the program. His anger has dissipated somewhat and has been partially redirected toward the victim of his crime, perhaps reflective of the impact of the Empathy program, even though he continues to still believe she lied in court. Yet, in this part of his narrative, we still see him struggling with this anger and incidents from the past in the face of all he has learned in the program:

I will probably make it [in the community], I think, pretty sure. I'm still, I guess, a little angry at the victim, you know, but I don't know. I wouldn't even talk to her again I think if I ever seen her on the street, you know, I would just ignore her. There was a time where I would have walked up and just punched her right in the teeth as hard as I could, you know? You know, she said that I dragged her off the street and I raped her . . . I didn't do that. It was all printed in the paper that I did do that and nobody ever unprinted that, nobody ever recanted that. I have never done anything that horrible, you know, by God's grace, never. So, to have somebody come out and say that and then, you know, it's all alright for them to say whatever they want about you, and they don't ever charge that individual with, you know, providing false evidence or, you know, perjury or anything along those lines. They just [say], oh, you know, you are a poor victim and she is a poor victim. But she had to have some cunning bloody mind in order to come up with a story like that and stick with it for eleven months. So, was she really as traumatized as she said? I am telling you there is no bloody way. You cannot come up with a story like that in a heartbeat, out of something like that that didn't even happen. So, who is deviant? Me or her? I hired her, she was a hooker, you know what I mean? But I knew that I had a serious anger, anger problems and stuff, and I still do. I still have to watch that even now, you know, even now as I talk about it I have got to be really careful because I get angry. I can be very angry. But I actually am taking this Empathy [program] and I thought, Oh man, you know what? Even if, you know, I will never get past what she said that I did, and I didn't do it. Even if I never get past that. But I get to the point where I hurt her and it wasn't even sexual, you know what I mean? I know that I got charged with sexual assault but there is nothing sexual [involved] . . . But, you can't tell these guys that because then they will automatically tell you, "You are in denial." . . . I mean regardless of whether I, you know, I drilled her in the back of the head with a tire iron or I screwed her or whether, you know, I made her give me a blow job or whatever it was, I was still offending, rape, regardless. I think the Empathy program was really good because, you know, it made me see that, if somebody did that to me, I would be very angry too. But I don't know if I could be that deviant to go out and say stuff like that, that never happened.

Though the influence of the program is clearly evident, Leon still fails entirely to speak of a future.

Like others, David appeals to the past in his initial interview with me, but he demonstrates a shift in the temporal dimension of his narrative when we meet again several months later. His intake narrative deals extensively with the past and present and only touches on the future, as he speaks about his own problems. David's sense of agency is indicated by the cautiousness that is clearly evident in his narrative, as he uses several "if" statements to suggest that a future without problems is contingent. For instance, he relates the following:

How do I see my life unfolding from this day forward? Well, if I use the program properly this time, if I use the skills that I can take with me, hopefully I see . . . a settled-down life. You know, my craving for alcohol and drugs is always there, doesn't matter if I've been away from them for a while now, it's still there. At times I'll be sitting there having a smoke and wishing that this was a nice big fat joint. That sort of adds to my . . . I don't know what you'd call them, my cycle to the . . . things that give me permission to do what I do. To assault. So if I can overcome some of these obstacles, which is very hard for me, I haven't done it yet, I think my chances of succeeding in a better lifestyle would be better. The skills that they teach you here, they can work. But it's up to the individual . . . I really think that's a big part of what I have to do. In order to feel empathy for my victims I have to learn how to feel myself. Otherwise, if I don't know how to feel, I'm not going to feel for anybody else. And I think that's part of why I continue . . . I'm not saying that's the whole reason why I continue to do the things I do, but that's part of the reason, because I don't feel. I don't allow myself to have these feelings of hurt, sadness. You know, I go strictly to anger. And if I can learn how to unscramble all these things I think it'd be much better for me to learn empathy, to feel more for the victims, the people that I've hurt.

This was David's third attempt in the treatment program, and his reference to using it "properly this time" betrays the fact that he has considerable knowledge about the program despite the fact that our interview is being undertaken during his first month on the unit. Here elements of David's Relapse Prevention Plan are evident, something he has worked on during previous treatment attempts, as is the impact of the program more generally, especially in his references to empathy. But his plans for the future are vague as he focuses yet again on the immediate task at hand, and he is clearly cautious about committing beyond that. David's exit interview has a considerably different tone, with real plans for the future and no time to dwell on the past:

> Well, once I leave prison I'm going to go home, live with my wife and my kids. From there on I'm just going to try and take it easy, settle down, work if I can, if I can find a job. With a past that I carry, it's kind of hard to find that job. If not, then I'd have to live on my disability for as long as I have to, I guess. And that's basically what I'd like to do, continue to take treatment, even out in the street. Maintenance groups, stuff like that. That's what I will be doing. That's my life after here, after institution time.

While the nuts and bolts of David's Relapse Prevention Plan are missing here, David does appeal to broader goals centered on the reconstitution of and support for his family. His temporal horizon extends beyond prison, and perhaps even beyond a period of time when elements of his Relapse Prevention Plan will be salient, to a stable future.

Given the level of public concern over the release of sexual offenders from prison, it is not surprising that the past and present intrude into prospective narratives about the future. Escaping the past and present, a goal of many inmates, is not seen as easily accomplishable. Yet, despite what many fear will be intense public scrutiny upon their release, concerns over reoffending are rarely evident in the prospective narratives. Only a few men express such concerns, and almost always in the intake interviews. Andrew speaks in this vein, saying, "I want to know I'm not ever going to be a threat to my kids. I don't think I will. I know I won't. But I want people to know that too. I want others to know. I don't want them to look at me, doubting me, mistrusting me." Harvey expresses a similar concern. "You know," he tells me, "I've got a family and friends passing away. I've got kids growing up. And you know, with the right motive, the right state of mind, I believe I can actually stay out of prison this time around. This is my first bad bit and I want it to be my last." And Steven too, emphasizing the problem he has had with sexual assaults involving his girlfriends, admits: "As for girlfriends, I don't want any right now. It's too hard on me. I really screwed up on my last one. I'm almost afraid of them, you know? And afraid what I'll do around them. So a girlfriend in the near future just doesn't seem proper to me or right at this moment in time."

Some inmates make only vague allusions to the possibility of reoffending, choosing to speak around that topic by focusing on the need to avoid particularly troublesome situations, situations that both they and the researcher know contributed to offending in the past, but about which the inmates are not willing to speak. Leon speaks generally about the need for structured release into the community as he ponders the likelihood of his own reoffending and the many obstacles that the program has taught him will be lying in wait:

> Like, I myself have asked for a slow, a slow release back into society. I mean I will be out [date], that's my SR [statutory release], right? So, to drop somebody off, you know? That's one thing I don't understand about this government, you know. You will incarcerate somebody for $184 a day, but then you just throw him out at the end, and you know, you all of a sudden got to come to the way of getting your own place, get a job . . . What they do is they throw you out and all of a sudden you have got to, you have to survive, right? And you don't know how to do that because it's been sometimes three, five, ten, fifteen years since you have done that. So unless they do that slowly, what are the chances of somebody going out there after they have been released instantaneously, of reoffending and not even, not just a sexual way, but you know breaking into somebody's house and, you know, stealing stuff or robbing somebody or, you know, armed robbery or whatever you name it. Just out of panic and out of survival. Because you really don't know what else to do, right? So, regardless, I think that I will make it whether I get, you know, tossed out in one day or whether I get to go to a halfway house for three months first, and then walk from there. I think regardless I will make it. Not because of, you know, anything special. But I think that if you have a plan, you realize that no matter what it is you do you are hurting people, and I think if you have the change of heart where you don't want to be out hurting people, I think you will make it because you don't want to be out there disturbing people or hurting people. No matter what the crime is, right. They all hurt people. I will probably make it, I think. Pretty sure.

An interesting link is also evident in some narratives, in which a desire to avoid reoffending is paired with a desire to live a "normal" life. Billy explains:

> I think I can do good here, and . . . I have a daughter now, since I've been in, she's seven months now, and I want to . . . take care of [her] when I get

out. And I'm still with my girlfriend too, her mom. Just want to stay sober, try and stay sober. For as long as I stay sober I can stay out of trouble, because I've never been in trouble while I was sober. I'll get a house, get a job, I don't worry . . . I don't know, just a simple . . . if I've been in jail for . . . I'm only twenty-five and I've been in jail for like almost thirteen years in my life. That's half of my life already that I've been inside or locked up somewhere. So it's a . . . I don't really ask for much, I just want to get out and live a normal life. You know? Go to sleep on a soft bed, not these little mats here. Just little things. Watch my kid grow up, make money so I can take care of her. Make sure you have everything, and just so she has a dad around, not like me, you know. I never really had my dad around, so . . . that's why I want to be around for her. So she knows me. And she knows that I cared enough for her to change my life around.

This subtext in many of the narratives, the desire to live a "normal" life, does not necessarily mean to *return* to a normal life, however, since most have come to realize that their lives were dysfunctional and related to their criminality. This "normal" is not what they aspire to. Rather, they wish for a normality that they perceive as lived by others, by noncriminals. This new "normal" life is full of joyous family relations, a good home and job, material goods, and a prosocial outlook. Yet the narratives do not stray too far into the overly fanciful. The "normal" life is somewhat humble. Notes Sam:

I really don't want to take any more victims, you know. I'm tired. You know, I want to live a nice normal life, you know? Like on my Relapse Plan I have here like, one of them is to . . . get back to work on a ranch and work the local cattle auction. I want to buy myself a home and own it outright and work on trying to get well, stay sober and conviction-free.

The concern over reoffending is dominated by two issues: first, to not take any more victims, as Sam explains; and second, to reunite with family and significant others. The program tends to focus on the former. The latter, in contrast, poses somewhat of a problem for many men. An inmate's past, like anyone's, is a matrix of personalities—family, friends, and associates—who appear in the Autobiography and subsequent narratives the men must produce and offer to the group. Yet since these individuals are in many cases linked to the aberrant behavior—as enablers or co-conspirators, for instance, or just bad influences—they are often targeted by treatment staff in any discussion of the future. Men struggle with this and often resist it, as these individuals are not simply criminal interlocutors but also key players in the social world of the inmate. During the program some inmates, such as Oren, are even denied contact with family on the grounds that it would interfere with their treatment, and they sometimes respond by protesting and employing various legal, and illegal, means to secure what they see is a fundamental right to remain in contact with others on the outside. This ongoing struggle is part of a larger process of cocooning: the treatment program dominates the lives of the inmates in such a way as to isolate them from others, both people on the outside and other inmates in the treatment center housed on different units.

So thinking in concrete terms about a future with family and friends is at least in some contexts actively discouraged. Nonetheless, in talking with me, a key element in many prospective narratives pertains to relational matters, the offender's concern or need to reconnect with family, friends, and community upon release. Andrew employs the metaphor of a debt to passionately explain the importance of family to him:

> But most of all I want to be able to spend time with my family, with my wife. I mean, my life out of here is going to go right back to . . . to my family, to my wife. Because I owe them a life now. They've been . . . without me for years now . . . You know, when you're with someone you love completely, you're one true love, crossed together, "across the crowded floor," you know, love at first sight, when you're with that person that's great. You know, when you're away from that person, it does get stronger. That absence makes the heart grow fonder, it's true. I miss her more, I love her more . . . And she visits me four times a week. And has for years. And I miss her more and more and more. My life from here on out . . . is just going to be dedicated to her. And my kids. Because I've been trying to catch up with the Joneses and grow up and all this crap, I didn't need to do that. I just needed to realize what was important and focus on that: my relationships. I mean I lost them earlier when I was young. My relationships were all lost through immature . . . I was too busy focusing on myself to realize there was another person in it. But now I realize, you know, what makes me happy is making my family happy. So when I . . . if I . . . well, when I . . . will eventually get out, my whole next ten years is going to be just focusing on paying back all the debts. I owe a lot of birthdays. I owe Christmases. I owe a lot to my family. I mean if I didn't have them I'd survive, wouldn't be nearly as happy, but I just feel . . . you know, I guess it's incredible I do have them. I keep having to do little checks, you know. If I didn't have them I'd be this way. Seems hard to believe I do. I see so many people . . . in this situation in prison. Families abandon them instantly. I spent an entire life being disposable.

A curious contradiction in the program that the men struggle to understand is between the need to disavow many dysfunctional relationships of the past while being encouraged to adopt prosocial lifestyles upon release. How does one construct a whole new social world from scratch, especially as a sexual offender? Some men recognize that to do so will require acquiring a whole new set of friends and romantic partners, and sometimes even relocation to a new community where they are not known. In effect, the program causes some men to think that they need to socially isolate themselves from familiar terrain if they are to avoid reoffending; a new "local social world" is in order. Yet since every man regardless of crime or sentence remains a part of a broader social web outside of prison, social isolation is somewhat problematic. Further, there are forces afoot to ensure that social isolation will by no means equate with invisibility.

"COMING TO A THEATER NEAR YOU"

As I have shown, for these sexual offenders the future cannot be contemplated without reference to the past, and this is contextually reinforced in the present when I ask them to contemplate a future while they are still in prison, and still in treatment. A key restriction on any conception of the future for the inmates, then, is their criminal record and especially the history of their sexual offenses. The inmates are acutely aware that this record will affect their futures. Billy expresses a very active agency in this passage, but one that also references his past and especially his current status as a sexual offender:

> I'm going to medium [security prison], and I'll finish my time and I'll get out and I'll go see . . . my girlfriend and my daughter, and we'll get a house and we're just gonna get a job. That's about it. That's the plans anyways. It's just to get out and we're going to get a place . . . somewhere where, like we've both never been before . . . Where . . . we don't know people, and they don't know us and . . . we can just raise our kid.

Billy's concern that he and his family locate to a place where they are unknown is suggestive of a need to hide, something that sexual offenders live with both in prison and in the community. A hoped-for future spent anonymously is articulated by many, a kind of public seclusion that, ironically, is almost impossible to achieve because of their criminal pasts. Oren, during our intake interview, expresses concerns that his record will make getting free of the justice system very difficult:

> From this day on I think there's going to be a lot of problems. Not so much with myself but with the way the system views me now. I'm basically viewed as a lost cause and somebody that shouldn't be released from prison. So I think that's going to cause a lot of conflict because . . . I'm on parole until

[a date more than a decade away], when I do get released from prison. So I think the system is going to interfere with my life as much as they can.

The "system," as Oren refers to it, often places restrictions on released sexual offenders that limit their mobility, residence, employment, and even their ability to have relationships, despite the emphasis of treatment on prosocial behavior and moral habilitation. Some sexual offenders, for instance, are required by law to inform potential employers or romantic partners of their criminal histories. The "system" is only part of the perceived problem, however. In many ways, dealing with parole officers and police after release is of less concern than dealing with the public, an angry and fearful civil society that rejects any notion that sexual offenders can be rehabilitated or in any way made safe for the community.

The past few decades have been witness to a continuing evolution of provincial, state, and federal legislation on sexual offender management in Canada and the United States, including sexual offender registries and community notification provisions (Murphy et al. 2009). Registration policies require individuals convicted of certain sexually based crimes to regularly inform their local police of their address, contact number, and any activity that will take them out of the jurisdiction for an extended period of time. Community notification is the public announcement of sexual offenders' relocation or release into a particular community. There is no singular form of legislation for community notification, but some allowances in privacy laws enable the release of personal information when the state deems the person to still be a risk to reoffend.

While registration and community notification are both contentious among offenders, criminologists, the state, and civil society, community notification tends to be the more controversial of the two. Critics of these policies have suggested that they were created for the political purpose of appeasing public outcry to "do something." Not surprisingly, community notification laws are not well received among sexual offenders. Ned, speaking during an interview, admits, "I got mixed feelings about it because I feel like it's almost like they're announcing a movie that's coming to a drive-in, or to a theater, you know? 'Sex Offender: Coming to a theater near you.'" He draws his hand through the air in front of his face as he speaks, as if to demonstrate the marquee of the theater. "You know," he continues, "they're advertising it . . . They can put your name and picture . . . on the web now, I guess too, and announce you like you're some kind of movie coming to a theater. And anybody that sees or hears that, knows to fear you, not to accept you and work with you. It's to fear you and keep you away, and that's the general message that I'm getting."

Community notification is handled by government in various ways. In Canada, as in the United States, some governmental services maintain websites with the names and photos of certain sexual and other offenders who are in the community. These websites offer typical statements of explanation such as this one:[2]

> These web pages have been established to provide information about high-risk offenders living in [our] communities. This information is provided to assist the public to take measures to protect themselves and their families.
>
> Only the most serious offenders, who are deemed to present a risk of significant harm, are included. Not all dangerous or serious offenders are included on this web site. The public must continue to be vigilant and use common sense to ensure their personal safety.

Further warnings are usually issued:

> Warning: Under no circumstances is the information contained on these web pages to be used in any manner to injure, harass, or commit a criminal act against any person named in the web site. Any such action could subject you to criminal prosecution.

The viewer is then invited to click on a box, agreeing, "I have read and understand the above warning and agree that I will not use the information to injure, harass, or commit a criminal act against any person named in the web site." Upon doing so, a new screen appears that lists the individuals currently on notification, along with links to frequently asked questions, statistics on sexual offenses generally, and tips for personal and family safety. Of paramount interest is the brief description of the risk the released offender is deemed to pose, including pertinent demographic descriptions of his previous victims. A list of conditions placed on the offender is also presented, including restrictions on mobility in the community. A typical entry concludes with the following warning (the capitalization is original to the site from which this text has been taken):

> THIS INFORMATION IS INTENDED TO ENABLE MEMBERS OF THE PUBLIC TO TAKE SUITABLE PREVENTION MEASURES, NOT TO EMBARK UPON ANY FORM OF VIGILANTISM OR OTHER UNREASONABLE CONDUCT DIRECTED AT THIS INDIVIDUAL.

Websites vary as to the disclosure of actual communities and addresses where released offenders are believed to be living. In the case of the inmates in my study who were subsequently released, specific community information was not always made public, although the town or city could be fairly easily inferred from other information contained on the site. Local, and sometimes national newspapers, however, often trumpet the release plan of certain offenders and identify the community. At this point, some members of the community, and beyond, may become alarmed and take matters into their own hands.

The message that Ned is "getting" from the public, as noted above, is clear: the public is not content solely with community notification and the accompanying newspaper releases and websites. The world of the Internet is now full of sites dedicated to identifying and locating sexual offenders, and in some jurisdictions maps showing their addresses are available. Some might suggest that social networking sites and the Internet more broadly have become important synoptic tools for citizens to utilize in an effort to protect themselves from sexual "predators." But ironically these sites have also been employed for outing, harassing, and punishing sexual offenders, so that the likelihood of their again threatening public safety possibly increases. One technology of surveillance, two dramatically different outcomes. The incongruity between state-sponsored polices for dealing with sexual offenders in the community and the actions of a frightened and enraged civil society is clear: the latter has commandeered its own technology to circumvent policies that the state has put in place to balance community and offender safety. The public, it seems, cares not a whit about offender safety.

In what might be thought of as a form of cyber-vigilantism that skirts the law protecting released offenders, when Wilson was released from the penitentiary a website sprang up almost as soon as the newspapers published his whereabouts. Within a few months this site had an astounding three thousand members! Many people, it seems, have no problem with threatening the offender in a public manner, including providing on the website their names and photographs along with some rather frightening comments. Here is a sample of the remarks made about Wilson (the spelling is original):

"I hope the devil is waiting with a rusty hot pitch fork up the ass for this pig!"

"Lets burn the motherfucker at the stake!!!!!!"

"People like this should be shot and pissed on. . . . obviously the so called justice system has failed yet again . . . shocking ain't it!"

"give me a hundrde buckk ill take em outttt hahahaha"

"id love to lynch mob this piece of shit"

"but he also is a fucking sex offender. he ahs no rights anymore"

"some one give me a drangerous weapon nd iill put him six feet under or better yet ten feet"

"I hope I see this sick fuck out on town . . . I actually want to pass by him because I don't give a shit where it happens . . . I will continuousley kick that grease ball in the nuts till he's pissing from his mouth!"

"Someone should kill this motherfucker."

"Rope. Tree. Some assembly required."

Other comments on the site involve surveillance, with eyewitness spotting of Wilson out in the community and reports of his address. Frustration with the justice system is rampant on the site, with many people expressing dismay that he was ever let out of prison. Perhaps the overall sentiment is summed up by one writer, who speculates that "maybe that's why they let him go, so the public can deal with him in a manner that the system can't."

Many comments of this ilk found on the site come not just from people living in the community where Wilson was released but from all over Canada and the United States, people who clearly are not at risk from this individual. The "folk devil" that is the sexual offender, to use Stanley Cohen's (1972/2002) expression, creates a moral panic that transcends jurisdictions, it would seem, confounding official government policy that necessarily must protect the rights of sexual offenders *as* members of the public. This latter point is particularly important, as our current legal system does not remove all rights from convicted criminals and affords them most, if not all, of the same rights as others when in our communities. It is as if the state must compensate through law and policy for the public's unruly discourse of abjection.

Ned's comments above reflect such a sense of abjection, feelings of horror or disgust that occur when the boundary between self and nonself is transgressed, as when a body part is detached (Beardsworth 2004; Diken and Laustsen 2005; Kristeva 1982). Abjection symbolizes chaos and disorder, thus threatening normality. It is for this reason that we are both repulsed and fascinated by the abject. But abjection is not only embodied. The concept has been extended to include social abjection— where collections or groups of people such as sexual offenders are cast off from the collective (Diken and Laustsen 2005)—which occurs as the result of public stigmatization. Men who have been convicted of a sexual offense—our modern-day lepers—occupy such a space in our communities, and they, along with those who would stigmatize them, reference opposite vantage points of moral experience, both "grappling with what makes social life and social worlds uncertain, dangerous, and terribly real" (Yang et al. 2007: 1534). Here abjection is exhibited through the ostracism and harassment by individuals or groups who want to make it known that the offender is unwanted. Community citizenship is thwarted, if not denied outright. The dread of being found out by others may dominate the day-to-day lives of sexual offenders. The feared become afraid.

Sex offenders are "matter out of place" (Douglas 1966), individuals ensconced in a liminality that is both polluting and dangerous. Their proper place, it seems in the eyes of many, is prison or, more gravely, a deathly hell. The distinction between the "truly evil" and the nonhuman blurs in the discourse surrounding sexual offenders (Waldram 2009b). "Evil," according to Alan Macfarlane (1985: 57), "in all instances, can be seen to represent a threat to the "integrity, the happiness and the welfare of 'normal' society and its moral order." "Evil is inexplicable," writes David Pocock (1985: 49), and "paradoxically, not human." Being "evil" suggests an inhumanity that seems to excuse actions as it denies the possibility of habilitation; abjection is a logical state for the truly evil. The irony is that while the public may be quick to label "evil" people—such as sexual offenders—as essentially nonhuman, these evil-doers generally and inevitably return to our communities *because* they are human. How they are treated when they do so speaks, essentially, to *our* humanity, a tough pill to swallow if you or a family member has been the victim of a sexual assault.

In being "out of place," sexual offenders challenge *as* they pollute our communities. And so some citizens seek to protect themselves by rejecting the panoptic methods of the state, which are deemed inadequate, in favor of a citizen-driven synoptic system of comprehensive, proactive surveillance; they utilize the full power of the "viewer society," as Mathiesen (1997: 219) describes it, to expand their capacity to surveil and, where necessary, intervene. But here the contradictions become clear. There is no evidence that community notification, sexual offender registries, or cyber- and other forms of synoptic vigilantism improve public safety in the context of sexual offenders, in part because most sexual offenders are known to their victims, especially in the case of crimes against children (Murphy et al. 2009). Sexual offenders—those as yet undiscovered as well as those released from prison terms—often fly under the radar, so to speak, because they are frequently already a part of our lives and communities and are not visibly remarkable in any way. Rather, the limited evidence suggests the opposite, that offenders' risk of reoffending increases when their visibility is heightened and they are subjected to the various forms of surveillance and freelance harassment that accompanies their abjection. The state, while bowing to public pressure, nevertheless seems to appreciate this and hence warns against such actions whenever it does publish a notification. Yet all such efforts by the state are largely toothless, since there are some very contemporary and effective forms of vigilantism that do not, as one commentator above suggested, necessarily involve a real rope and tree. Some people, not happy with the extent to which the state is willing to control sexual offenders in the community, and perhaps furious that they are allowed out of prison at all, take matters into their own hands and create the conditions for greater, rather than lesser, harm. In so doing, ironically, they also turn the state's panoptic lens onto themselves, as these citizens frequently use open-access websites—which may publish their names and photos—to utter threats against the offenders in violation of the law. And the lessons of CBT and all the psychoeducational sessions seem to have little to offer the offender when faced with this kind of community response.

. . .

A prospective narrative provides individuals with an opportunity to project into the future, to articulate without constraints or boundaries the story of a life as yet unlived. Such prospective narratives often contain elements of both pragmatism and romanticism; yet while constrained by the past and articulated in the complex present, as narrative theorists suggest, the future is, in some ways, wide open when the narrator is provided such an opportunity to project. Perhaps surprisingly, then, this group of prison inmates rarely journey into the territory of the fanciful. Their narratives are largely of two types: those that offer a fairly realistic assessment of the future and concentrate on the reestablishment of family, shelter, and employment; and those that largely fail to look beyond their daily existence in prison, or beyond the length of their prison terms. Among those who foresee release from prison, a future in the community is not without fear. The future is a time of both hope and apprehension.

Most men recognize that they will not simply be able to pick up where they left off, rejoining their families and communities. Rather, they appreciate that their crimes and their status as not only prison inmates but a special kind of prison inmate, a sexual offender, will affect the kind and extent of reintegration. They know that they will have to work to regain the trust of those who are most meaningful to them. And they are aware, to some extent, of both state regulations and civil society maneuverings designed to keep them under surveillance and, in effect, to regulate and even inhibit their ability to reintegrate into society. Most have lived their prison lives as invisibly as possible, because of the nature of their crimes, but their ability to do so upon release is a matter of considerable concern. "After institution time" is not utopian by any means. In phenomenological terms, to return to both Ricoeur (1980) and Mark, for many sexual offenders the future does look "like a pretty shitty place."

CHAPTER 9

"It's All in the Head"

"Everything they teach us is all in the head," David tells me one day. He has only a few days before he departs for the penitentiary. He has been judged "successful" in his program by his primary nurse and the treatment team, but, as typically happens, he must return to his home institution to await the justice system's own judgment of the meaning of "success" in his case. Our final interview affords him the opportunity to look back upon his experience on the unit.

"It's all things for cognitive thinking," he explains further. "But what the program doesn't do is, it doesn't give you a change of heart." David taps his chest as he speaks. "Which is where you have to basically have the change in order to bring in the head, right?" He moves his hand as he speaks, and lays three fingers across his temple. He continues. "If you still want to go out and do those things, you are going to go out and do them regardless of what they teach you."

David seems to be referencing the key issue of treatment assessment, that is, the extent to which inmates sincerely embrace what they have been taught and launch themselves on a new, more prosocial life course. In many ways, the treatment program does speak both to changes in the "heart" and changes in the "head," but David speaks to an enduring imbalance. After all, the program is dominated by the detection and correction of "thinking errors" or "cognitive distortions," and intensive cognitive instruction in how to properly think, express oneself, control oneself, and relate to one's self and to others, or, in other words, be moral. The treatment paradigm *is* Cognitive Behavioral Therapy, after all, and lessons of the heart are much less direct. These come attached to messages about emotions, morality, empathy, and what it means to be a prosocial individual. These messages pervade the entire program, yet appear rather subtle alongside the often confrontational attention paid to cognition and memory, with the exception, perhaps, of the Empathy module. David's assessment is intriguing, then, for he suggests that the emphasis of the treatment program may be somewhat misplaced: too much thinking, not enough feeling. Therapeutic change, in David's assessment, requires more than education, it requires an emotional response. How does David's assessment fit with the ethnographic material I have presented here? Can morality be taught, or is it simply "felt"? Is being moral an enduring part of one's adult personality, or is it more developmental and malleable? And can an "unreflective" (Zigon 2007) state of morality be achieved through a psychoeducational program that encourages the inmate to think carefully about the moral implications of each and every intersubjective act?

Looking back to our understanding of narrative as developed in chapter 1 and then throughout, I have argued that the original narrative of men's lives is characteristically—even paradigmatically—found wanting by definition. The theory of treatment suggests that, at the outset, their narratives are not "broken," as Kirmayer (2000) uses the term, so much as essentially false, full of lies and discourses of minimization, justification, and denial. These narratives contain cognitive "distortions," according to the theory, errors in thinking about the world and relationships with people that somehow contribute to criminal activity. Such narratives are seen to have little therapeutic value other than as windows into what is wrong with the individual. Further, the narratives are seen within the treatment theory less as autobiographical explanations of a life lived, "efforts after meaning" (Bartlett 1932), than as forms of disclosure that, while rendered in narrative form, are not judged according to narrative standards. This, I would suggest, is the essence of the problem faced by inmates in this program.

THE "TRUTH" OF SEXUAL OFFENDER HABILITATION

"Now, given the nature of your offenses," I ask, "a lot of people try and keep that sort of thing quiet, keep it secret. And yet you're expected to stand up in front of a group of inmates you're just getting to know, and talk openly about it. Did you find that difficult?" Oren responds to my question without thinking. "I knew I was going to be asked to do that," he says. "So at the very beginning of the program I just made up my mind that I would just do it, get it out in the open, and get it over with, so I could move on. I convinced myself this would be the best approach, and that's what I did. I didn't beat around the bush. I didn't try to minimize it or cover it up or hide it. I just got it out there."

"It seems to me it would be natural to hold some things back at that early stage in the program," I continue. "You didn't hold anything back?" "No," he answers in a serious tone. "And the reason I didn't hold it back is because I am smart enough to know that these people have copies of the police report, the court reports and everything else . . . To hold things back or to hide things would certainly work against me. So I was in a position where I thought, I might as well be honest. Just . . . just do it."

Eddy is only weeks away from leaving the treatment program, an official "success." Looking back, he reflects upon the many tasks he has been asked to perform, the many times he has stood before the group and talked about his life, and how much that he has said and done, both in the sessions and during nonprogram time, has been observed and recorded. He feels strongly that he should be a very well-known commodity by this point. He has "bought" into the program in hopes it would help him and, in his mind, has cooperated fully and disclosed all. Was it all for naught, he wonders? "The thing that I am disappointed about is about the parole officers here," he laments during an interview. "You are here for eight and a half months. They don't know jack squat! They know everything that is on your file, but that's it."

Oren and Eddy express similar sentiments about the treatment program. Oren, appreciating that everything about his life that is deemed meaningful is already known, decides to deliver as much as he can recall of that information in hopes of obtaining a positive outcome. He is clearly willing to relinquish a considerable degree of agency over his narrative, his life story, in order to do so. Eddie likewise feels that he has worked hard, done what was asked of him, and met the standards of "truthfulness" demanded in the program, but he is shocked and angry to learn that those individuals that are of greatest importance to him and his goals—the parole officers—have, as he interprets it, apparently paid no attention to what he has learned and accomplished in his program. In Eddie's view, they already knew what they needed to know to pass judgment, the treatment program notwithstanding.

I set before me three major goals for this ethnography. First, I wanted to fill what I refer to as a forensic "black hole" by providing an ethnographically rich account of the experience of treatment for imprisoned sexual offenders. Employing a variety of ethnographic approaches and techniques over an eighteen-month period of fieldwork, I was able to track the experiences of four cohorts and intensively interview thirty-five men at various points in their eight-month program. The ethnography, like the program itself, is built around three seminal performative, retrospective, and prospective narrative events: the Autobiography, the Crime Cycle, and the Relapse Prevention Plan. These are bookended and interrupted by various other psychoeducational programs and contextualized in a therapeutic community "total institution" that includes program time and off-time that are both considered therapeutic spaces where evidence of "working the program" is sought by therapists. The greatest difficulty in any ethnography is trying to represent lived experience in textual form and to honor the temporal dimension of that experience while freezing it so that it can be textually shared. The chapterettes and vignettes I have employed throughout reflect my effort to give the reader a feel for the broader experience of treatment—its jaggedness, if you will—and the many social encounters that both define and influence those experiences.

My second goal was to provide a critical analysis of Cognitive Behavioral Therapy (CBT) as it is employed on the unit. This attention to therapeutic pragmatics acknowledges the intersubjective nature of therapy and the role that significant others—including co-patients—play in the treatment of any given individual. It also demonstrates how the theory of treatment is employed in actual therapeutic encounters, where dynamic human factors come into play, including personalities and interpersonal relations, skill level of therapists, educational level and previous treatment experience of inmates, and broader institutional factors that influence how treatment ensues, how new therapeutic ideas are communicated and received, and how inmates and therapists get along in their moral community. This includes an overt engagement with relations of power and competing regulatory regimes. The fact that my research emanates from a prison clearly represents a key dynamic factor in understanding the therapeutic pragmatics at work.

My critical examination of CBT itself centered on the theoretical idea of cognitive distortion as the essential "problem" of inmates that requires "rehabilitation." Since this is a therapeutic prison, operating partly under a health regulatory regime, it is necessary for inmates to have some diagnosable condition to be admitted. Given that few fit the criteria for a *DSM* diagnosis of a sexual disorder, the tendency to use the broad diagnosis of antisocial personality disorder is noteworthy. The treatment program itself, with an emphasis on group work, approaches the treatment of this problem globally, with a variety of psychoeducational groups across various themes employed in conjunction with the three performative narratives noted above. My ability to observe the manner in which CBT was employed in these group sessions in particular demonstrates the precariousness of relying on the somewhat abstract notion of cognitive distortion and broader cognitive issues as both *the* key problem and one that, within the context of a unit composed of prison inmates, is amenable to treatment. The dynamic created on the unit—what I refer to as the therapeutic pragmatic—works to some extent at cross-purposes to the treatment theory and goals of the program.

I am not in a position, professionally or otherwise, to judge whether cognitive distortions "really exist," as I examined in chapter 3, or to claim that they do or do not explain specific criminal acts. But there are some troubling inconsistencies. If human psychology has an essentially narrative structure, as Jerome Bruner (1986), Sarbin (1986), and others suggest, and if, over time, memory loss with regard to details is predictable, as cognitive science demonstrates, and if fabulation and confabulation in narrative is normative, as Berrios (1998) argues, and if the "truth" and internal consistency of narrative are characteristically soft, as theorists such as Rubin (1995), Jackson (2002), Spence (1982a) and of course Jerome Bruner (1986) among many others argue, then both the way inmates render their stories and their resistance to the disemplotment and reemplotment of their narratives through therapeutic laundering are themselves likely normative and certainly not unique to their situation as convicted criminals and prison inmates. This in turn challenges a fundamental idea of CBT: that the inmates uniquely suffer from thinking errors or cognitive distortions that cause them to commit sexual crimes, at least as these may be evidenced by the stories they are required to tell. The fact that it is not always easy to distinguish sexual offenders from other criminals, or even noncriminals, on the matter of the existence of cognitive distortions compounds the issue. In many ways, sexual offenders look like everyone else (Marshall. 1996), and, I would suggest, in prison they behave narratively no different than anyone else probably would in such a circumstance. This is not to discount the significance and impact of their crimes, but rather to emphasize that to view these inmates solely or even primarily in the context of their criminal acts serves to oversimplify human existentiality and hence poses a risk to public safety, the opposite of the intended goal of prison treatment.

It is in this context that the idea of habilitation, rather than rehabilitation, takes on salience. In forensic discourse, rehabilitation is a concept so ubiquitous that one is hard pressed to find an actual definition beyond recidivism. I have argued that a strict definition of rehabilitation, which implies intervention to return the person to a previous, undisordered, noncriminal state, makes little sense for the lifeworlds of the inmates in my study. There is no "happyland" waiting for them when they are released from prison. To suggest that there is no restore point is not to say that they have always been criminals, of course, but rather that the idea that they can, and would want to, return somehow—physically, morally, cognitively, existentially, or whatever—to an earlier time or place is naive and nonsensical. Rather, "happyland" is an ideal, a perhaps mythical place that they are encouraged to seek out but that, by definition, they can never find.

The intended cumulative effect of the treatment program, and disciplinary institutions more broadly, therefore, is to attempt to create in the inmates a new sense of morality, to make them "fit" or, in Foucault's (1979: 210) terms, "useful" as members of society should they be released; in forensic circles, this is usually referred to as being "prosocial." This process of intentional habilitation references Rose's (2007: 27) notion of "ethopolitics," that is, "attempts to shape the conduct of human beings by acting upon their sentiments, beliefs, and values—in short, by acting on ethics." The idea of habilitation allows for the complexities of life in the penitentiary and in the community for sexual offenders, in which moral decision making and moral and ethical acts are laden with the cross-cutting tensions and conflicts inherent in sociality, and in which moral reference involves interactions with actual people—friends, family, antagonists—and not interaction with an ideal model of prosociality. Habilitation speaks not to restoration but to transformation, a process that seeks to inculcate in others, through the overt use of power and control, that which we most admire or wish to emulate morally, ethically, and socially, and to do so by glossing over the complexities of human sociality to make being moral seem as unambiguous as possible. Therapy is offered to inmates, not so much to make *their* lives better, as to make *our* lives better, and this is the essence of habilitation. This represents a curious form of therapy for sure, in that the measures of successful treatment of the patient are largely extracorporeal. It is telling that an inmate in this treatment program can receive a "successful" treatment evaluation and still not necessarily attain a reduction in security status, a lower risk-to-reoffend score, or parole.

Nonetheless, while the official goal of treatment—to promote public safety—is laudable, two major problems are evident. First, if the inmates are to be believed, the moral beings that the program seeks to create are to varying degrees dysfunctional in a prison context, where the custody mandate and con code are dominant, yet this is where the vast majority of the inmates will live for varying amounts of time following completion of the program. To expect them to retain the lessons of treatment for future use in the community seems implausible. Second, perhaps surprisingly, it would seem that such moral beings may well also be dysfunctional in a community context, especially a community that, in the end, does not actually want them. The latter supposition is conjecture at this point, of course, as I have not explored what happens to the men once they are released, with the exception of Wilson in the previous chapter. However, I have shown how the lessons they are exposed to represent an idealized, unnuanced, morally imbued, even utopian "happyland" that not only is a caricature of actual society but fails ultimately to deal with the fact that these are sexual offenders who will emerge into a community still *being* sexual offenders, a status they will never lose, and that they will be subject to varying rules and regulations that will keep them within the synoptic gaze of a wary, even frightened public. Theirs is a stigma not easily shed, a status not easily hidden.

The above two goals combined point me toward my third goal, to explore the impact of the paradigmatic mode and truth discourse on treatment, with an emphasis on the generation and performance of narrative. Therapeutically speaking, the ultimate modus operandi of treatment seems to be to challenge individual inmates' narratives of their lives and crimes, to break them down through attention to detail, in preparation for replacement by institutionally supported and theoretically compatible narratives (an approach that is common in many forms of psychotherapy). This form of "narrative asymmetry" serves to silence inmate stories while simultaneously supporting the status quo of the treatment paradigm (Ochs and Capps 1996: 33–34). The disclosure of their crimes, as the dominant point of the Autobiography, represents a form of "forced confession," reflecting "the principle that human beings must divulge their sinful acts and thoughts to avoid damnation" (Ochs and Capps 1996: 34). The similarity between this form of disclosure in therapy and confession in religious contexts is striking (Rose 1992), and even though the program lacks such overt religious referents, the centrality of moral instruction represents a parallel: beginning with the Autobiography, inmates must confess or be removed from the program and returned to what they often see as the "damnation" of the penitentiary.

Initially, as a result of instructions provided by the therapists and the Patient Manual, inmates interpret the Autobiographical exercise as an invitation to offer "their" stories, but as my discussion shows they come to realize the challenges to narrative agency that will characterize their residency. These challenges are significant and emanate from a treatment theory which assumes that, from the outset, inmates will lie about their lives and crimes and employ cognitive distortions—such as justification, minimization, and denial—especially as they engage with their criminal histories. Their stories are presumed to be error filled, false, and outright wrong, dysfunctional in their meaning, and hence in need of repair if not complete replacement. The reparation of their stories carries across all three narrative performances, supported by the more content-oriented psychoeducational sessions on how to be moral, assertive, empathetic, and so on. As is compatible with CBT, at each step on the therapeutic journey the inmate's stories are judged by peers and therapists, with the latter obviously holding especially significant power to determine therapeutic success or failure and the consequences that these will have for the inmate.

I have argued in this book that the judging of narrative represents a case in which standards of truthfulness and falsifiability usually associated with what Jerome Bruner has referred to as the paradigmatic mode of cognition have intruded into the narrative mode. The CBT treatment modality, built upon a scientific platform with its appeal to empirically established and verifiable "evidence-based" and "best practices" ideology, occupies a position as the singular authority for judging. The practitioners of this therapeutic modality—the psychiatric nurses, psychologists and psychiatrists—have been trained within a scientist-practitioner tradition that pays appropriate allegiance to these standards. The therapeutic program itself, while hospital based, also operates within a forensic context that has its own understanding of the importance and definition of acceptable evidence. Theory "truth" and legal "truth," while not identical, do seem to conflate and together represent the truth discourse that dominates the program.

The inmates themselves, experts in neither the theory of treatment nor the legal world, nonetheless learn how to employ snippets of truth discourse and raise issues of verifiability and falsification as they challenge each other's narratives in an effort to represent themselves as therapeutically progressive. Indeed, it is quite a bit easier for them to challenge each other's story details and memory than it is to grasp the complexities of the CBT paradigm. While together the actions of the therapists and inmates may constitute "misplaced verification," to use Jerome Bruner's (1986: 14) expression, insofar as they involve the inappropriate application of paradigmatic standards to the evaluation of narrative, these actions reflect a mode of verification that has institutional and theoretical support and hence are hegemonic. Within the program, such standards for verification are not at all viewed as "misplaced"; since narrative expression is in effect conceptualized as inherently reconstructive, as opposed to constructive, as narrative theorists suggest, the search for verifiability seems entirely logical. The emphasis in the program is on historical truth, as Spence defines it (1982a), and when the inmates appeal to narrative truth—to verisimilitude—which seems entirely appropriate to them, they open themselves to challenge. Let me explore this dynamic further.

The "institutional memory" (Linde 1999) within the correctional system is substantial, consisting of all the information about the inmate's life, crimes, and prison experiences that is, as Eddie suggests earlier in this conclusion, considered worthy knowledge. Such information can be seen as a textual elaboration of panoptic principles, in which not only is the inmate continually observed but such observations are frozen in time as they are recorded and then become available for future purposes of surveillance. This information is accrued over many years, and until documents were converted to electronic files, some paper sets of correctional files for the men in my research could easily reach several feet high. As Rose (1998: 75) suggests, this process effectively translates the individual "into the domain of knowledge [that] makes it possible to govern subjectivity according to norms claiming the status of science, by professionals grounding their authority in an esoteric but objective knowledge." This science, in turn, can be seen to advocate for the objective existence of an "historical truth" (Spence 1982a) about the individual that is contained within the files, a truth that the inmate is unlikely to know much about, or is unlikely to recall, or is unlikely to agree with. No matter, the historical truth of his life *is* known to others, individuals with substantial legislative power over him, and establishes that important benchmark from which to judge both initial narrative offerings and progress in the treatment program. And significant elements of this historical truth form the core of assessments of recidivism risk.

But there is also another standard applied to the narratives of these inmates. This one derives from the CBT theory upon which the treatment program is based. In this case, the inmate must not only accurately relate the details of his life and crimes as already known and legally validated but also learn to interpret these criminal experiences appropriately, by expressing both criminal episodes and the larger narrative in terms of thoughts and emotions compatible with his lifestyle and crimes; in other words, he must demonstrate an emerging morality compatible with CBT theory (which, it is implicitly assumed, reflects the broader moral code of society as a whole). These thoughts and emotions, of course, are unlikely to be known by anyone, including the inmate, and therefore recourse to treatment theory becomes crucial. The men learn from the program, and from each other, what thoughts and emotions are considered compatible with the commission of such acts as understood in CBT theory, and they in turn offer them up to the group as a means of participating in the establishment of their own treatment benchmarks. An affective statement such as "I was angry at women" carries great currency when uttered as part of a narrative of a crime, whether or not the inmate really believes this. Subsequent narrative renderings must demonstrate that the inmate appreciates the error in thinking contained within such an utterance if he is to be successful. These new interpretations do not necessarily settle in the "heart," as David notes, and their very cognitive nature allows for, even encourages, a shallow acceptance and manipulation.

To reiterate, I am arguing that the validation of inmate narratives—their narrative truth—is subject to standards that are most appropriate to matters of both historical and theoretical truth and, as such, are influenced by concerns about accuracy, consistency, replication, and theoretical compatibility characteristic of the paradigmatic mode as outlined by Jerome Bruner (1986). There is little value accorded to narrative truth, for this is seen, in effect, to be so full of cognitive distortions as to be invalid for anything other than a demonstration of the existence of cognitive distortions!

That inmates will resist to varying degrees the treatment program and efforts to "fix" or replace their narratives is entirely predictable. Those experiencing illness or treatment routinely find themselves engaged in a struggle to maintain control and to resist the imprinting and labeling directed at them by the professionals who exist as authoritative experts on their condition and who have the power to silence them or interpret their resistance as noncompliance or, in the case of psychotherapy, a lack of insight (Fox 1999; Price 1995; Saris 1995; A. Young 1990). As I have described, prisons in particular exist as unique "institutional landscapes" (Saris 1995), sites of both power and resistance dynamically negoti- ated in an intensely social and moral context (Waldram 1998, 2010). The legislated loss of autonomy experienced by inmates also applies to how they experience treatment programs. They are "socially positioned" (Miller 1995) in unique ways to each other, as fellow inmates, and to their jailers, and this position invariably shapes their experiences and the narratives they offer. An analysis of prison treatment simply cannot evade the fact that, by intent, control over the doctrines of treatment and definitions of success, and control over the evaluation of inmates, rests entirely in the hands of employees of the correctional system and representatives of the broader judicial system, including psychiatrists, psychologists, psychiatric nurses, and social workers. This is what being an inmate means. And resistance on the part of inmates is both morally "correct"—from the perspective of the con code—and inevitable; as sexual offenders, even when housed altogether in the Hound Pound, they feel that resistance and suspicion are the keys to their survival, and no amount of attempted indoctrination into the discourse of hospitalization will change the fact that they are still in prison and are still inmates.

While issues of power and legitimacy are central to understanding the narrative process generally (E. Bruner 1986; Kirmayer 2000), it is not a stretch to say that this is considerably more acute in carceral contexts. This can be taken for granted. However, inmate resistance in this case can also be fruitfully seen as the normative product of an engagement between the narrative and paradigmatic modes (J. Bruner 1986: 11), an area largely ignored by psychological and medical anthropologists who otherwise employ Bruner's notion of narrative. As noted earlier, while narrative emphasizes the creative process of story making, the paradigmatic mode focuses on the generation of reproducible truth statements within a positivist tradition. Insofar as they exist side by side in any context-specific domain, like this treatment unit, confusion and conflict can be anticipated, even more so when the standards of validation characteristic of one are applied to the other. I would suggest further that such a circumstance is not unique to the prison context and that we need to better explore the many and varied ways that the two cognitive modes influence each other. The two modes interact in any clinical encounter involving science-based therapeutics, including when any of us consults with our family physician.

But what we do see in this prison treatment program is that the power differential between the inmates and staff is also reflected in the broader power differential between the narrative and paradigmatic cognitive modes. Inmate narratives are subordinate to staff paradigmatic interpretations, and while it is certainly possible to view CBT as a "narrative," or even "metanarrative," as narrative scholars might, this would be to miss the point that CBT is representative of the broader paradigmatic mode, a science-based mode of inquiry and validation. Its metanarrative form does not emanate from the bottom up, that is, from an assemblage of individual narratives, but rather from the top down, from a treatment theory. The inmates' narratives, then, "replete with whimsy, metaphor, wishful thinking, and distorted memories" (Gergen and Kaye 1992: 171), cannot compete with the scientific narrative of CBT, with its "seal of professional approval." Both the inmates and the therapists express a mode of cognitive functioning relevant and relative to how they are situated in the therapeutic context—one narrative and experiential, the other paradigmatic and theoretical—that can be seen to duel for control of the therapeutic process. But only the professionals have a science-based paradigm, with the power that it implies and, to be metaphorically blunt, the keys to the front gate. Inmates experience this power differential early and often in their treatment program and must learn to accommodate it if they are to receive a successful evaluation. My sense is that this accommodation may be at the expense of some therapeutic progress, as many inmates come to concentrate not so much on the value of what they are being taught as on the instrumental goal of demonstrating progress in the program in the hope that it will, one day, help them gain release from custody.

BROKEN NARRATIVES OR BREAKING NARRATIVES?

The distinction made by Donald Spence (1982a) between "historical truth" and "narrative truth," despite its critics (see Sass and Woolfolk 1988, for instance), remains heuristically useful. To reiterate, "historical truth" refers to what "really happened," whereas "narrative truth" refers to the story that is told about those events, both the details selected for inclusion and the story's meaning or interpretation. Narrative truth allows for fabulation and confabulation in the interests of making the story "good"; historical truth, of course, does not. The ideas of narrative and historical truth, however, fail to deal cleanly with notions of cognition and affect related to the events being told: namely, what the inmate was thinking and feeling at the time of the experience being narrated. Since these are intensely subjective mental processes that presumably only the narrator can know, these are not "knowable" in any empirical sense, that is, not open to external verification or falsification. They do not exist in the empirical world the way an event does and hence can be known to others only through disclosure or narrative expression.

While the memory of events erodes over time, as gist replaces rote recall of details, and while there are vagaries involved in what constitutes not only a significant "event" but also one that is "memorable," cognition and affect seem less prone to imprinting and therefore remembering, if accurate recall is even possible. Indeed, it is conceivable that cognition and affect related to specific events can be "known" to the individual only in a post hoc manner through narrative construction. One might think that the narrator would have considerable, even absolute, agency in relating cognitive and affective dimensions, since there is no other witness, but in fact this is not the case. These dimensions, like the details of the events themselves, are subject to a kind of process of verification. The standard for evaluating them is drawn from the treatment theory and aims for both what is plausible given the circumstances and what is "appropriate" in compatibility with the treatment theory. This theory is grounded in the psychological sciences (i.e., the paradigmatic mode), and therefore the standards of validity from this mode slide over to become those for narrative more broadly. Hence, not only historical and narrative truth are at play here but also theoretical truth, "truth" of human cognition and behavior as known to a body of theory.

Donald Spence (1982b: 43) writes that "as we discover that narrative truth lies at the heart of insight and therapeutic change, we are also learning that historical truth is less accessible than we are taught to believe." Why, then, is there such an emphasis on this historical truth in forensic treatment? Because in this context it is not possible to escape the theoretically and emotionally powerful assumption that criminals lie and, in therapeutic terms, will by definition engage in cognitive distortion. This is seen as such a normative state—even an inherent one—for those who break laws and are caught and convicted that the forensic system is compelled to continuously drive the point home with them for fear they will quickly revert to their usual lying ways. From the forensic perspective, then, to engage with narrative, and especially narrative truth, as Spence and others employ the concept, is to risk allowing the criminal to continue in these antisocial thoughts and behaviors—their cognitive distortions—and, by extension, to maintain the risk they pose to the rest of us.

My analysis, however, suggests that the current approach of CBT misplaces attention and, therefore, may underachieve in terms of the forensic standard of program efficacy, recidivism. While looking at a person's life, as narrative, through the lens of paradigmatic empiricism engenders resistance, something as fundamental as denial of the crime seems less correlated to potential success in treatment or recidivism than often assumed (Marshall, Anderson, and Fernandez 1999; Metzner, Humphreys, and Ryan 2009). So why focus so intently on the details of inmate narratives? It seems that the forensic approach—group based and confrontational—goes considerably beyond the "reframing" of narrative typical of cognitive psychology (Kirmayer 2000: 154). And if, as Bruner and others suggest, narrative is an inherent capability of humans, one that we are compelled to employ, does it make sense to so forcefully challenge it in therapy? We are not simply talking about changing some of the content of narrative, nor are we even talking about altering the meaning of life events for the inmate. What we are talking about is a sustained critical engagement with narrative and its use as a vehicle for meaning making, dismantling it fact by fact, detail by detail, affect by affect, recalled thought by recalled thought, in preparation for its replacement by a new prosocial and therapeutically healthier narrative.

But the evidence that this is happening here is suspect. Instead, it seems most inmates either resist to varying degrees the imprinting of a new, theoretically compatible narrative, instrumentally adopt elements of the new narrative to appear therapeutically progressive, or become doubt-ridden or confused about their own understanding of their life, about the understanding of their life that the therapists want them to embrace, and about the practical utility of what they have been taught given their life circumstances (cf. Rose 1990: 239). Most seem to demonstrate all three types of engagement with the program, to varying degrees. If the inmate's narrative was not "broken" when he arrived, there is a good chance it will become so at some point during treatment, unless, of course, he intrinsically detects the threat of this process to his own self-sense and employs various means to resist while pretending to acquiesce. This process is never fully or completely resisted, it seems, and many inmates in group sessions and in interviews do demonstrate some program impact, at the very least in a discursive sense. There is, then, considerable risk of incomplete adoption of a new narrative as the tension between agency and resistance, on one hand, and compliance on the other, plays out. The risk is compounded in the many cases where the inmate is removed from the program midstream, possibly now with a truly "broken" narrative and no recourse to having it fixed.

As Gergen and Kaye (1992: 174) have put it, "There is no justification outside the narrow community of like-minded therapists for battering the client's complex and richly detailed life into a single, pre-formulated narrative, a narrative that may be of little relevance or promise for the client's subsequent life conditions." While I can appreciate the problematic issues inherent in utilizing metaphors of violence and victimhood to speak about the experience of sexual offenders, the use of the descriptor *battering* does resonate with what I observed in the group sessions. These new therapeutic narratives, "precariously insinuated into the life circumstances of the individual," may well be so fragile as to fall quickly to the wayside when the individual is confronted with real-world problems of both an existential and an intersubjective nature. Many of the men in this study detail with great ease how what they are learning is of little utility as long as they remain in prison, and indeed could be quite dangerous. Few, however, seem to fully appreciate that the utility of these new ways of thinking and acting once inmates are released out on the street is also questionable, since the therapeutic model by definition must emphasize a somewhat utopian world of uniformly moral, law-abiding, and prosocial individuals if it is to have any draw at all. The model must in effect present an alternative "good life." But this is not a life most inmates have ever really known, and it may not be achievable. Further, the challenges and contradictions of forensic treatment, when combined with an angry and fearful civil society that is suspicious of claims of rehabilitation however defined, combine to ensure that the physical and moral reintegration of sexual offenders into society will be fractured and difficult no matter how closely they can be said to reflect the moral ideals communicated during their treatment.

I am not attempting to lay out a course for a new approach to CBT or broader forensic treatment, as this is beyond the scope of the book and, indeed, my expertise as an anthropologist. Nor am I prepared to render final judgment one way or another as to the value of prison-based therapeutic intervention, as it seems to me that to simply throw up our hands at the futility of habilitation/rehabilitation and do nothing but warehouse would be a step backwards. There is evidence that current prison therapeutic programs do reduce recidivism, after all. However, I do think my critique here, bolstered by the data, suggests the need for a healthy reconsideration of the therapeutic status quo, one that would engage more positively with the normative processes of narrative construction and meaning making, perhaps through a narrative therapy approach (White and Epston 1990). Forensic specialists are constantly seeking new avenues of treatment, and this is my contribution to that discussion, one that, I hope, will work for both treatment staff members and the sexual offenders who undergo these programs. I believe it is possible for both *our* lives and *their* lives to be better.

FINAL THOUGHTS ON AN ANTHROPOLOGY OF THERAPEUTIC INTERVENTION

This ethnography is many things. It is an exploration of the treatment experiences of sexual offenders housed in a special prison unit, the "Hound Pound." It is a critical examination of the form of Cognitive Behavioral Therapy used on this unit. And it is an engagement with the ideas of narrative and paradigmatic cognitive modes as relational and not independent as many narrative theorists have inferred. But this is also a work in what I have termed the anthropology of therapeutic intervention.

Therapeutic intervention refers to health-related contexts in which there is a largely unwelcome intrusion into the lifeworld of the patient. Typically in these cases, patients may not recognize or accept that they have a medical or psychological problem, or they may accept that they have a problem but reject the official diagnosis, or they may not accept that treatment is needed, or they may reject the kind of treatment offered or imposed. Or they may simply be powerless—cognitively or legally—to offer a viewpoint. Recourse to power and authority is central to the concept: social, political, and economic structures, including legal structures, establish a jurisdictional right to intervene, to determine what is in the best interests of the patient and society more broadly, and they support a capacity to force or otherwise coerce therapeutic measures. Involuntary commitment may be employed. But more subtle pressures can also be brought to bear, situated within family and social webs of significance. And an active civil society can take matters into its own hands and act in what it sees as its best interests by identifying and targeting individuals whose physical presence is seen as a threat to their health or morality. An *anthropology* of therapeutic intervention employs a central concern with cultural process to understand the dynamics, at all levels, at work in such cases, from the macro-level examination of structures of power to the quotidian experience of a daily life lived out within a particular social context.

An anthropology of therapeutic intervention seeks to provide phenomenologically rich description of the tussle for control over meaning and experience as it plays out on a daily basis in many therapeutic contexts, including intersubjectively among patients and between patients and therapists. It recognizes formal and informal structures of authority and power yet is also able to explore the dynamics of within-group intersubjectivity that is created by the therapeutic context, how family and significant others, including "peers," often act in support of the broader goals of those structures and against the wishes of the patient. This includes a concern with how those co-sharing the position of "patient" can act in ways that do not express group solidarity or a classlike consciousness so much as validate and support the structures that they otherwise might interpret as oppressive. It encourages us to examine how even in the voluntary relationship between doctor/therapist/healer and patient, issues of authority and control are pertinent: for instance, how a health practitioner authorizes the expression of narrative in the clinic (e.g., "Tell me what the problem is") then acts to alter it, judge it, even dismiss it, all on the basis of the authority of medical science or some regulatory body.

An anthropology of therapeutic intervention, then, is a critical phenomenology that explores experience in any therapeutic context or pretext in which the patient's participation is not consciously self-motivated or voluntary. What is created is not so much an individual with a disorder as a class of disordered individuals, with each individual diagnosed, treated, and received as representative of the class. This deindividualization makes it easier to use whatever legislative or other means is needed to impose diagnosis and treatment; somewhat ironically, this deindividualization makes it harder to hide for those who threaten by virtue of their "disorders." Those targeted for intervention represent our contemporary "folk devils," dysfunctional, abnormal, or in other ways behaviorally problematic individuals whose comportment is medicalized. In all cases, it is the threat posed to others that leads to the intervention. This threat—real or imagined, medical, behavioral, or moral—is the essence of therapeutic intervention: concern for the well-being of the patient is easily confused with concern for the well-being of the population and may even be clearly subordinate. It is only through the invocation of power and authority that the intervention can ensue. Therapeutic intervention is ultimately about protecting the dominant social and moral order. As I have shown in this ethnography, while treatment in the Hound Pound is centered on the habilitation of individuals, their transformation into morally sound citizens reflective of our ideals, the crucial evidence of success in this process is not their health or well-being but ours. Indeed, the viability of the program is based on demonstrating improvements in public safety, not improvements in cognitive or emotional functioning or morality of the inmates. The offender may well be released into the community and thereafter engage in severe alcohol or substance abuse, have episodes of depression, perhaps commit suicide, yet if he does not commit another sexual offense he will, ironically, be considered a treatment "success" because he has harmed only himself, not others. The public good outweighs the private, the collective is more important than the individual. This, to my mind, is what habilitation, and many other forms of therapeutic intervention, are all about.

While I have focused here on the therapeutic prison, there are many other historical and contemporary examples of therapeutic intervention. Leper colonies obviously spring to mind, as does the historic persecution of witches in Europe and North America. More contemporary examples also abound: individuals involuntarily committed to psychiatric institutions; children diagnosed and medicated for ADHD because of their behavior in the classroom; those convicted of impaired driving who are ordered into alcohol education programs; employees that are required to undergo medical or psychological assessment or treatment in order to obtain or keep jobs; abusive and neglectful parents who must enter and graduate from therapeutic programs in order to get their children back; offenders forced to undergo court-ordered drug abuse treatment or face prison time; individuals quarantined with contagious diseases; HIV-positive individuals under court order to disclose their conditions to sexual partners. I am not suggesting that any of these actions and restrictions is unwarranted, nor am I arguing against the importance of a public health and safety strategy. The effectiveness of any such strategy, however, must be understood in relation to how those targeted as problematic respond to such targeting and imposed efforts to diagnose, treat, rehabilitate, habilitate, or isolate. An anthropology of therapeutic intervention explores contexts in which the patient is reluctant or unwilling, the diagnosis is imposed, the treatment is in some manner coerced, the therapeutic goals are less pertinent to the patient than to the community or the state, and resistance to imposed treatment is itself often seen as a disorder or a crime.

An anthropology of therapeutic intervention represents a new direction in the fields of medical and psychological anthropology, one that brings together the theoretical and conceptual frameworks of both to focus our attention on the therapeutic implications of the cognitive, social, religious, economic, and political creation of monsters, deviants, folk devils, and other human contaminants for the social and moral world in which we inhabit. It blurs the patient/healer and victim/ victimizer dichotomies by viewing them all as subject to broader forces of power that, while positioning them differently in the therapeutic context, nevertheless articulate with each other. It encourages us—scholars included—to extend humanity to those we fear, those we dislike, those we disrespect, those who harm us, those who threaten us, because they share our world too. For anthropology as a discipline to continue to be relevant in an increasingly violent world, it must be willing to "go down with the Hounds."

Where Are They Now?

As readers come to the end of this ethnography, having met many different characters in the Hound Pound, some will no doubt want me to conclude with information on what has happened to them since my research. I cannot provide that information in specific. Further, I remind that my aim here is not to evaluate the overall effectiveness of the treatment program: among other issues, the sample size is simply too small to allow for any meaningful assessment even where data on recidivism are available. Yet if I provided information on known criminal trajectories of my participants since my research such problematic inferences would no doubt be drawn. I have offered a critical appraisal of the experience of sexual offender treatment here, and that in itself suggests that I believe that there are ways in which that experience could be improved with an eye toward reduced recidivism or improved psychosocial development for the individuals involved, or both.

That being said, I have watched with interest as several individuals with whom I worked came to the attention of the media over the past few years. At least seven have been subject to public notification—and I am not necessarily aware of notifications tendered in far-off jurisdictions where the released inmates may have landed. There have been several cases of parole violation, but not involving a sexual crime; one participant lasted barely twenty-four hours before being arrested for carrying a prohibited item. At least two have been charged with a new sexual offense, involving patterns that look surprisingly like those of their previous offenses. One participant has been charged with the murder of an adult female victim. And of course some participants remain behind bars. Those who may have been released and have managed to avoid reoffending (or managed to avoid being caught) do not show up on the public and media radar, and hence I know nothing about them. One did write to me from a halfway house last year to tell me how well he was doing.

To say that these men are no angels is an absurd understatement. They committed reprehensible crimes that caused great suffering, and the fact that some have reoffended sexually or otherwise is not surprising. They represent, after all, the most difficult of inmates, and this is why they were in the Hound Pound in the first place. In my efforts to understand and communicate their experiences of treatment, I never lost sight of this fact. Unlike many anthropological encounters, this research did not result in career- or lifelong relationships of respect and trust. It did, however, afford me the opportunity to tread where I was told not to go, and to gain insight into a (re)habilitative process that has otherwise garnered scant attention from anthropologists. For that opportunity, I will forever remain grateful.

Notes

PREFACE

1. I will use the term *victim* in this book as it is the term used in the treatment program to refer to those who have been offended against. I appreciate that many believe this is a term that further disempowers these individuals.

2. In Canada, Indigenous peoples are often subsumed under the broad label *Aboriginal* despite significant cultural, linguistic, and historical differences. In the United States, such individuals might be referred to as "American Indian" or "Native American."

1. A MAN WHO NEEDS NO INTRODUCTION

1. In this book, I use *Autobiography* to refer to the rendering of the life story required by the treatment program as a core element, and I use *autobiography* to refer to the more general notion of telling one's life story. As I shall argue, these are not identical processes in this treatment program.

2. From this point onward, I will use the terms *rehabilitation* and *rehabilitate* to refer to the approach characteristic of mainstream forensic treatment. This will be contrasted throughout by my use of the terms *habilitation* and *habilitate*.

3. For instance, in a recent examination of Jerome Bruner's work published in the psychological anthropology journal *Ethos* (Mattingly, Lutkehaus, and Throop 2008), none of the contributing authors mentioned the paradigmatic mode.

4. I am referring here to what Foucault (1988: 18) described as "technologies of the self," how individuals "effect by their own means or with the help of others a number of operations on their bodies or souls, thoughts, conduct and way of being, so as to transform themselves in order to attain a certain state of happiness, purity, wisdom, perfection or immortality."

2. GOIN' DOWN WITH THE "HOUNDS"

1. However I am not suggesting here that these two mandates are uniquely distinct, for as Foucault (1979) suggests, and I shall demonstrate, the therapeutic mandate also involves the control of the inmates, but for different purposes.

2. As Stanley Cohen (1985) argues, it is impossible to discuss punishment and prisons today without citing Foucault. However, like Rhodes (2004: 15), I see my work here not as an "application" of Foucault to prisons but rather as an ethnography in which Foucault's ideas, and especially those of Foucault-influenced scholars such as Nikolas Rose, carry some resiliency and insight. Further, I owe as much if not a greater debt to the ethnographic approach and ideas expressed in *Asylums* by Erving Goffman (1961).

3. I refer to "pragmatic" rather than "praxis" not simply to emphasize the application of a theoretical paradigm but also to recognize the intersubjective and contextual nature of that application. CBT with an adult nonoffender suffering from, say, obsessive-compulsive disorder will present a very different set of challenges to a therapist than would CBT with an incarcerated sexual offender.

3. DISORDERED SEX

1. The assessment of psychopathy in the criminal system is typically done with the Hare Psychopathy Checklist, Revised Version, a commercially available tool. A common assertion is that psychopaths cannot be treated and will never change, that it is who they "are." A recent article suggests that there is no strong evidence one way or the other that diagnosed psychopaths benefit from sexual offender treatment, unlike other sexual offenders (Doren and Yates 2008). See also Hare (1993).

2. The *DSM* employs a "multiaxial" system of five levels or categories in which to assess and diagnose a patient:

Axis I: Clinical disorders, including major mental disorders such as depression, anxiety disorders, bipolar disorder, and learning disorders

Axis II: Personality disorders and mental retardation

Axis III: Acute medical conditions and physical disorders

Axis IV: Psychosocial and environmental factors contributing to the disorder

Axis V: Global Assessment of Functioning

Axes I and II are of primary concern in forensic treatment as they represent the diagnosable conditions around which treatment is focused.

3. It is not my intent to wade deeply into the debates—often methodological—over studies of CBT's effectiveness, but they are extensive.

4. MORAL CITIZENSHIP

1. A shank is a homemade knife, and hence to "be shanked" means to be stabbed.

2. Hank is referring to the posters that I placed on the bulletin boards in each lounge, explaining who I was and what I was doing on the unit.

MORAL HABILITATION 1. "STINKIN' THINKIN'"

1. In this and subsequent chapters and chapterettes I make the distinction between the "Treatment Manual," and the "Patient Manual." The former is a photocopied, unpaginated manual that is designed for the therapists and other officials and provides an overview of the program. It is not published. The latter is not a manual per se but rather consists of a series of photocopied handouts that the men are expected to collate and, in effect, use to create their own treatment manual.

5. "IT'S *YOUR* LIFE STORY"

1. Indeed, the men are largely discouraged from confessing to possible offenses for which they have never been charged, as this would compromise the treatment staff and invoke a different regulatory regime, with the inmate possibly removed from the program and returned to his home penitentiary to await another trial in court.

2. I remind the reader that I was not allowed to record or take notes during these group sessions. Immediately afterward, I returned to my research office in the institution and wrote down as much as I could recall. In effect, I attempt here to reconstruct the events and their tone. The quotes that appear are, I am confident, accurate.

3. I have lived in northern communities where the local police station is not locked at all sometimes or where the cells themselves do not lock. It is a different way of life there!

4. This has now changed. The entire institution is smoke-free.

5. Members of the treatment staff do not like references to a "hot seat" because of the hostile connotations, which are antithetical to the treatment paradigm. Inmates, however, routinely refer to the presenter as "being on the hot seat."

6. As noted earlier, the men must submit a final Autobiography to treatment staff, who may then deal with any remaining issues during occasional individual sessions. The Autobiographies are placed in the inmate's institutional file, to be reviewed if necessary in the future.

MORAL HABILITATION 4: "THE MOST EMOTIONALLY DRAINING THING I HAVE EVER DONE IN MY LIFE"

1. I will use *Empathy* to refer to the training module employed in the program, and *empathy* to refer to the psychological and emotional experience as defined in the literature and discussed here.

2. This letter has been edited and altered to protect the inmate who wrote it as well as the victim.

3. I am not suggesting that all sexual offenders have experiences of sexual abuse that parallel those of their victims. Indeed, some seem to stretch the parallels beyond credibility in some cases, and others simply have not experienced sexual or physical abuse prior to the commission of their offenses. I am also not suggesting that the experience of abuse justifies its perpetration.

8. "A PRETTY SHITTY PLACE OUT THERE"

1. Since this interview the Government of Canada has in fact implemented a national sexual offender registry.

2. The text in this example is taken from an actual website maintained by a government agency.

Works Cited

Abel, Gene, Judith Becker, and Jerry Cunningham-Rathner. 1984. "Complications, Consent and Cognitions in Sex between Children and Adults." *International Journal of Law and Psychiatry* 7 (1): 89–103.

American Psychiatric Association. 2000. *Diagnostic and Statistical Manual of Mental Disorders.* 4th ed. Text Revision. Washington, DC: American Psychiatric Association.

Auburn, Timothy. 2005. "Narrative Reflexivity as a Repair Device for Discounting 'Cognitive Distortions' in Sex Offender Treatment." *Discourse and Society* 16 (5): 697–718.

Auburn, Timothy, and Susan Lea. 2003. "Doing Cognitive Distortions: A Discursive Psychology Analysis of Sex Offender Treatment Talk." *British Journal of Social Psychology* 42:281–98.

Bambonyé, Manassé. 1996. "Mental Health and Psychosexual Disorders among Federal Sex Offenders." *Forum on Corrections Research* 8 (2). www.csc-scc.gc.ca.

Bartlett, Frederick. 1932. *Remembering: A Study in Experimental and Social Psychology.* Cambridge: Cambridge University Press.

Beardsworth, Sara. 2004. *Julia Kristeva: Psychoanalysis and Modernity.* Albany: State University of New York Press.

Beck, A., and Weishaar, M. 1989. "Cognitive Therapy." In *Comprehensive Handbook of Cognitive Therapy,* edited by A. Freeman, K. Simon, L. Beutler, and H. Arkowitz, 21–36. New York: Plenum Press.

Becker, Gay. 1997. *Disrupted Lives: How People Create Meaning in a Chaotic World.* Berkeley: University of California Press.

Becker, Gay, Yewoubdar Beyene, and Pauline Ken. 2000. "Memory, Trauma, and Embodied Distress: The Management of Disruption in the Stories of Cambodians in Exile." *Ethos* 28 (3): 320–45.

Berrios, German E. 1998. "Confabulations: A Conceptual History." *Journal of the History of the Neurosciences* 7 (3): 225–41.

Biehl, Joao. 2005. *Vita: Life in a Zone of Social Abandonment.* Berkeley: University of California Press.

Bourgeois, Philippe, and Jeff Schonberg. 2009. *Righteous Dopefiend.* Berkeley: University of California Press.

Brainerd, C. J., and V. F. Reyna. 2002. "Fuzzy-Trace Theory and False Memory." *Current Directions in Psychological Science* 11 (5): 164–69.

Brockmeier, Jens. 2010. "After the Archive: Remapping Memory." *Culture and Psychology* 16 (1): 5–35.

Bruner, Edward. 1986. "Ethnography as Narrative." In *The Anthropology of Experience,* edited by Victor Turner and Edward Bruner, 139–55. Urbana: University of Illinois Press.

Bruner, Jerome. 1986. *Actual Minds, Possible Worlds.* Cambridge, MA: Harvard University Press.

———. 1990. *Acts of Meaning.* Cambridge, MA: Harvard University Press.

———. 1991. "The Narrative Construction of Reality." *Critical Inquiry* 18:1–21.

———. 2002. *Making Stories: Law, Literature, Life.* Cambridge, MA: Harvard University Press.

———. 2008. "Culture and Mind: Their Fruitful Incommensurability." *Ethos* 36 (1): 29–45.

Busch, Noël Bridget, Norma Hotaling, and Martin A. Monto. 2002. "Male Customers of Prostituted Women." *Violence against Women* 8 (9): 1093–1112.

Butler, Andrew, Jason Chapman, Evan Forman, and Aaron Beck. 2006. "The Empirical Status of Cognitive-Behavioral Therapy: A Review of Meta-Analyses." *Clinical Psychology Review* 26:17–31.

Chase, Gillean. 1983. "An Analysis of the New Sexual-Assault Laws." *Canadian Woman Studies* 4 (4): 53–54.

Cohen, Stanley. 1972/2002. *Folk Devils and Moral Panics.* 2nd ed. New York: Routledge.

———. 1985. *Visions of Social Control: Crime, Punishment and Classification.* Cambridge: Polity Press.

Cordilia, Ann. 1983. *The Making of an Inmate: Prison as a Way of Life.* Cambridge, MA: Schenkman.

De Leon, George, Gerald Melnick, George Thomas, David Kressel, and Harry Wexler. 2000. "Motivation for Treatment in a Prison-Based Therapeutic Community." *American Journal of Drug and Alcohol Abuse* 26 (1): 33–46.

Desjarlais, Robert. 2005. "Movement, Stillness: On the Sensory World of a Shelter for the 'Homeless Mentally Ill.'" In *Empire of the Senses: The Sensual Culture Read,* edited by David Howes, 369–79. Oxford: Berg.

Diken, Bullent, and Carsten Bagge Laustsen. 2005. "Becoming Abject: Rape as a Weapon of War." *Body and Society* 11 (1): 111–28.

Doren, Dennis M., and Pamela Yates. 2008. "Effectiveness of Sex Offender Treatment for Psychopathic Sexual Offenders." *International Journal of Offender Therapy and Critical Criminology* 52 (2): 234–45.

Douglas, Mary. 1966. *Purity and Danger: An Analysis of Concepts of Pollution and Taboo*. New York: Routledge and Kegan Paul.

Durkheim, Emile. 1912/1965. *The Elementary Forms of Religious Life: A Study in Religious Sociology*. Translated by Joseph Ward Swain. New York: Free Press.

Ellis, Albert. 1989. "The History of Cognition in Psychotherapy." In *Comprehensive Handbook of Cognitive Therapy*, edited by A. Freeman, K. Simon, L. Beutler, and H. Arkowitz, 5–19. New York: Plenum Press.

Feldman, Allen. 1991. *Formations of Violence: The Narrative of the Body and Political Terror in Northern Ireland*. Chicago: University of Chicago Press.

Fisher, D., A. Beech, and K. Browne. 1999. "Comparison of Sexual Offenders to Non-Offenders on Selected Psychological Measures." *International Journal of Offender Therapy and Comparative Criminology* 43 (4): 473–91.

Foucault, Michel. 1979. *Discipline and Punish: The Birth of the Prison*. New York: Vintage.

———. 1982. "The Subject and Power." In *Michel Foucault: Beyond Structuralism and Hermeneutics*, edited by Hubert Dreyfus and Paul Rabinow, 208–27. Chicago: University of Chicago Press.

———. 1988. "Technologies of the Self." In *Technologies of the Self*, edited by L.H. Martin, H. Gutman, and P.H. Hutton, 16–49. London: Tavistock.

Fox, Kathryn. 1999. "Changing Violent Minds: Discursive Correction and Resistance in the Cognitive Treatment of Violent Offenders in Prison." *Social Problems* 46:88–103.

Foxen, Patricia. 2000. "Cacophony of Voices: A K'iche Mayan Narrative of Remembrance and Forgetting." *Transcultural Psychiatry* 37 (3): 355–82.

Frank, Arthur. 1995. *The Wounded Storyteller*. Chicago: University of Illinois Press.

Garro, Linda. 1992. "Chronic Illness and the Construction of Narratives." In *Pain as Human Experience: An Anthropological Perspective*, edited by M-J. Delvecchio Good, P. Brodwin, B. Good, and A. Kleinman, 100–137. Berkeley: University of California Press.

———. 1994. "Narrative Representations of Chronic Illness Experience: Cultural Models of Illness, Mind, and Body in Stories Concerning the Temporo-Mandibular Joint." *Social Science and Medicine* 38:771–74.

Garro, Linda C., and Cheryl Mattingly. 2000. "Narrative Turns." In *Narrative and the Cultural Construction of Illness and Healing*, edited by Cheryl Mattingly and Linda C. Garro, 259–69. Berkeley: University of California Press.

Gay y Blasco, Paloma, and Huon Wardle. 2007. *How to Read Ethnography*. London: Routledge.

Geertz, Clifford. 1973. "Deep Play: Notes on the Balinese Cockfight." In *The Interpretation of Cultures: Selected Essays*, edited by Clifford Geertz, 412–35. New York: Basic Books.

———. 1976/1984. "From the Native's Point of View: On the Nature of Anthropological Understanding." In *Culture Theory*, edited by Richard Shweder and Robert A. LeVine, 123–36. Cambridge: Cambridge University Press.

Genders, Elaine, and Elaine Player. 1995. *Grendon: A Study of a Therapeutic Prison*. Oxford: Clarendon Press.

Gergen, Kenneth J., and Mary M. Gergen. 1986. "Narrative Form and the Construction of Psychological Science." In *Narrative Psychology: The Storied Nature of Human Contact,* edited by T. R. Sarbin, 22–44. New York: Praeger.

Gergen, Kenneth J., and John Kaye. 1992. "Beyond Narrative in the Negotiation of Therapeutic Meaning." In *Therapy as Social Construction,* edited by Sheila McNamee and Kenneth J. Gergen, 166–85. Newbury Park, CA: Sage Publications.

Goffman, Erving. 1961. *Asylums: Essays on the Social Situation of Mental Patients and Other Inmates.* New York: Anchor Books.

———. 1963. *Stigma: Notes on the Management of a Spoiled Identity.* New York: Simon and Shuster.

———. 1969. *The Presentation of Self in Everyday Life.* New York: Penguin.

Good, Byron. 1994. *Medicine, Rationality and Experience: An Anthropological Perspective.* Cambridge: Cambridge University Press.

Gunn, Rita, and Rick Linden. 1997. "The Impact of Law Reform on the Processing of Sexual Assault Cases." *Canadian Review of Sociology and Anthropology* 34 (2): 155–74.

Halpern, Jodi. 2001. *From Detached Concern to Empathy: Humanizing Medical Practice.* New York: Oxford University Press.

Haney, Lynne A. 2010. *Offending Women: Power, Punishment, and the Regulation of Desire.* Berkeley: University of California Press.

Hanson, R., A. Gordon, A. Harris, J. Marques, W. Murphy, V. Quinset, et al. 2002. "First Report of the Collaborative Outcome Data Project on the Effectiveness of Psychological Treatment for Sex Offenders." *Sexual Abuse: A Journal of Research and Treatment* 14:169–94.

Hare, Robert. 1993. *Without Conscience: The Disturbing World of the Psychopaths among Us.* New York: Guilford Press.

Harris, Monica J. 1991. "Controversy and Culmination: Meta-Analysis and Research on Interpersonal Expectancy Effects." *Personality and Social Psychology Bulletin* 17 (3): 316–22.

Hinton, Alexander Laban. 2005. *Why Did They Kill? Cambodia in the Shadow of Genocide.* Berkeley: University of California Press.

Hollan, Douglas. 2008. "Being There: On the Imaginative Aspects of Understanding Others and Being Understood." *Ethos* 36 (4): 475–89.

Hollan, Douglas, and C. Jason Throop. 2008. "Whatever Happened to Empathy? Introduction." *Ethos* 36 (4): 385–401.

Howard, George S. 1991. "Culture Tales: A Narrative Approach to Thinking, Cross-Cultural Psychology, and Psychotherapy." *American Psychologist* 46 (3): 187–97.

Jackson, Michael. 2002. *The Politics of Storytelling: Violence, Transgression and Intersubjectivity.* Copenhagen: Museum Tusculanum Press.

Jefferson, Andrew M. 2003. "Therapeutic Discipline? Reflections on the Penetration of Sites of Control by Therapeutic Discourse." *Outlines* 1:55–73.

Kafka, M., and J. Hennen. 2002. "DSM-IV Axis I Comorbidity Study of Males with Paraphilias and Paraphilia-Related Disorders." *Sexual Abuse* 14:349, 366.

Kerby, Anthony P. 1991. *Narrative and the Self.* Bloomington: Indiana University Press.

Kirmayer, Laurence. 1996. "Landscapes of Memory: Trauma, Narrative and Dissociation." In *Tense Past: Cultural Essays in Trauma and Memory,* edited by Paul Antze and Michael Lambek, 173–98. New York: Routledge.

———. 2000. "Broken Narratives: Clinical Encounters and the Poetics of Illness Experience." In *Narrative and the Cultural Construction of Illness and Healing,* edited by Cheryl Mattingly and Linda C. Garro, 153–80. Berkeley: University of California Press.

Kleinman, Arthur. 1992. "Local Worlds of Suffering: An Interpersonal Focus for Ethnographies of Illness Experience." *Qualitative Health Research* 2 (2): 127–34.

———. 1995. *Writing at the Margin: Discourse between Anthropology and Medicine.* Berkeley: University of California Press.

———. 1997. "Everything That Really Matters: Social Suffering, Subjectivity, and the Re-Making of Human Experience in a Disordering World." *Harvard Theological Review* 90 (3): 315–26.

———. 1999a. "Experience and Its Moral Codes: Culture, Human Conditions, and Disorder." In *The Tanner Lectures on Human Values,* edited by G.B. Peterson, 20:357–420. Salt Lake City: University of Utah Press.

———. 1999b. "Moral Experience and Ethical Reflection: Can Ethnography Reconcile Them? A Quandary for 'The New Bioethics.'" *Daedalus* 128 (4): 69–97.

Kristeva, Julia. 1982. *Powers of Horror: An Essay on Abjection.* Translated by L.S. Roudiez. New York: Columbia University Press.

Kurosawa, Akira, dir. 1950. *Rashômon.* Tokyo: Daiei Tokyo Studios.

Landau, Mark J., Jeff Greenberg, and Sheldon Solomon. 2008. "The Never-Ending Story: A Terror Management Perspective on the Psychological Function of Self-Continuity." In *Self Continuity: Individual and Collective Perspectives,* edited by Fabio Sani, 87–100. New York: Taylor and Francis.

Langton, Calvin M., and William Marshall. 2000. "The Role of Cognitive Distortions in Relapse Prevention Programs." In *Remaking Relapse Prevention with Sex Offenders: A Sourcebook,* edited by D. Richard Laws, Stephen Hudson, and Tony Ward, 167–85. Thousand Oaks, CA: Sage Publications.

Lee, Julian C.H. 2005. "The Narrative Imperative." *Anthropological Forum* 15 (2): 115–30.

Lees, J., N. Manning, and B. Rawlings. 1999. *Therapeutic Community Effectiveness: A Systematic International Review of Therapeutic Community Treatment for People with Personality Disorders and Mentally Disordered Offenders.* York: National Health Service Centre for Reviews and Dissemination, University of York.

Lehne, Gregory K. 2009. "Phenomenology of Paraphilia: Lovemap Theory." In *Sex Offenders: Identification, Risk Assessment, Treatment and Legal Issues,* edited by Fabian Saleh, Albert Grudzinskas, John Bradford, and Daniel Brodsky, 11–24. New York: Oxford University Press.

Lester, Rebecca J. 2007. "Critical Therapeutics: Cultural Politics and Clinical Reality in Two Eating Disorder Treatment Centers." *Medical Anthropology Quarterly* 21 (4): 369–87.

Levy, Robert I., and Douglas Hollan. 1998. "Person-Centered Interviewing and Observation in Anthropology." In *Handbook of Methods in Cultural Anthropology*, edited by H. Russell Bernard, 333–64. Walnut Creek, CA: Altamira Press.

Leyton, Elliott. 2001. *Hunting Humans: The Rise of the Modern Multiple Murderer.* Toronto: McClelland and Stewart.

Liebling, Alison. 1999. "Doing Research in Prison: Breaking the Silence?" *Theoretical Criminology* 3 (2): 147–73.

Linde, Charlotte. 1999. "The Transformation of Narrative Syntax into Institutional Memory." *Narrative Inquiry* 9 (1): 139–74.

Lockwood, Dorothy, James Inciardi, Clifford Butzin, and Robert Hooper. 1997. "Therapeutic Community Continuum in Corrections." In *Community as Method: Therapeutic Communities for Special Populations and Special Settings,* edited by George De Leon, 87–96. Westport, CT: Praeger.

Loftus, Elizabeth. 1992. "When a Lie Becomes Memory's Truth: Memory Distortion after Exposure to Misinformation." *Current Directions in Psychological Science* 1 (4): 121–23.

Lösel, F., and M. Schmucker. 2005. "The Effectiveness of Treatment for Sexual Offenders: A Comprehensive Meta-Analysis." *Journal of Experimental Psychology* 1:117–46.

Luhrmann, T.M. 2000. *Of Two Minds: The Growing Disorder in American Psychiatry.* New York: Alfred A. Knopf.

Lutz, Catherine. 1986. "Emotion, Thought and Estrangement: Emotion as a Cultural Category." *Cultural Anthropology* 1 (3): 287–309.

Lyn, T.S., and D.L. Burton. 2004. "Adult Attachment and Sexual Offender Status." *American Journal of Orthopsychiatry* 74 (2): 150–59.

Macfarlane, Alan. 1985. "The Root of All Evil." In *The Anthropology of Evil,* edited by David Parkin, 57–76. Oxford: Basil Blackwell.

Mann, Ruth E. 2004. "Innovations in Sex Offender Treatment." *Journal of Sexual Aggression* 10 (2): 141–52.

Marques, Janice K., David M. Day, Craig Nelson, and Mary Ann West. 1994. "Effects of Cognitive-Behavioral Treatment on Sex Offender Recidivism." *Criminal Justice and Behavior* 21 (1): 28–54.

Marshall, William. 1996. "The Sexual Offender: Monster, Victim, or Everyman?" *Sexual Abuse: A Journal of Research and Treatment* 8 (4): 317–35.

Marshall, William, Dana Anderson, and Yolanda Fernandez. 1999. *Cognitive Behavioural Treatment of Sexual Offenders.* New York: John Wiley and Sons.

Marshall, William, and A. Eccles. 1993. "Pavlovian Conditioning Processes in Adolescent Sex Offenders." In *The Juvenile Sex Offender,* edited by H. Barbaree, W. Marshall, and S. Hudson, 118–42. New York: Guilford Press.

Marshall, William, and Sharon Williams. 2000. "Assessment and Treatment of Sexual Offenders." *Forum on Corrections* 12:41–44.

Maruna, Shadd, and Ruth Mann. 2006. "A Fundamental Attribution Error? Rethinking Cognitive Distortions." *Legal and Criminological Psychology* 11 (2): 155–77.

Mathiesen, Thomas. 1997. "The Viewer Society: Michel Foucault's 'Panopticon' Revisited." *Theoretical Criminology* 1 (2): 215–34.

Mattingly, Cheryl. 1994. "The Concept of Therapeutic 'Emplotment.'" *Social Science and Medicine* 38 (6): 811–22.

———. 1998a. *Healing Dramas and Clinical Plots: The Narrative Structure of Experience.* Cambridge: Cambridge University Press.

———. 1998b. "In Search of the Good: Narrative Reasoning in Clinical Practice." *Medical Anthropology Quarterly* 12 (3): 273–97.

———. 2008. "Reading Minds and Telling Tales in a Cultural Borderland." *Ethos* 36 (1): 136–54.

Mattingly, Cheryl, Nancy Lutkehaus, and Jason Throop, eds. 2008. "Troubling the Boundary between Psychology and Anthropology: Jerome Bruner and His Inspiration." Special issue, *Ethos* 36 (1).

McCorkel, Jill. 1998. "Going to the Crackhouse: Critical Space in Total Institutions and Everyday Life." *Symbolic Interaction* 21:227–52.

McCulloch, Trish, and Lynn Kelly. 2007. "Working with Sex Offenders in Context: Which Way Forward?" *Probation Journal* 54 (1): 7–21.

Metzner, Jeffrey, Scott Humphreys, and Gail Ryan. 2009. "Juveniles Who Sexually Offend: Psychosocial Intervention and Treatment." In *Sex Offenders: Identification, Risk Assessment, Treatment and Legal Issues,* edited by Fabian Saleh, Albert Grudzinskas, John Bradford, and Daniel Brodsky, 241–61. New York: Oxford University Press.

Millar, Sarah. 2011. "Police Officer's Remarks at York Inspire 'SlutWalk.'" March 17. www.thestar.com/news/article/955682--police-officer-s-remarks-at-york-inspire-slutwalk.

Miller, Peggy J. 1995. "Personal Storytelling in Everyday Life: Social and Cultural Perspectives." In *Knowledge and Memory: The Real Story,* edited by R. Wyler, 177–84. Advances in Social Cognition 8. Hillsdale, NJ: Lawrence Erlbaum.

Monahan, Ken, Joseph Marolla, and David Bromley. 2005. "Constructing Coercion: The Organization of Sexual Assault." *Journal of Contemporary Ethnography* 34 (3): 284–316.

Motiuk, Larry, and Ray Belcourt. 1996. "Profiling the Canadian Sex Offender Population." *Forum on Corrections Research* 8 (2). www.csc-scc.gc.ca.

Murphy, Lisa, Daniel J. Brodsky, S. Jan Brakel, Michael Petrunik, J. Paul Fedoroff, and Albert J. Grudzinskas Jr. 2009. "Community-Based Management of Sex Offenders: An Examination of Sex Offender Registries and Community Notification in the United States and Canada." In *Sex Offenders: Identification, Risk Assessment, Treatment and Legal Issues,* edited by Fabian Saleh, Albert Grudzinskas, John Bradford, and Daniel Brodsky, 412–24. New York: Oxford University Press.

Ochs, Elinor, and Lisa Capps. 1996. "Narrating the Self." *Annual Review of Anthropology* 25:19–43.

Olver, Mark, and Stephen Wong. 2010. "A Comparison of Static and Dynamic Assessment of Sexual Offender Risk and Need in a Treatment Context." *Criminal Justice and Behavior* 38 (2): 113–26.

Olver, Mark, Stephen Wong, and Terry Nicholaichuk. 2009. "Outcome Evaluation of a High-Intensity Inpatient Sex Offender Treatment Program." *Journal of Interpersonal Violence* 24 (3): 522–36.

Olver, M.E., S.C.P. Wong, T.P. Nicholaichuk, and A.E. Gordon. 2007. "The Validity and Reliability of the Violence Risk Scale-Sexual Offender Version: Assessing Sex Offender Risk and Evaluating Therapeutic Change." *Psychological Assessment* 19:318–29.

Ong, Aihwa. 1996. "Cultural Citizenship as Subject-Making: Immigrants Negotiate Racial and Cultural Boundaries in the United States." *Current Anthropology* 37 (5): 737–62.

———. 1999. *Flexible Citizenship: The Cultural Logics of Transnationality.* Durham: Duke University Press.

O'Shaughnessy, Roy J. 2009. "The Role of Personality Disorder in Sexual Offending." In *Sex Offenders: Identification, Risk Assessment, Treatment and Legal Issues,* edited by Fabian Saleh, Albert Grudzinskas, John Bradford, and Daniel Brodsky, 144–55. New York: Oxford University Press.

Parhar, Karen K., J. Stephen Wormith, Dena M. Derkzen, and Adele M. Beauregard. 2008. "Offender Coercion in Treatment." *Criminal Justice and Behavior* 35 (9): 1109–35.

Pocock, David. 1985. "Unruly Evil." In *The Anthropology of Evil,* edited by David Parkin, 42–56. Oxford: Basil Blackwell.

Polkinghorne, Donald E. 1995. "Narrative Configuration in Qualitative Analysis." *Qualitative Studies in Education* 8 (1): 5–23.

Presser, L. 2004. "Violent Offenders, Moral Selves: Constructing Identities and Accounts in the Research Interview." *Social Problems* 51 (1): 82–101.

Price, Laurie J. 1995. "Life Stories of the Terminally Ill: Therapeutic and Anthropological Paradigms." *Human Organization* 54 (4): 462–69.

Raymond, N., E. Coleman, F. Ohlerking, G. Christenson, and M. Miner. 1999. "Psychological Co-Morbidity in Pedophilic Sexual Offenders." *American Journal of Psychiatry* 155 (6): 786–88.

Reyna, Valerie F. 2008. "A Theory of Medical Decision Making and Health: Fuzzy Trace Theory." *Medical Decision Making* 28:850–65.

Rhodes, Lorna A. 2000. "Taxonomic Anxieties: Axis I and Axis II in Prison." *Medical Anthropology Quarterly* 14 (3): 346–73.

———. 2001. "Toward an Anthropology of Prisons." *Annual Review of Anthropology* 30:65–83.

———. 2004. *Total Confinement: Madness and Reason in the Maximum Security Prison.* Berkeley: University of California Press.

Ricoeur, Paul. 1980. "Narrative Time." *Critical Inquiry* 7 (1): 169–90.

———. 1988. *Time and Narrative.* Chicago: University of Chicago Press.

Robbins, Joel. 2004. *Becoming Sinners: Christianity and Moral Torment in a Papua New Guinea Society.* Berkeley: University of California Press.

Rose, Nikolas. 1990. *Governing the Soul: The Shaping of the Private Self.* London: Routledge.

———. 1992. "Engineering the Human Soul: Analysing Psychological Experience." *Science in Context* 5 (2): 351–69.

———. 1998. *Inventing Our Selves: Psychology, Power and Personhood.* Cambridge: Cambridge University Press.

———. 2007. *The Politics of Life Itself: Biomedicine, Power and Subjectivity in the Twenty-First Century.* Princeton: Princeton University Press.

Rubin, David C. 1995. "Introduction." In *Remembering our Past: Studies in Autobiographical Memory,* edited by David C. Rubin, 1–15. Cambridge: Cambridge University Press.

Sarbin, Theodore R. 1986. *Narrative Psychology: The Storied Nature of Human Conduct.* New York: Praeger.

Saris, A. Jamie. 1995. "Telling Stories: Life Histories, Illness Narratives, and Institutional Landscapes." *Culture, Medicine and Psychiatry* 19:39–72.

Sass, Louis A., and Robert L. Woolfolk. 1988. "Psychoanalysis and the Hermeneutic Turn: A Critique of Narrative Truth and Historical Truth." *Journal of the American Psychoanalytical Association* 36:429–54.

Scheper-Hughes, Nancy. 1995. "The Primacy of the Ethical: Propositions for a Militant Anthropology." *Current Anthropology* 36 (3): 409–40.

———. 1997. "People Who Get Rubbished." *New Internationalist,* no. 295. October. www.newint.org/issue 295.

———. 2004. "Parts Unknown: Undercover Ethnography of the Organs-Trafficking Underworld." *Ethnography* 5 (1): 29–73.

Shuker, Richard, and Elizabeth Sullivan, eds. 2010. *Grendon and the Emergence of Forensic Therapeutic Communities: Developments in Research and Practice.* Chichester: Wiley-Blackwell.

Spence, Donald P. 1982a. *Narrative Truth and Historical Truth.* New York: Norton.

——— 1982b. "Narrative Truth and Theoretical Truth." *Psychoanalytic Quarterly* 51:43–69.

Strauss, Claudia, and Naomi Quinn. 1997. *A Cognitive Theory of Cultural Meaning.* Cambridge: Cambridge University Press.

Stueber, Karsten R. 2006. *Rediscovering Empathy: Agency, Folk Psychology, and the Human Sciences.* Cambridge, MA: MIT Press.

Taussig, Michael. 1999. *Defacement: Public Secrecy and the Labor of the Negative.* Palo Alto: Stanford University Press.

Thomas, Jim. 1993. *Doing Critical Ethnography.* Newbury Park, CA: Sage Publications.

Throop, C. Jason. 2010. *Suffering and Sentiment: Exploring the Vicissitudes of Experience and Pain in Yap.* Berkeley: University of California Press.

Toch, Hans. 1998. "Psychopathy or Antisocial Personality in Forensic Settings." In *Psychopathy: Anti-Social, Criminal and Violent Behavior,* edited by Theodore Miller, Erik Simonsen, Burket Smith, and Roger B. Davis, 144–58. New York: Guilford Press.

Turner, Victor. 1967. *The Forest of Symbols: Aspects of Ndembu Ritual.* Ithaca: Cornell University Press.

Vincent, Gina M., Shannon M. Maney, and Stephen D. Hart. 2009. "The Use of Actuarial Risk Assessment Instruments in Sex Offenders." In *Sex Offenders:*

Identification, Risk Assessment, Treatment and Legal Issues, edited by Fabian Saleh, Albert Grudzinskas, John Bradford, and Daniel Brodsky, 70–88. New York: Oxford University Press.

Viney, Linda, and Lynne Bousfield. 1991. "Narrative Analysis: A Method of Psychological Research for AIDS-Affected People." *Social Science and Medicine* 32 (7): 757–65.

Wacquant, Loïc. 2002. "The Curious Eclipse of Prison Ethnography in the Age of Mass Incarceration." *Ethnography* 3(4): 371–97.

Waitzkin, Howard, and Theron Britt. 1993. "Processing Narratives of Self-Destructive Behavior in Routine Medical Encounters: Health Promotion, Disease Prevention, and the Discourse of Health Care." *Social Science and Medicine* 36 (9): 1121–36.

Waitzkin, Howard, and Holly Magana. 1997. "The Black Box in Somatization: Unexplained Physical Symptoms, Culture, and Narratives of Trauma." *Social Science and Medicine* 45 (6): 811–25.

Waldram, James B. 1993. "Aboriginal Spirituality: Symbolic Healing in Canadian Prisons." *Culture, Medicine and Psychiatry* 17:345–62.

———. 1994. "Aboriginal Spirituality in Corrections: A Canadian Case Study in Religion and Therapy." *American Indian Quarterly* 18 (2): 197–214.

———. 1997. *The Way of the Pipe: Aboriginal Spirituality and Symbolic Healing in Canadian Prisons.* Peterborough: Broadway Press.

———. 1998. "Anthropology in Prison: Negotiating Consent and Accountability with a Captured Population." *Human Organization* 57 (2): 238–44.

———. 2004. *Revenge of the Windigo: The Construction of the Mind and Mental Health of North American Aboriginal Peoples.* Toronto: University of Toronto Press, Anthropological Horizons.

———. 2007. "Everybody Has a Story: Listening to Imprisoned Sexual Offenders." *Qualitative Health Research* 17 (7): 963–70.

———. 2008. "The Narrative Challenge to Cognitive Behavioral Treatment of Sexual Offenders." *Culture, Medicine and Psychiatry* 32 (3): 421–39.

———. 2009a. "Challenges of Prison Ethnography." *Anthropology News,* January, 4–5.

———. 2009b. "'It's Just You and Satan, Hanging Out at a Pre-School': Notions of Evil and the Rehabilitation of Sexual Offenders." *Anthropology and Humanism* 34 (2): 219–34.

———. 2010. "Moral Agency, Cognitive Distortion, and Narrative Strategy in the Rehabilitation of Sexual Offenders." *Ethos* 38 (3): 251–74.

Waldram, James B., D. Anne Herring, and, T. Kue Young. 2006. *Aboriginal Health in Canada: Historical, Cultural and Epidemiological Perspectives.* 2nd ed. Toronto: University of Toronto Press.

Ward, Tony, Stephen Hudson, Lucy Johnston, and William Marshall. 1997. "Cognitive Distortions in Sex Offenders: An Integrative Review." *Clinical Psychology Review* 17 (5): 479–507.

Ware, Jayson, Andrew Frost, and Anna Hoy. 2010. "A Review of the Use of Therapeutic Communities with Sexual Offenders." *International Journal of Offender Therapy and Comparative Criminology* 54 (5): 721–42.

Weinstein, Raymond M. 1982. "Goffman's Asylums and the Social Situation of Mental Patients." *Orthomolecular Psychiatry* 11 (4): 267–74.

Wertsch, James V. 2011. "Beyond the Archival Model of Memory and the Affordances and Constraints of Narratives." *Culture and Psychology* 17 (1): 21–29.

Wesson, Marianne. 1984/85. "Historical Truth, Narrative Truth, and Expert Testimony." *Washington Law Review* 60:331–54.

White, Michael, and David Epston. 1990. *Narrative Means to Therapeutic Ends.* New York: Norton.

Wikan, Unni. 2000. "With Life in One's Lap: The Story of an Eye/I (or Two)." In *Narrative and the Cultural Construction of Illness and Healing,* edited by Cheryl Mattingly and Linda Garro, 212–36. Berkeley: University of California Press.

Winnipeg Free Press. 2011. "Rape Victim 'Inviting," So No Jail." February 24, 2011. www.winnipegfreepress.com/local/rape-victim-inviting-so-no-jail--rape-victim-inviting-so-no-jail-116801578.html.

Wong, Stephen, Mark Olver, Terry Nicholaichuk, and Audrey Gordon. 2003. "Violence Risk Scale: Sexual Offender Version." Unpublished.

Yang, Lawrence Hsin, Arthur Kleinman, Bruce G. Link, Jo C. Phelan, Sing Lee, and Byron Good. 2007. "Culture and Stigma: Adding Moral Experience to Stigma Theory." *Social Science and Medicine* 64:1524–35.

Young, Alan. 1990. "Moral Conflicts in a Psychiatric Hospital Treating Combat-Related Posttraumatic Stress Disorder (PTSD)." In *Social Science Perspectives on Medical Ethics,* edited by George Weisz, 65–82. Dordrecht: Kluwer.

Young, Myla H., Jerald V. Justice, and Philip Edberg. 2010. "Sexual Offenders in Prison Psychiatric Treatment: A Biopsychosocial Description." *International Journal of Offender Therapy and Comparative Criminology* 54 (1): 92–112.

Zigon, Jarrett. 2007. "Moral Breakdown and the Ethical Demand: A Theoretical Framework for an Anthropology of Moralities." *Anthropological Theory* 7 (2): 131–50.

Index

abjection, 216–17

Aboriginal inmates: Autobiographies of, 1–7, 106, 107, 114–21, 122–28; Crime Cycles of, 147–50; Elders, ix, 41, 67, 118, 170, 177; Relapse Prevention Plans of, 169–78; sexual offenders, 52, 63, 72–74, 81–82, 86, 87–88, 96–97, 201, 210

American Psychiatric Association, 53, 54

Anger Management module, 135–36

antisocial personality disorder, 56–57, 224

Assertiveness module, 136–37, 139

Auburn, Timothy, 61, 62

Autobiographies: assumed to be wrong from the outset, 227; audience influence on shaping of, 3–5, 6, 108–9, 111–12, 119–21, 131; challenges to as major aspect of treatment experience, 15–16, 20; as core narrative around which treatment is built, 109; Curtis', 114–21; difficulty in presenting, 70–71; as disclosure, not narrative, 110, 133; as disemplotment of life story, 132–33; "fixing"of, 19; as "forced confession," 226–27; Franklin's, 122–28; instructions for, 112–13, 132; judged by "truth," 16, 18, 110–11, 133; as measure of success in program, 133; primary nurse helps prepare, 2, 114; Sam's, 1–7, 106, 107; Steven's, 1

28–32; as stressful event, 111; varying factors affecting presentation and receipt of, 127. See also narrative/narrative mode

Bambonyé, Manassé, 55–56

Brockmeier, Jens, 144, 145

Bruner, Jerome: comparison of paradigmatic and narrative modes by, 13–14, 16, 17, 19, 108; on inappropriateness of falsifiability criteria to narrative, 18, 19, 227, 228; on narrative as inherent capability of humans, 12–13, 233

Busch, Noël Bridget, et al., 54

Capps, Lisa, 19, 226–27

Caucasian inmates: Autobiographies of, 122–32; Crime Cycles of, 151–61; Relapse Prevention Plans of, 178–83; sexual offenders, 52, 72, 78, 80, 83, 89, 90, 91, 92, 95, 96, 120, 130

Cognitive Behavioral Therapy (CBT), 1–2, 9; assumes inmates will lie or omit details, 111, 221, 227; basic arguments of, 59, 60; as challenge to personal narrative, 15–16; "choice" as central element in, 138; cognitive distortion as key problem of, 59–62, 223–24, 229; constructed upon paradigmatic mode, 13, 14; inmate resistance to, 233–34; and Relapse Prevention, 167; success of, 62–63 cognitive distortions (thinking errors), 59–60; assumed of criminals, 232–33; concept usually new to entering inmates, 71; criticism of concept of, 61, 62, 224; denial as, 60; examples of, 60, 146; focus on in treatment may be misplaced, 61; inconsistency with idea of, 224; as key problem of Cognitive Behavioral Therapy, 59–62, 223–24, 229; not unique to criminals, 224; regarding women, 54–55

Cognitive Strategies program, 101–3

Cohen, Stanley, 216, 242n2

Correctional Service of Canada, ix

Crime Cycles, 145–46; audience influence on, 148–49, 153–56, 158–59; Curtis', 147–51; Eddie's, 157–61; reinterpreting life in, 149; reworking of reality in, 142; Tom's, 151–57; "truth" not stable in, 162

criminogenic: factors, 12, 133; needs, 92

Desjarlais, Robert, 8

Diagnostic and Statistical Manual of Mental Disorders (DSM), 53, 55, 56–57, 242n2

disclosure, 62, 67, 110–13, 132–33, 190, 221, 226–27, 232

emotions, 6, 55, 56, 59, 60, 61, 69, 71, 93, 96, 101, 113, 143–44, 146, 153, 154, 162, 184–96, 221, 229, 232, 237

empathy, 165, 191; as a relationship, 184–85, 193

Empathy module: complications of, 191, 194; controlled emotionality emphasized in, 194–95; evokes inmate's past experiences, 186, 191–93; as habilitation, 196; letters written to victim in, 187–90; may fail to create empathy, 195; potential benefit of, 193–94; risks of, 195–96

emplotment, 107, 132

ethnographer/interviewer (author): access to inmate files of, 39, 44; adjunct therapeutic role of, 36–37; anomalous status of, 45; attempt to present views of inmates as accurately as possible by, xii–xiii; difficulty of participant observation by, 34–35; efforts to protect identities of inmates by, xiii–xiv; first encounter with sexual offender of, viii; goals of, 8–12, 223; inmates ask opinions of, 40; interview methods of, 37–39; minimal contact with staff of, 43–44; participant in group treatment sessions of, 39–40; person-centered interviews of, 37–38; rejection of original proposal to study sexual offenders of, ix; suspicions by inmates and prison personnel of, 35–36, 40–42; watching of, 34, 42

ethnography: importance of personal relationships in, xii, 37; issue of representation in, xi–xiii; "social suffering" paradigm of, xi

evil, x, 64, 217

exit interviews, 38, 73, 220–22

Feldman, Allen, 34

folk devils, 216, 236, 238

Foucault, Michel, 29, 34, 225, 241n2, 241n4

fuzzy trace theory, 143

Garro, Linda, 198

Geertz, Clifford, 42, 185

Gergen, Kenneth J., 14, 15, 231, 234

Goffman, Erving, xii, 31, 43, 40–41, 44, 76, 89

habilitation, 10–12, 225, 237; Empathy training as, 196; moral, 66, 101

Halpern, Jodi, 195

Haney, Lynne A., 53

Hinton, Alexander Laban, ix

Hollan, Douglas, 184–85, 191

Hound Pound, defined, 8

inmates/patients: accommodation to paradigmatic mode may be at the expense of therapeutic progress of, 231; affect of record on future of, 212–18; alcohol and drug problems of, 6, 71, 72, 74, 81, 117, 126, 177, 207; assumed to lack empathy, 185; claims of innocence not taken well by other inmates, 206; difficult transition from inmate to patient of, 31–32; drug tests on, 45; files as "historical truth" about, 140–42, 228–29; "happyland" as ideal to seek, 138, 225–226; medication of, 28, 52–53, 151; present-only approach of, 200, 202–3; "problems" identified by, 71–74; quasi-authority of, 30; reasons for getting into treatment program of, 95–96; reconciling differing moral world by, 79; reject idea that they are "sick," 71; resist blanket admission of culpability, 94; resist efforts to "fix" narratives, 229–30; term "cure" not used by, 72; treatment contracts of, 92–95, 97–98; view of outside of, 197–98; view of staff by, 90–91. *See also* Autobiographies; Crime Cycles; exit interviews; narratives, prospective; Relapse Prevention Plans

Jackson, Michael, 107, 142
Jefferson, Andrew M., 9, 30

Kaye, John, 14, 15, 231, 234
Kirmayer, Laurence, 132
Kleinman, Arthur, xi, 76, 99
Kurosawa Akira, viii-ix

Landau, Mark J., et al., 198–99
Leyton, Elliott, viii
Loftus, Elizabeth, 143
Luhrmann, T. M., 56, 58, 62

Macfarlane, Alan, 217
Marshall, William, viii
Marshall, William et al., 64, 65, 107, 145
masturbation, 172, 175
Mattingly, Cheryl, 17
medical anthropology, x, xi, 12, 238
memory: archive model of, 143–45; institutional files as, 15, 140–42, 228; mistakes, 144–45; as mingling of past and present experience, 144; verbatim vs. gist, 143
Monahan, Ken et al., 54
moral communities, 76–77, 79, 87–88, 99–100
morality, ix, 11, 57–58, 71, 72, 85, 92, 100, 102, 110, 193, 196, 221, 225, 229, 235, 237

narrative/narrative mode: is about violations of "shared ordinariness," 13; is affected by listener's reaction, 108–9; asymmetry, 226; challenges to can terminate, 20; cognition and affect of past events only knowable through construction of, 232; compelled, 107; is contextual, 108; functions of, 12–13; inappropriate to apply falsifiability criterion to, 18; inherent voluntariness of, 106; intersubjectivity of, 108; paradigmatic mode as standard to judge, 18; paradigmatic mode intrudes on,

20; patients account replaced by that of therapist, 15, 17, 226; as process of negotiating events, 109; relationship with paradigmatic mode of, 10, 13–14, 16–17, 230–31; seen as form of disclosure, 221; success based upon reemplotment of life story, 133; truth of not judged by perfect correspondence with past events, 18–19. *See also* Autobiographies
narratives, prospective, 183, 198–99, 218–19; concern over reoffending in, 208–10; desire to live "normal" life in, 210; examples of present-only approach to, 200–203; inability to escape the past in, 204; need to reconnect with family and friends in, 208, 211. *See also* exit interviews

Ochs, Elinor, 19, 108–9, 198, 226–27
Ong, Aihwa, 76

panoptics, 23, 27, 34, 45, 77, 198, 217, 218, 228
paradigmatic mode, 10; Cognitive Behavioral Therapy constructed upon, 13, 14; conflict in therapeutic treatment with narrative mode, 230–31; definition of, 13; intrudes on narrative mode, 20; relationship to narrative mode of, 10, 13–14, 16, 17, 19; as standard to judge narratives by, 18
paraphilia, 53, 72
pedophilia, 49, 53–55, 71
phallometric assessment, 163–65
Pocock, David, 217
power: differential between inmates and staff of, 15, 98, 231, 237; surveillance and assessment as mechanisms of, 65–66
prisons: institutional memory of, 228; as involuntary communities, 76; lessons of treatment program incommensurate with life in, 82–84, 138; one-way research tradition in, 43; provide degree of comfort and security, 198; public assumptions about, vii; sexual offenders in Canadian federal, 48
psychology: 8, 18, 19, 32, 33, 141, 224, 227; forensic, xiv, 57, 69; cognitive, 132, 233
psychological anthropology, x, 54, 238
psychopaths, 57, 58, 131, 242n1

psychiatry, 8, 18, 19, 32, 47, 53–55, 62, 141, 227

rape, 50, 131
Raymond, N. et al., 55
recidivism: assessment of risk of, 69–70; inmate concern about, 208–10; as measure of success of treatment program, 62–63, 69; Static 99 assessment tool, 69; Violence Risk Scale–Sex Offenders Version (VRS-SO) assessment tool, 69; See also Relapse Prevention Plans
rehabilitation, 10–11; corrections officers discount likelihood of, 33; makes little sense, 225. See also habilitation
Relapse Prevention Plans, 166–67; Alfred's, 174–78; audience input into, 171–72, 173, 175–77, 179–80, 181–82; Crime Cycle particularly relevant to, 167, 168–69; Sam's, 169–74; Steven's, 178–83
Reyna, Valerie F., 143
Rhodes, Lorna A., xi–xii, 9, 35, 43, 57
Ricoeur, Paul, 198, 201
Robbins, Joel, 58
Rose, Nikolas, 19, 29, 225; on correctional files, 228; definition of therapeutics by, 58; on disclosure, 110; on relapse prevention, 167–68
Rubin, David C., 108

sexual crimes: against children, 51–52, 71–72, 89, 102, 104–5, 152; against sex trade workers, 78, 80; against wives, 117–18, 147; alcohol involvement in, 4, 51, 52, 90, 120, 124, 146, 158–59, 180, 181–82; definitions of, 48–49, 50; double standard in, 105; issue of consent and, 79; not necessarily evidence of sexual disorder, 54; not psychological disorders or sickness, 53; socially patterned, 54–55
sexual offenders: antisocial personality disorder as common diagnosis for, 56–57; average sentence length for, 49; in Canadian federal institutions, 48; community notification about released, 50, 213–15; crimes committed by inmates interviewed, 51–52; Criminal Code regarding, 48–49; failure to remember details of crimes by, 4–5, 124, 131, 152, 158, 160–61; idea of reintegrating into society seems unlikely, 234; laws

relating to released, 213–14; as "matter out of place," 217; means of release of, 49–50; mental disorders of, 55; as monsters in public discourse, vii–viii; moral boundaries of, 105; negative attitude towards sex trade workers of, 78; not different from general population, 55–56, 224; ranking by inmates of, 90; registration, 213; remain so upon release, 226; social abjection of, 216–17. See also inmates/patients
sex trade workers, 51, 78, 80
Spence, Donald P., 231, 232
sweat lodge (sweat), 170, 177, 179
synoptics, 34, 45, 67, 77, 198, 215, 217, 226

therapeutic intervention: anthropology of, x–xi, 235–38; defined, 235; deindividualization in, 236; examples of, 237; power and authority allows, 237; success measured by improvement in public safety not in patient, 237. See also therapeutic treatment program
therapeutic prison, xvii, 1, 9, 21, 23, 26, 29, 30, 45, 48, 53, 57, 65, 75, 223, 237
therapeutics, 58
therapeutic pragmatic, 9, 20, 45, 61, 63–64, 223, 224, 242n3
therapeutic treatment program: assessment of recidivism risk in, 69–70; attrition of cohorts in, 98; compared with religious beliefs, 226–27; compelled narrative in, 107; complexity of power and resistance in, 9; conflict between narrative and paradigmatic modes in, 230–31; consequences of refusing to attend, 99; constructed on paradigmatic mode, 13, 14; creation of a moral community by, 76–78, 99–100; determination of success in, 68; "dynamic" and "static" factors in, 58; full openness and disclosure in, 67; goal of reintegrating offenders into society seems unlikely, 234; goal to make our lives better, 225; greater emphasis upon thinking than feeling in, 220–21; group sessions supposed to be confidential in, 67; habilitation as goal of, 11–12; incommensurability of many lessons with life in prison, 138; inmate disappointment with, 222; inmates usually returned to prison after, 68; intent of to make inmates prosocial, 225; little known

about experience of being in, 8–9; misplaced verification in, 228; as moral community, 76–77, 79, 87, 99–100; parole unstated goal of, 151–52; power imbalance as essence of, 15, 98; recidivism as main measure of efficacy of, 62–63, 69; replacement of clients narrative by therapists in, 15, 17, 226; "therapeutic community" approach of, 65, 66; as "therapies of normality," 19; three central components of, 66; truth discourse dominates, 10, 13, 227. *See also* Cognitive Behavioral Therapy (CBT); inmates/patients; therapeutic intervention

therapeutic unit: arrival of new inmates in, 79–82; "con code" in, 67, 77–80, 90, 204; contrast with prison of, 82–84; description of, 23–28; difficulties of integrating new inmates in, 79–89; drug use in, 146; economy of, 91–92; fluidity of patient-inmate statuses in, 29–33, 46; patients view of, 30–31; power of inmates/patients in, 29; problems of adaptation to, 85–91; ratting in, 84; searching of inmates "house" in,
186–87; self-regulation and self-governance in, 77, 83–84, 88; staff of, 63–64, 70, 91; state of flux of, 84–85; surveillance and assessment as mechanisms of power in, 65–66; tensions between security and treatment mandates of, 29, 30, 32–33; watching by and of staff in, 27–28, 34. *See also* therapeutic treatment program

Thomas, Jim, xii

Throop, C. Jason, 184–85, 191

treatment contract, 92–100, 108, 111, 204

truth, historical vs. narrative, 231–32

truth discourse, 13, 16, 227

Turner, Victor, 202

Values, Attitudes and Beliefs program, 103–5

Ware, Jayson et al., 8, 65

Wertsch, James V., 111–115

Yang, Lawrence Hsin et al., 217

Young, Myla H. et al., 55

Zigon, Jarrett, 78, 101

TEXT
10/13 Sabon

DISPLAY
Sabon (Open Type)

COMPOSITOR
Toppan Best-set Premedia Limited

PRINTER AND BINDER
Maple-Vail Book Manufacturing Group